BINDING THE GOD:

URSINE ESSAYS FROM
THE MOUNTAIN SOUTH

BINDING THE GOD

URSINE ESSAYS FROM
THE MOUNTAIN SOUTH

JEFF MANN

[signature: Jeff Mann]

[handwritten inscription: 5/14/11 for Lewis, Here's hoping you enjoy these Surly Bear essays!]

BEAR BONES BOOKS
NEW LONDON, CONNECTICUT, USA

Bear Bones Books, New London, CT
An imprint of Lethe Press, 118 Heritage Avenue, Maple Shade, NJ 08052
BearBonesBooks.com / lethepressbooks.com / lethepress@aol.com

Cover photo by Matt Hill
Book design by Toby Johnson

1-59021-219-3 / 978-1-59021-219-6

Library of Congress Cataloging-in-Publication Data

Mann, Jeff.
 Binding the god : ursine essays from the mountain south / Jeff Mann.
 p. cm.
 ISBN 1-59021-219-3 (alk. paper)
 1. Bears (Gay culture) 2. Gay men--Identity. 3. Gender identity. 4. Gay men--United States--Biography. 5. Appalachian Region, Southern. I. Title.
 PS3563.A53614B56 2010
 814'.54--dc22
                                        2010039569

ACKNOWLEDGMENTS

"How to be a Country Leather Bear" appeared in *Second Person Queer*, edited by Lawrence Schimel and Richard Labonté.

"The Mountaineer Queer Ponders His Risk-List" appeared in *Appalachian Journal*.

"Valhalla in the Redwoods" appeared in *Chiron Review*.

"'Till The Ductile Anchor Hold': An Appreciation of Appalachian Folk Culture" appeared, in a shortened form, in *Traditions: A Journal of West Virginia Folk Culture and Educational Awareness*.

"Here and Queer" appeared in *Now and Then: The Appalachian Magazine*.

"Unreconstructed Queer" appeared in *Callaloo*.

"Plantation Fantasies; or, One Hillbilly's Journey to the Tidewater and Back" appeared in *Identity Envy: Wanting to Be Who We're Not*, edited by Jim Tushinski and Jim Van Buskirk.

"Beards, Body Hair, and Brawn: Reflections of a Muscle Bear" appeared in *White Crane*.

"Leather Bear Appetites" appeared in *Bears: Gay Erotic Stories*, edited by Richard Labonté.

"715 Willey Street" appeared in *On the Meaning of Friendship Between Gay Men*, edited by Andrew Gottlicb.

"Binding the God" appeared in *Queer and Catholic*, edited by Amie Evans and Trebor Healey, and in *Best Gay Stories 2009*, edited by Steve Berman.

Portions of "Country Boys, Butch Queers, and *Brokeback Mountain*" appeared in *The Charleston Gazette*.

"Loving Tim; or, My Passionate Midlife Affair" appeared in *Arts and Letters: Journal of Contemporary Culture*.

"Surviving Winter's Woods" appeared in *Connotation Press*.

The poem "Maple Syrup," a portion of which appears in "'Till the Ductile Anchor Hold'," was published in *Loving Mountains, Loving Men* and appears here by permission of Ohio University Press.

I have many people to thank:

Steve Berman and Ron Suresha, for kindly publishing this book, and Toby Johnson for formatting the finished product.

Cynthia Burack, for very helpful editorial suggestions and for thirty years of top-notch friendship.

Katie Fallon, for gentle critical commentary, avian gossip, and luscious teas.

Tiffany Trent, for Araporn, Southern understanding, and many a fine meal.

Lisa Norris, for good advice, and for introducing me to "Brokeback Mountain."

Joni Mitchell and Tim McGraw, for the inspiration.

Richard Labonté, Lawrence Schimel, Sandy Ballard, George Brosi, Nathan Jackson Tucker, Karen Salyer McElmurray, Andrew Gottlieb, Doug Imbrogno, Amie Evans, Trebor Healey, Dan Vera, Bo Young, Jim Tushinski, Jim Van Buskirk, Randall Sanders, Judy Byers, Paul J. Willis, Greg Herren, Sean Meriwether, Jamison Currier, Andrew Beierle, Wayne Courtois, Shane Allison, Patrick Califia, Sven Davisson, and Dorothy Allison, for their ongoing support of my work.

Bobby Nelson, Ken Belcher, Darius Liptrap, Farron Allen, Laurie Bugg, Donna Ross, Joe and Charlene Eska, Angelia Wilson, Dan Connery, and Phil Hainen, for their friendship.

For John Ross, Cynthia Burack, and Laree Martin.

TABLE OF CONTENTS

Acknowledgments 5

Beards, Body Hair, and Brawn 11

The Mountaineer Queer Ponders His Risk-List 21

Valhalla in the Redwoods 27

Country Boys, Butch Queers, and *Brokeback Mountain* . . *39*

"Till the Ductile Anchor Hold" 61

Here and Queer 79

Southern (LGBT) Living 85

Bondage Tape in Budapest 97

Unreconstructed Queer 109

Plantation Fantasies 119

How To Be a Country Leather Bear 135

Leather-Bear Appetites 141

715 Willey Street 153

Negative Capability in the Mountain South 167

Surviving Winter's Woods 183

Loving Tim 195

Binding the God 217

About the Author 230

BEARDS, BODY HAIR, AND BRAWN:
REFLECTIONS OF A MUSCLE-BEAR

Awriter's obsessions are more obvious than most. Other folks, if they have any self-control or acting ability at all, can veil their eccentric fascinations, their quirky fixations, but for us writers, if we are true to ourselves in what we compose, our obsessions are there on the page, ready to be conned by any discerning reader. I learned this fact early in my publishing career, at a book party thrown to celebrate my third chapbook of poems, *Flint Shards from Sussex*. I feasted on Chinese food, chatted with friends, and signed books, delighted to be the center of attention. One attendee bought my chapbook, had me sign it, flipped through it, grinned, and said, "You're *really* into chest hair, aren't you?" It had taken him about six seconds of scanning to figure that out.

Yes, indeed, that obsession fills my work, whether poetry, creative nonfiction, or fiction. When I was working on my book of memoir and poetry, *Loving Mountains, Loving Men*, one of the editors even suggested that there might be too many references to chest hair in the book, though she didn't press the point. And that volume is by far the least erotic of my books. In my erotica, my fur fixation borders on the compulsive. I half-jokingly, half-dismissively describe my Lammy-winning fiction collection, *A History of Barbed Wire*, as a book about "big, bearded, beefy, hairy guys getting tied up."

I have been worshiping the Holy Bear Trinity of Beards, Body Hair, and Bulky Brawn since I was an adolescent (a bear cub, if you will) in the 1970's. I was a bear longing for bears well before the present gay subculture existed. How did my desire for furry men develop? How and when did my bear identity coalesce? I don't know...but in the writing of this essay, I hope to figure a few answers out.

Where we grow up has a lot to do with who we become and what we desire. I grew up in the Mountain South, where there is a discernible masculine look I learned early on to lust after. Call it country, redneck, blue-collar, hillbilly. (One warning here: though "redneck" and "hillbilly" are terms we mountain folks might use to describe ourselves, we don't much like to be called those words by supercilious outsiders.) It's how lots of men look around here, in small-town Appalachia. There's bulk, there's brawn. The bellies are built up by bourbon, beer, biscuits, and other tasty, fattening, down-home cooking. The muscles are built up by physical labor, sports, or weightlifting. There's a good bit of body hair, simply because many mature male bodies naturally sprout it. (Ah, the sweet gifts of testosterone and secondary sex characteristics.) There's a lot of facial hair, whether full beards or goatees. There are a goodly number of tattoos. The comfortable, relatively inexpensive, and not particularly fashionable clothes that conceal and reveal these physiques are pretty consistent: jeans, cargo shorts; work boots and cowboy boots; lots of baseball caps, occasional cowboy hats; A-shirts, tank tops, T-shirts, muscle-shirts, and flannel shirts. The presence of such men makes Appalachia an especially scenic region for me, though the unwelcome fact that 90-some percent of these men are heterosexual makes for daily erotic frustration. The auburn-goateed guy working in Lowe's plant department, the scruffy-faced cub with the thick furry calves who delivers the mail...Appalachia brims with straight bears I'd love to bed.

I spent my childhood and adolescence around men like this, and that proximity in those formative years has influenced both what I find desirable and how I myself look, act, and dress. By the time I got to college, I was a confirmed aficionado of furry masculinity who aspired to resemble the men I craved. Because I found beards, body hair, and brawn hot on other men, I figured they might make a shy and insecure loner like me somewhat more appealing, and so I began growing my first attempt at a beard during my freshman year at West Virginia University and have worn some version of facial hair since then. During my twenties,

I watched in hopeful suspense as my chest and belly slowly began to sport the dark hair my legs had worn since I was sixteen. When hair-growing products like Rogaine began to hit the market, I was more interested in rubbing them on my chest than on my receding hairline, though their high cost and my student poverty discouraged such experimentation. Since I found masculine men attractive, and since part of traditional masculinity is strength, and since strength is manifested physically in size, bulk, and muscle, I began lifting weights in my sophomore year and have been lifting on and off ever since. I was indeed a Cub in Training, many years before I learned to name that identity "bear."

Certain college classmates only inscribed these passions deeper. I began my years at West Virginia University as an English major, but, afraid that an English degree wouldn't make me marketable enough, after one semester in college I decided to work for a second degree as well: Nature Interpretation, an option in the Forestry Department. Quite a few guys in my botany, forestry, ornithology, and wildlife management classes were butch, bearded, and exceedingly desirable, albeit apparently straight. They inspired in me many a sweaty-furred bondage fantasy set in a mountain cabin or a forest ranger's isolated eyrie, and their style of manhood was one I found worth emulating. From them I picked up the habits of wearing baseball caps, jeans, and what I call lumberjack boots (very useful attire during our outdoor dendrology and ornithology labs, during which we trekked through all sorts of weather over rocks and through woods in the Core Arboretum and Cooper's Rock State Forest). In warm weather, we wore T-shirts (including one with the slogan "Foresters Do It in the Woods"); in cool weather, we wore flannel shirts with the sleeves rolled up. As for outerwear, the Levi jacket was ubiquitous in Percival Hall, the home of WVU's Forestry Department, though my budding enthusiasm for BDSM led me to wear leather jackets too. This informal manner has been so engrained in me after several decades that I only learned to knot a tie in my mid-forties, and, to this day, wearing khakis or dress shirts makes me feel uncomfortably overdressed.

This style, developed in emulation of the men of my hometown and my buddies in the Forestry Department, was one in deliberate defiance of what I found in the gay bars I frequented during my college years.

There I was, a bear cub before that concept had been invented, surrounded by gay men much sleeker and urbane, witty men in dress pants, polo shirts, and loafers. They were gay in a different way than I was. Now, possessing the terminology, I would simply say that they were members of the gay mainstream, while I was a bear cub, and *vive la différence*. But then, without the benefit of that terminology, that comforting self-identification, I simply felt unpolished, provincial, clumsy, rough, heavy, and unattractive. I was very unpopular in such contexts; I spent those college barhopping years almost always celibate, because my scruffy forestry-major look, combined with my shyness, drew few men my way.

This sense of inadequacy was heightened by the models in gay porn magazines I bought and gay skin flicks I borrowed from friends. These supposed acmes of male beauty were, for the most part, nothing like me. They were young, slender, sculpted, and smooth-chested. I was still young, but I was never slender, having been bequeathed a metabolism that, to use the colorful colloquial, runs to fat, and I was increasingly hairy. This great gap between what I was and what the gay world implied that I should be only added to my insecurity. True confusion, too, discovering that the mainstream gay ideal aesthetic so contradicted mine, for I found very few of these supposed sex gods of photo- and video-porn particularly appealing. Almost all of them lacked the Holy Trinity of Beards, Body Hair, and Brawn. Only Al Parker, whose chest was sadly hairless but whose face was handsomely bearded, stands out in my memory as being a 70's porn star who heated me up.

Meanwhile, I felt like a lumpish Caliban among lithe, acerbic Ariels. One tall, lean acquaintance, studying the guys I cruised in the local gay bar, joked that all the men I wanted "either looked like Grizzly Adams or escapees from *Wilderness Family Robinson*." Combine my taste for BDSM with my taste for furry, beefy guys, and I felt like a freak among freaks. Since I never quite fit into the typical gay bar or the average gay gathering, I tended to hang around with lesbians, who were more tolerant of my oddities than most gay men I knew.

Discovering the leather community during my infrequent visits to Washington, DC helped me out of this isolation. By the early 1980's I'd nervously entered my first leather bar, had found magazines like *Drummer* and *Honcho*, with their occasional photos of the bearded beefcake I craved and the BDSM I fantasized about, and had begun identifying as a leather man. Though most city-dwelling gay men were too slick, fashionable, and clean-shaven for my taste, in the leather bars I visited during my urban forays I found men who looked like me, men who appealed to my hirsute aesthetic. By 1990 (I have confirmed these dates by digging, with many a sneeze, through my dusty, long-boxed-up porn stash), I had discovered the developing bear community through *Bear Magazine*. Here were the sex gods I favored, sprawled heftily and hairily in centerfolds; here were gay men who found beautiful what I found beautiful; here were gay men who resembled the straight men I grew up around, the straight guys I admired in my forestry classes: similar furry faces and bulky bodies, similar country-boy clothes.

Though I don't recall identifying as a bear during the tumultuous affair that consumed me during the early 1990's, a relationship with an already espoused man whom I would now describe as a muscle-cub, in the agonized aftermath of that relationship I took a lot of comfort in the company of a couple of big, bearded, hairy men in Roanoke, Virginia, with whom I made an occasional frolicsome third. I'd met Keith and Tony at Roanoke's Pride in the Park celebration, where they manned a bear-club booth. Keith was a tall redheaded Top, Tony a short, black-bearded butch bottom. They gave me a lot of what I needed at such a bleak time in my life: lots of good food and beer, lots of rough sex. During the occasional weekends I spent at their house, I felt desirable, cared for, among my own kind. It was, I suppose, during my friendship with them—the mid-1990's—that I first identified myself as a bear. One of the most regularly worn objects in my closet began to be a black corduroy *Bear Magazine* baseball cap. Having adopted the identity, I was now advertising it to celebrate my sense of belonging.

By the time I met John, in June of 1997, I was describing myself as a leather bear. The travels we've shared during our ten years together have often involved visits to bear bars like San Francisco's Lone Star, cooking-and-drinking evenings with other bear couples, and social events with bear clubs in West Virginia and Virginia. In one of our Mountain State buddies, Bob, I first consciously noticed something I'd unconsciously admired

in Keith and Tony and have seen since in many bears, something I find
exceptionally appealing. When it came to looks, dress, and mannerisms,
Bob was very masculine, but he also embodied sweetness, gentleness,
domesticity, and kindness, more traditionally feminine characteristics.
Butch, brawny, and thickly hairy Bob certainly was—on a drunken lark,
he even posed once for *Bear Magazine*—but he nevertheless kept a cozy,
attractive home and treated lucky friends like us to many home-cooked
meals. This combination of yin and yang is quite a beautiful balance,
a fine median between the obnoxiously effeminate on one end and the
obnoxiously masculine on the other. (I've often said that, in either sex,
extremes of femininity are ridiculous, extremes of masculinity downright
dangerous.)

At this point in my midlife, not only do I regularly wear baseball caps,
tank tops, and T-shirts that sport bear slogans and symbols, but several
colleagues of mine in Virginia Tech's English Department even call me
"The Bear," much to my amusement. I have, in other words, enthusiastically
joined a subculture, a folk culture defined, as all folk cultures are, by
similar modes of dress, shared customs, codes, symbols, and language.
Growing up in Hinton turns out to have been good training for my adult
bear-identified years, for the attire worn by Appalachian country boys and
that worn by bears both urban and rural are almost identical. The first
time John and I visited the Lone Star, I was grunting with admiration over
the virile scenery when John whispered in my ear, "They all look like
guys from West Virginia." (The late Eric Rofes hypothesizes about this
similarity in his essay "Academics as Bears: Thoughts on Middle-Class
Eroticization of Workingmen's Bodies," found in the superb and thought-
provoking volume *The Bear Book: Readings in the History and Evolution
of a Gay Male Subculture*, edited by Les Wright.)

Then there is the language, expressions and terminologies that mark
one as an insider. Along with "bears," there are, of course, "cubs" (young
bears), "otters" (young lean, hairy guys), and "wolves" (older lean, hairy
guys). "Daddy bears" are guys like me, with a good bit of silver in the
facial and body hair. One's partner is one's "husbear." "Woof!" is the
conventional bear expression for "Oh-yum-Good-Gawd-I'd-like-to-fuck-
that!" (though "Grrrr!" is also useful in this regard), while sexy men

are described as "woofy." And these are only the basics. Ray Kampf's informative and funny *The Bear Handbook* contains several pages of "Fur-nacular."

Like language, visual symbols also serve to help a community coalesce. I occasionally take a break from writing this essay by flirting online, and the bear website I frequent is full of such symbols: bear-paw images, as well as the colors of the bear flag, stripes that grade from brown into red, then yellow, beige, white, gray, and black. If you see those colors, that bear-paw print, or a sticker that says "Woof!" on a car, you can be pretty certain that the driver sports the Holy Trinity mentioned above. Through such codes and symbols have members of minorities and oppressed groups identified one another throughout history.

Events and festivals further contribute to the definition of a subculture. Along with the myriad small "runs" sponsored by local bear groups, there are national bear weekends in such homo-friendly spots as Provincetown, Key West, and Chicago, as well as the huge International Bear Rendezvous in San Francisco. When I attended the latter in 2005 to read some of my erotica at the kind invitation of noted bear writer and editor Ron Suresha, I stumbled around in a haze of lust, for the Holy Trinity was everywhere I looked. Bears in groups are said to create and enjoy an easy camaraderie, and that was certainly there. This unselfconscious ease might be due to a general lack of the wittily caustic, critical attitudes found in some other gay contexts. Since we bears have bucked the prevailing aesthetic judgments that one must be thin, hairless, and young to be desirable and have learned to accept ourselves, we are less likely to judge and snub others who are different or those who don't measure up to some standard. This friendly, accepting attitude has, I suspect, contributed to the organized and jovial solidarity of our hirsute tribe.

(Amusing aside on my IBR experience: when a taxi driver picked John and me up to leave for the airport, he nervously studied the milling pack of big, shaggy, intimidating men in front of the hotel, and then asked us if we were part of a wrestlers' convention. "Sort of," I replied. You can imagine the wrestling I had in mind.)

Confirmed member of this clan I certainly am, yet, even after these many years of desiring bears, ravishing bears, hanging out with bears, and being a bear, I'm still trying to discern deeper meanings inside my hairy aesthetic, my attraction to the Holy Trinity. As an artist, I want to feel as profoundly as possible, but I also want to understand as profoundly as possible. Why is anything eroticized? Eros remains a mystery, and that's all right: the world of the 21st century needs more mystery. Still, when I see a good-looking goateed guy on the street, muscle-shirt showing off his big chest, a bit of beer belly, a few biceps tattoos, and some dark fur curling over his collar, I wonder at my wonder, at my usually unconsummated ache to touch, smell, and taste him, however briefly to possess him. Wondering, I probe. I use writing to probe. So, here are a few last attempts at comprehension.

My taste in men is broader than it used to be. There are many lean and furry guys who catch my eye: the country-music star Tim McGraw, case in point, my candidate for Most Desirable Man in the World. There are even a few thin, beardless, smooth-chested men I wouldn't mind owning for an evening. I must also admit, at this point in my Daddy Bear years, there are many, many scruffy country-boy cubs, young enough to be my sons, who bring out the (both tender and stern) Top in me. This is an Eros based on difference (as, I assume, heterosexuality is): this cub is smaller and younger than I, this Daddy/boy power inequality is erotic. But I continue to be most often attracted to men like me: burly, furry men in their midlife prime. Many might call this narcissism. I would simply say that some perfectly valid versions of Eros are based on similarity. Your lover is the brother, the twin, the image in the mirror; you are loving yourself, to some extent, but there's nothing wrong with that. I would opine that loving yourself is sometimes the greatest challenge the heart can face.

When I examine the Holy Trinity of Beards, Body Hair, and Brawn, and the fascinations those have always held for me, two essences come to mind: maturity and animality. Furriness and heft are indicators of the mature masculine. The gay mainstream's valorization of thinness and smooth-faced, smooth-chested hairlessness is an attempt to return to youth, when being thin was easier and a hairless face and body were simply due to immature hormones. That goatee, that torso pelt, and that solid physique I admire on bears signify manhood, not boyhood. Testosterone gives us the fur, aging nudges us toward the heft. When I make love to bears, I am rejoicing in ripeness.

As for animality, I remember the exact moment I realized that several physical features I find most arousing in men are simply those that make them mammals. It was the first day of a Mammalogy course in the Forestry Department I took my senior year of college. As soon as I entered the classroom, I noticed and began longing wildly after a classmate, a broad-shouldered, big-chested guy named Kevin with shaggy black hair and a full midnight-black beard. Just about the time I focused on the sight of Kevin's nipples barely and temptingly visible through the fabric of his tight T-shirt, the professor began discussing the traits that made mammals unique. Warm blood, fur, and nipples were the ones that grabbed me; needless to say, I didn't care about live birth. Kevin's naked body warmth, hard and tasty nipples, black beard, and vividly imagined chest hair were already the objects of fantasy. It was then that the amateur biologist in me had this revelation: Kevin's mammality, his animality, were what was firing me up.

Not for nothing that the bear clan is named after a wild animal, for we are simply more honest about our beast-bodies than most. As many have pointed out, furriness represents on some level our inner beast, our inner wildness so fenced in and domesticated by civilization, our Id so frequently scolded stupid by our Superego. The fur on other men and on myself reminds me of that animal, its needs, the wisdom of making peace with it, of celebrating it. Dismissing the beast is impossible. Jung pointed that out when he discussed the Shadow and the imperative need of incorporating and facing it, not banishing it. Bear sex, leather sex, rough sex are all ways of coming to terms with the odd mixture of wild and domesticated, animal and human, we all are, so it makes simple sense that what I find most sexually appealing in men is what most marks them as animals.

These observations might also help to make sense of an odd sign often posted in bear or leather bars: NO COLOGNE. Many bears I know, including myself, detest perfumes and colognes as artificial blights; the scents leap from our noses to our tongues and nauseate us. Many of us love instead the musky natural smell of a man: it's an aphrodisiac, a true pheromone. A ripe and furry armpit becomes an erotic adventure. Biology again: what's attracting us is animal aroma. (To me, man-musk smells like cumin. I remember once entering a friend's kitchen, catching an arousing armpit whiff, thinking to myself, "Um, yum! Some ripe man's in here somewhere!" only to discover that what I was randily snuffling after was a bag of cumin seeds on the kitchen counter.)

What is essential in animals is, finally, flesh and appetite. A New York City bear-chaser buddy I know recently told me that when he thought of bears, he thought of satisfied appetites. This may be because, when he visits me here in the mountains of Virginia, in what I jokingly call my B&D B&B, his hungers for good food, drink, and sex are entirely sated. (Sorry—I can't help but boast.) Still, he has a point. If bears are honest animals, animals are honest hedonists. The animal flesh has urges; the animal satisfies those urges if circumstances permit.

As a Wiccan, I'm not much on transcendence and the Christian denial of the flesh. Joy, it seems to me, should be explored here, on this physical plane, in this corporeal form. "All acts of love and pleasure are my rituals," states the Moon Goddess in Doreen Valiente's "The Charge of the Goddess," one of the primary Wiccan texts. Being a bear, for me, means respecting and answering the body and its appetites, taking full advantage of mortal existence while it lasts, and honoring the spiritual by honoring the physical. Certainly there are intellectual and spiritual pleasures—good books, thick forests, staunch friends, starlight—but these only complement the body's sensory focus rather than negating or surpassing it. I want to sip as many bourbons, devour as many doughnuts, and savor as many hairy, bearded men as my luck, chance, time, and reason allow. Skeletal, ascetic monasticism I leave to others. I am convinced that we live this earthly life so that our souls may learn; our souls experience the world through our bodily senses; our senses lead to passions; through the satisfaction and the occasional and inevitable disappointment of our passions we evolve. In other words, when I spy that bearded, hairy, brawny man on the street or in the bar and I mutter "Woof!" what I'm saying is, "Thank you, whatever gods there be, for beauty, for hunger, for the body."

THE MOUNTAINEER QUEER
PONDERS HIS RISK-LIST

"Activist." It's an odd word I'm pondering this morning at my desk in Pulaski, Virginia. How can such a word be applied to me, a college professor who has seen few picket lines and political rallies? Activism is surely about ideological battle, and there is much in my nature not cut out for such conflict. In many respects I am the polite sort my Southern mother raised me to be, the kind of man who bends over backward to avoid giving offense. I detest confrontation; it makes me squirm with discomfort. Instead, I am well practiced at putting folks at ease and adept at smoothing over social disjunctions. ("Slopping sugar," my colleague Alice Kinder would call my manipulative use of charm.)

Identifying myself as an activist at the same time that I'm going up for tenure makes me nervous. I feel confident that I've done all the right things to achieve tenure: I've published a lot (in particular a university press book, which is the kind of publication that tenure committees most respect); I've received fairly high teaching evaluations; and I've done my time on assorted committees (partly because it's the politic thing to do, partly because I have an overdeveloped sense of professional responsibility).

Friends tell me I have nothing to be concerned about, but I worry nevertheless. Perhaps being an outspoken member of two minority groups—I'm gay and Appalachian—has made me paranoid. Still, as the saying goes, just because you're paranoid doesn't mean that someone isn't gunning for you. I've received a few anonymous, hateful e-mail notes railing against the queer, and occasionally erotic, nature of my publications, though I doubt that such hysterical, reactionary objections would influence those committees deciding on my tenure bid. As part of a fairly liberal academic community, I feel insulated against attack (though I know full well that any risks I've taken have been trivial compared to some, those whose race or socio-economic status or gender behavior has worked not for them but against them). Nevertheless, with my professional future on the line, I am sharply aware of all I have done and said, in person and in print, which might be used against me.

This very day—a clear, warm day, mid-September 2006—my department's Personnel Committee is meeting to examine my long-labored-over C.V. and my several-times-revised Personal Statement. If I pass muster, there are college and university committees to come. I won't know the final decision till Summer 2007. That gives me a long time to contemplate both what risks I've taken and why.

My risk-list? I'll use here the same categories in which my above-mentioned Personal Statement is organized: creative activities, teaching, and service/outreach.

Many of my publications are intensely autobiographical, depicting a life lived far from middle-class respectability. My first book of poetry, *Bones Washed with Wine,* describes a secretive affair I had in the early nineties with a man already partnered. My second, *On the Tongue,* moves from that exciting, guilt-soused adulterous relationship to its break-up, then through the kinky promiscuities and fantasies I used to distance myself from that loss, and so on to the beginning of the solid relationship in which I find myself now. My memoir *Edge* covers similar material, along with travel essays that make explicitly clear my physical and emotional insecurities, my frustrated lusts, my occasional one-night-stands and brief affairs, and even my attraction to a straight student during a Study Abroad trip. My volume of memoir and poetry, *Loving Mountains, Loving Men,* is particularly frank about my constantly present and often barely suppressed rage at fundamentalist Christians, gay-bashers, and mountaintop removal.

And my fiction? *Devoured,* my gay-Appalachian-vampire novella (that phrase always gets a laugh at readings) and *A History of Barbed Wire,* my collection of short fiction, are both graphic in their depiction of both violence and BDSM eroticism. (That's bondage/discipline/dominance/submission/sadomasochism for you innocents.)

Despite my determination to be detailed and truthful in my writing, when I think about the possibility of my students, my students' parents, university administrators, or even the majority of my colleagues reading my work, I cringe. Luckily, few of them are likely to. There are advantages to being a not-particularly-well-known writer. Still, the work is out there for those who care to read it, and it is all part of my C.V. being examined by the Personnel Committee today. My favorite musician Joni Mitchell once said of the emotional honesty of her lyrics on the 1971 album *Blue*, "At the time I was absolutely transparent, like cellophane" (Garbarini 128). I can relate. It is hard, sometimes frightening, to be so open, especially since, instead of retreating to a more liberal urban area, I've stayed in Appalachia, where the conservative and pious would regard me as a dangerous, subversive freak. On the other hand, the literature that has most moved me and most changed the ways I look at the world has been equally frank. Art without emotional urgency and a dangerous honesty seems to me not worth the effort to create.

On to teaching, which these days means creative writing classes both introductory and advanced. At the same time that I try to make each classroom a comfortable and enjoyable space in which students might learn, I am also exceedingly open about who I am, despite Virginia's conservative political climate. Right-wingers who fear that liberal teachers might serve as dangerous role models for the young are right to worry. In fact, I have come to joke recently about attempting in my classes to "normalize the monstrous" by both who I am and what I teach.

I must appear ordinary enough, striding into the classroom with my bushy goatee, baseball cap, cowboy boots, flannel shirt, jeans, and duster. Most of my students are upper-middle-class kids from Northern Virginia's suburbs, and to them I probably come across as just another Southwest Virginia redneck. Still, even my appearance can shake up their simple categories: "The guy's a backwoods hillbilly *and* a writer/professor/scholar?" Soon enough, via my illustrative anecdotes, my students hear about my small-town/West Virginia background, my enthusiasm for country music, down-home food, and pickup trucks. Not long thereafter, with humor and an apparent casualness that conceals a deliberate calculation, I shake up their assumptions further when they hear about my partner John, or a drag queen acquaintance of mine who carries a brick in his purse, or my crush on country-music star Tim McGraw. Many of my students are simply entertained by this array of apparent contradictions. Some, I hope, learn something about how to value diversity, complexity, and nonconformity. A few, I suspect, are quietly horrified, and only my likeable nature and their grudging obedience to a prevailing political correctness keep them from complaining to their parents or campus authorities.

How I come across—my pedagogical persona—is only the beginning. Determined to teach my students not only about creative writing but about the richness of both Appalachian and Lesbian/Gay/Bisexual/Transgender literature, I supplement the exemplary works of mainstream writers in our texts with readings from mountain writers like Denise Giardina, Irene McKinney, Lee Smith, and Maggie Anderson, as well as queer authors like Andrew Holleran, Dorothy Allison, and Mark Doty. Encountering such work, the majority student's powers of empathy are, ideally, deepened, and the minority student's identity is affirmed.

Final category: service/outreach. Virginia Tech is supposedly committed to diversity, but its definition of diversity is often limited to race. My avowed purpose on any number of committees is to remind everyone that mountain kids and queer kids represent minorities often neglected, ignored, or subjected to frequent outrageous prejudice on and off campus. I supplement this crusade by giving discussions for civic groups in which I extol the richness of Appalachian writing and by organizing departmental discussions on how to incorporate both mountain and LGBT literature into class curricula.

I am, in brief, a very open, very vocal Mountaineer Queer in George W. Bush's America, in a state that will be voting this fall on an amendment that would ban same-sex marriage. Yes, I suppose the word *is* "activism," these words and acts in support of unpopular minorities, these attempts to nudge the world in the direction I want it to go by improving the lot of the marginalized. Why—I ask myself occasionally—do I—despite my precariously untenured position, despite my hatred of conflict and fear of offending—keep pushing, publishing, refusing to shut up?

Because my father, to my mother's genteel embarrassment, as early as the 1950's began attacking racism, conservatism, and fundamentalism in published op-eds and letters to the editor and continues to do so at age 85. It's a common and oft-accurate expression, the one about apples falling not at all far from the tree.

Because I have come to an age at which my mortality is ever evident, many of my long-entertained dreams are looking a mite trivial or apparently impossible, and it is increasingly clear that all I will leave behind is the hopefully salutary effect my words and deeds have had on those around me and might have on those to come.

Because, despite my Southern politeness, what Loyal Jones in "Appalachian Values" calls "personalism," the desire "to relate well with other persons" and the willingness to "go to great lengths to keep from offending others" (511), I possess an inborn Celtic orneriness that delights in going against the grain and standing up for underdogs. From an early age a King Arthur enthusiast, a devourer of heroic epics like *The Iliad* and *Beowulf,* and, more recently, Irish and Icelandic sagas, as well as battle films like *The Lord of the Rings, Troy, Alexander,* and *Gladiator,* I have a fierce and pugnacious protective streak when it comes to defending friends and relations, those I regard as members of my clan. In fact, sometimes I think my entire personality is predicated on defiance and resistance, and, had I nothing to resist, were I somehow to find myself in the privileged majority, I would lose my sense of self entirely.

Because, once, my freshman year in college at West Virginia University, a lesbian friend and I ended up in a bar-brawl with two huge homophobic thugs who, we later discovered, were a Mafioso's bodyguards. Before anyone was seriously injured, the bartender called the cops. The thugs departed. When I went to the door to stand guard—a scruffy-bearded, scrawny, bespectacled boy from a small West Virginia town who had never struck anyone—the thugs reappeared across the street and made for me. How I wanted to turn around and return to the relative safety of the bar. But I could not, for then I would have been a coward in my own eyes and in the eyes of my foes. I discovered, in those frightening seconds as they slowly approached, that I was more afraid of my own fears than of anything else. Young, prideful, and stupid? Perhaps. Luckily, when only three yards separated me from the worst beating of my life, or worse, policemen appeared, and I survived with both skull and honor intact.

Here is a secret. Under the façade of confidence and courage I cultivate along with most men, I am very often afraid. Afraid of disease, dishonor, humiliation, and a meaningless death. Afraid of my own incompetence, weakness, and gracelessness. Afraid of abandonment, confusion, the dwindling of physical and mental capacities. Afraid for the many women and men I care about. The frightened little boy is so close, so perpetually present, though few would look at my burly frame, tattooed arms, and stubble-rough cheeks (all careful camouflage) and ever suspect that child was anywhere around. I take the risks I do as a grassroots activist, writer, and teacher for two basic reasons. Altruistically, I hope to improve this world before I leave it. Selfishly, I hope to avoid the scalding self-hatred and self-contempt I would suffer if fear forced me to ignore the voices of passion and conviction and cravenly to refrain from doing what needs to be done.

WORKS CITED

Garbarini, Vic. "Joni Mitchell is a Nervy Broad." *The Joni Mitchell Companion: Four Decades of Commentary.* Ed. Stacy Luftig. New York: Schirmer, 2000. 113-133.

Jones, Loyal. "Appalachian Values." *Voices from the Hills: Selected Readings of Southern Appalachia.* Second Edition. Ed. Robert J. Higgs and Ambrose N. Manning. Dubuque, Iowa: Kendall/Hunt, 1996. 507-517.

VALHALLA IN THE REDWOODS

I

I've been devouring Nordic mythology lately: *The Poetic Edda*, *The Prose Edda, The Saga of the Volsungs*. I suppose this reading jag got started because I developed a powerful crush on Aragorn, as played by Viggo Mortensen in the recent *Lord of the Rings* film trilogy, and thus my taste for big, scruffy, bearded warriors swinging swords was sharpened considerably. Then a colleague of mine at Virginia Tech taught an independent study course in Celtic and Nordic literature, which he invited me to sit in on, and soon I was hooked. These days I'm wearing a Thor's cross around my neck and buying various *Lord of the Rings* memorabilia on-line: Aragorn's Ranger sword, his ring, and, most recently, his elven hunting knife. My partner John is accustomed to my strange enthusiasms—I also have a decent number of *Dark Shadows* collectibles—so, instead of chiding my silliness, he's helped me mount both sword and knife on my apartment wall.

I've also been writing poems based on Nordic mythology, and it's here that they begin to come in—Guerneville, a small California town on the Russian River, and its Eagle, sadly closed the last time I visited, in the summer of 2003. Believe it or not, something about that bar and that town remind this Appalachian/queer/leatherman/Wiccan/poet of Valhalla.

According to the Eddas, those prime repositories of Northern mythology, warriors who have died in battle are taken to their reward by female spirits called Valkyries, to a great banquet hall where they spend

27

the afterlife together. During the days, they fight one another, and during the nights, they feast side by side on roast boar and mead.

What's missing from this picture? I thought, reading the details in Snorri Sturluson's *Edda* and in various lays in the anonymous *Poetic Edda* while preparing to write a poem based on my own vision of Valhalla. Well, if paradise is all about finding one's pleasures in one place, then, in my version of the Scandinavian afterlife, along with fighting and feasting, there would be fucking too.

Fighting: that appeals to my violent streak, my free-floating hostility, my love of swords and dirks and punching bags, my taste for revenge, so often thwarted in this law-and-order world. It also appeals to my taste for intensity, for rough sex. I still remember the chestful of bruises a particularly tough Top left me with, during my last stay in Fife's Guest Ranch. He collared, blindfolded, and bound me, and then he worked me over with his fists. I flexed my pecs and he punched. Hard. Again and again. I was proud I could take it. Someday, especially now that I'm learning how to box, I'd like to return the favor. Touch, like a blossom, is such an evanescent thing. Touch that leaves marks? Like the purple petals of the clematis, which keep their form and their color for a good long while.

Feasting: that appeals to my big-bear/country-boy appetite. I love German and Scandinavian food, so how about that roast boar and mead to start, then maybe some *rinderroulanden*, red cabbage, or cabbage rolls, or Swedish meatballs? Maybe some starch. Potato dumplings, or spaezle, or bread dumplings? For dessert, there's apple strudel, or German chocolate cake, or Black Forest cherry cake, or Danish rum pudding. The possible menus are endless, but endlessness is what heaven's all about.

And then there's fucking: big, hairy-chested warriors going at it. In my BDSM Valhalla, there would be lots of pit-musk and beards, lots of rope and gags, some flogging and caning, hairy asses getting roughly fucked, furry nipples getting sweetly hurt, dark goatees wrapped eagerly around cocks. In fact, it's recently occurred to me, musing over Odin's battle-scarred heaven, that my idea of the perfect afterlife would involve making love to all the men I've yearned for in life but which circumstances or my own shyness and self-doubt have denied me.

Little Gisli, for instance, as I've christened a guy at my gym here in Blacksburg, Virginia. Around the time I was reading *The Saga of Gisli,* about an Icelandic outlaw who escapes his pursuers for many years, I started noticing this kid. Just the sort that brings out the Top in me big-time. Mid-twenties, I'd say. Short, about 5'8". Stocky: broad shoulders, chunky ass, thick thighs and calves. Muscular: finely formed delts, biceps and triceps, with big pecs pushing out the front of his shirt. Hirsute: golden-brown hair in his armpits when he stretches up into an overhead press; chest hair roiling over the collar of his tank top like golden smoke. Very pale, which makes the contrast between white skin and honey-colored fur all that more arousing. And scruffy, the way a Viking ought to be: little goatee, cheek stubble, a golden-brown ponytail that gleams in the harsh gym light the way new leaves shimmer in spring, the way dawn makes rich texture of pond waters. I glimpsed him naked once, in the locker room, that beautiful hair loose, falling around his white shoulders, a line of fur bisecting his slightly rounded belly, his broad white ass heading for the shower. He'd left his underwear on the bench, and to this day I regret the cowardice that prevented me from stealing a souvenir.

But I see Little Gisli in the Fallen World, the Quotidian, in the relatively small town of Blacksburg. Here we are far from Bay Area liberalism, redwoods and leather bars. Here we are embedded in the conservatism of Southwest Virginia, the mountains where I grew up and where I live still. This is the world I am long accustomed to, where the laws of probability dictate that Little Gisli is most likely straight, most likely not interested in becoming my boy. This is what makes the world fallen: it rarely accommodates our desires. I want to hog-tie Little Gisli with about ten yards of rope, wrap a few feet of bondage tape over his mouth, and spend the afternoon like an indecisive bee, moving back and forth among the honeysuckle blooms of his fur-rimmed nipples and bobbing cock while he grunts, sweats, struggles, and sighs. Later, perhaps, a position that will allow me access to his beefy butt. The kid would learn a lot from a good hard ride, from submitting to the vacillations between roughness and tenderness.

The frustrating impossibility of all this is what makes me—here, typing in Appalachia, where there are few leather bars—think of

Guerneville and its Eagle as, relatively speaking, a queer Valhalla, a Paradise of Appetite. There, such scenarios might be much more easily arranged, a leatherman's fantasies might be more easily translated into reality. Were I to meet Little Gisli, or a boy like him, in such a setting, I might be bolder, luckier, in my element. After a few bourbons, I might have him in my rented room, hands tied behind his back, on his knees, choking on my length, his long hair—color of sourwood honey—falling around his shoulders like Christ's, showers of gold, like Danae's, I gather up in my hands, praising the ways the world shares its wealth.

Others might prefer the Eagle in DC, the Eagle in Atlanta, the Eagle in San Francisco, all fine bars I have patronized and hope to see again. But for this hillbilly, that rare amalgam one finds in Guerneville—the combination of small town, countryside, and queer life, those usually mutually exclusive things I love—is as close to Valhalla as I can imagine.

I have an identity conflict. I am an Appalachian, one who loves his native region—its painful history, its flora and fauna, its dialect, its folk culture, its food. I do not want to live in a city, as much as I relish visiting them with regularity, wonderful cities like Washington, D.C, San Francisco, New Orleans, or, overseas, Vienna, Munich, Edinburgh, Athens. I love my mountains, I love the countryside. I am happiest, I think, driving alone on some Appalachian back road, in any season, with no cars before me and no cars behind, with my Major Country-Music Boyfriend Tim McGraw (please, oh please, Tim, won't you be my boy?!) on the stereo of my—yes, you guessed it—four-wheel-drive pickup truck.

But I am also a writer, a scholar, a Wiccan, a gay man, a leather enthusiast. None of these identities feels at home here in the mountains, where I have spent my life, first—as a queer adolescent—unwillingly, and now—as a man in his forties, a man who has tasted cities and preferred country—very much willingly. Still, behind my fairly content existence, there is the nagging sense that I am at home nowhere.

These are tensions that make for a richer, more complex existence than many, but they are still tensions, ones that I can escape for a few days when I visit Guerneville and its leather bars: the Russian River Eagle in 2000, the Rainbow Cattle Company in 2003. There, I find myself amidst all the disparate elements I love, so rarely found together: beautiful countryside, small-town life, queer community, and leather venues. Somewhere else, I suspect, the same unusual combination can be found, but that other place I have yet to discover.

John and I discovered Guerneville and its Eagle in July 2000. As soon as I saw the great redwoods about the town, the clear, jade-green Russian River flowing by, and the modest main street, with its odd combination of down-home establishments and upscale boutiques, I felt at home. Physically, it was somewhat like my hometown of Hinton, West Virginia—mountains, river, trees. But Guerneville's denizens were significantly more simpatico. Here was a host of fellow queers rather than the Southern Baptists that infest Appalachia and make gay/lesbian life there far more difficult than it should be.

We stayed at a gay guesthouse, Paradise Cove, up the road a little ways, where, the only apparent mid-week guests, we relished silence by the pool and the surrounding forest green before unpacking and then heading out to hit the tasting rooms of a few local wineries. Back to Guerneville for good cheap Mexican food at the Taqueria, then a drive out to the coast, along a small road that wound through the emerald light of forests, through looming redwood trunks. As we neared the ocean, the bright California sunshine was slowly eclipsed by sea mist. Jenner was entirely swathed in white fog, that tiny coastal town where the Russian River takes one last loop and empties into the booming waves of the Pacific, amid sea-stranded rock outcrops. As beautiful and dramatic a landscape as any on earth.

When we returned to town, it was time for a drink, and so we headed for the Russian River Eagle. For an Appalachian like me, it was amazing to see a leather bar right on the main street of such a small town. In West Virginia, my native state, many gays and lesbians must drive for hours to spend time with their own kind in a queer bar. Needless to say, the only queer venues are in cities like Huntington, Charleston, Morgantown, or Parkersburg. If you're into leather, there's only one in-state alternative: the Tap Room, in the state capital of Charleston. Otherwise you have to drive to DC, Pittsburgh, or Columbus, Ohio, all many hours away. Difficult to imagine, then, after a lifetime of relative isolation, how it might be to live in a scenic town where access to leather brethren could come so easily.

We entered, John fetched some beers, and we soon found a corner from which to watch the action and size up the other patrons. What I remember of the surroundings, what notes I later made in my travel journal, are sketchy. It was like the interior of many bars, and thus unremarkable. Low ceilings, dim light, too-loud music. About a third of the patrons were discernibly into leather; the rest were folks you might see in any drinking hole, clad in T-shirts and shorts. There was a smelly biker—the nasty, not the sexy sort—with a bone through his nose, talking up a hot guy with white A-shirt (fuck, those are sexy garments), tanned shoulders and arms, broad lats, and a sweet clipped-close beard I would have liked to taste. There were a very sexy man with a thick black moustache, wearing a black-leather cap and jacket, and a few beefy guys with shaved heads, dark goatees, tattoos, and hoop earrings—exactly my look—causing John to make his usual joke: "Ah, a leather bar! Where half the men look like Jeff!" (As if I need another reminder of what a clone I've become.)

I was halfway through my first Sierra Nevada when I fell in love with the bartender. Like most leather bar bartenders, he was sexy, My Type par excellence. Like most leather bar bartenders, he was bare-chested. With a chest like that, he should have been. For men like that, shirtlessness is their civic duty.

I wish my memory were clearer. I wish I had photographs, rather than these scrawled travel-notes, this vague visual that, this morning spent over my laptop, breaks free of the mud in the bottom of my brain and floats to the surface, dim, blurry-edged, translucent.

He was beautiful the way the landscape surrounding the town was beautiful. If heaven is the presence of God, then it is also the locus of the whitest light, the matrix (patrix?) of unmitigated loveliness, and so, again, the Russian River Eagle seemed like Valhalla. Or, rather, the presence of that bare-chested bartender did—in that scenic little town, among the primeval greatness of those redwoods, that clear river, those forested hills. Beauty layered upon beauty, splendor cupped inside splendor.

This litany of dimly remembered details I create with words, as I have for so many men I have seen, desired, and described, as if listing the elements of beauty might be a way to somehow possess it. Paltry possession indeed, compared with the solid, sticky facts of ravishing. So:

Honey-brown goatee. Handsome baby face. Short brown hair. Broad shoulders, tanned skin, hard-muscled arms. Big pecs and belly matted with brown fur. And, beneath that torso pelt, tattoos. Beneath his skin were parallel lengths of inked-in chain, carefully delineated links running down his torso, over his pec mounds, over his belly, finally disappearing beneath the waist of his jeans, a vanishing point that thwarted the eyes and maddened the imagination.

I must have spoken to him, at least to order a second beer. My guess is that I smiled and stammered and shyly looked away, as I—cursed with self-doubt and insecurity—always do around men I find incredibly desirable. Like Paradise, with its multifarious beauties. But not Paradise, for there, surely, I would not be paralyzed by beauty but galvanized by it, laved, immersed, adored by hirsute male houris like my goateed bartender, willing slavery etched into his chest.

I was thoroughly besotted and disturbed. Though John swears that he can look at a sexy man without the terrible urge to touch, I cannot say the same. Observing human beauty, male beauty, is instantly followed by a longing to touch, to possess entirely. To kiss, stroke, suck, bind, gag, fuck. Even in my forties, far from my hormonal peak, it is an urge that, most often frustrated by circumstance, my own shyness, or heterosexual surroundings, becomes painful, becomes a curse, reminds me of the agonizing gap between the possible and the probable, reminds me of what I must live without. After all these years of frequently futile yearning, I still cannot reconcile myself to the fact that I cannot make love to any man I want.

Distraction from that discomfort came from an unusual source. I hardly had the time to begin constructing fantasies—what, in other words, I might do to such an arousing man in the best of all possible worlds— when the karaoke began.

Karaoke in a leather bar? I was amazed, and, very soon, amused. I had never see karaoke before (or since, I might add), never seen the funny screen with the lyrics and the bouncing ball, the crazily varying range of talent, the utter lack of inhibition or shame. The contestants all seemed to be locals, none of them leathermen. A few fine voices, a few banshees that made my musically trained partner wince with pain. One of my recent favorites, Tim McGraw's "Just to See You Smile" (oh Tim, I want so badly to see you shirtless and smiling). Several good folk/rock songs I had loved in my youth and had not heard for years, like Michael Martin Murphy's "Wildfire," which I used to play pretty well on my guitar, and Jackson Browne's "In the Shape of a Heart." "Try to think of a word for the burning," sang the contestant, "I guess I never knew what she was living without," as I stared at the bartender's fur-nested nipples, at the chains beneath the chest hair.

And then a new contestant seized the mike and my brooding erotic longing was derailed entirely. He appeared to be a local favorite, for, as his name was announced, the crowd erupted with enthusiastic hoots and applause. Wanda was easily 300 pounds, easily 65 years old, with a crinkled apple-doll face and frizzy hair pulled back into pigtails. The tune, "Que Sera, Sera," instantly evoked images of Doris Day, but instead a huge wrinkled man was skipping animatedly around the bar, singing loudly (and very well, I should add), slapping leather-clad friends on the shoulders, his pigtails bouncing merrily. The contrast between the macho leather patrons and this huge, theatrically effeminate, and obviously-much-adored performer was delicious. What a myriad odd flowers in our Queer Garden.

John and I enjoyed several other songs by Wanda before the long day caught up to us and we headed back to our cabin at Paradise Cove, unfortunately without the bartender. We shared a big bed, a little single malt we'd brought along, some play with the soft black-leather straps I'd bought the day before at Mr. S in San Francisco. Cool mountain night, flickering logs in the fireplace, warm, furry bodies cuddling against one another. And, outside, towering about our brief, briefly melded lives, the redwoods, fog-shrouded, encompassing centuries.

II

TODAY IS AN UNUSUAL DAY. First I receive a note from a gay/lesbian listserv informing me that the General Assembly of the great state of Virginia, this state where I was born and where I have spent many years living and working, has just passed the "Marriage Affirmation Act," which prohibits the state from recognizing civil unions and also outlaws any "partnership, contract or other arrangements that purport to provide the benefits of marriage."

Grim, I go to class, read to my students Mark Doty's poem "Charlie Howard's Descent," about a young gay man thrown off a bridge by gay-bashers and drowned, then rein in my rage long enough to lead creative writing workshops. In between the first class and the second, I go to the bathroom, where I see FUCK YOU FAGGOTS in large letters inked on the door of a stall.

Near the afternoon's end, I guest-lecture in a course focused on "The Appalachian Family and Its Environment." As I discourse about Appalachian food and food habits, discussing brown beans and cornbread, ramps, creecy greens, and chowchow, all the regional foods I grew up on, the down-home cuisine that makes me feel safe and at home in these hills, I wonder what sort of meals the members of the General Assembly will be enjoying this evening, wonder how many of them are Tidewater bluebloods and how many of them are mountain-bred men like myself.

After that lecture, I walk back to my office, admiring a few bare-chested students playing basketball in the spring warmth. I press my face into the white, fragrant blooms of an apple tree and stand there for a while, beard nuzzling the flowers, breathing in the rich scent. I'm thinking of escape, thinking of the Celtic paradise, Avalon, the Isle of Apples, and the Nordic paradise, Valhalla, where pleasures will surround us, where every appetite will be sated only to eagerly rise again, where our enemies cannot follow us.

At home, after dinner with friends and a visiting writer's reading, I polish Aragorn's elven hunting knife, a scimitar-shaped blade etched with an elvish phrase meaning "Foe of Morgoth's Realm." My fantasies have always run toward extremes: love and death, sex and murder. The knife

is very sharp; I am a tolerably big, and, occasionally, a very angry, man.
Between the two of us, we could do some damage.

It is a warm evening. A breeze blows the gauzy curtains in. I light a
candle, strip, then lie on the bed. Tomorrow, I will drive up to Charleston
to spend a few days with John, but tonight I am alone. I place the knife
on my chest, in the patch of silvering hair between my pecs, and close my
eyes.

In middle age, reality has become decidedly unaccommodating: too
restrictive of my passions, in need of constant imaginative revision. More
and more, my writing, poetry and prose, edges toward wish fulfillment.
More and more, fantasy has become significantly more appealing, a space
with much more room for my loves and hates, much more room to swing
a sword.

So, tonight, a good crop's gathered, the heads of enemies. The elven
hunting knife comes down again and again. I toss the sticky souvenirs in
a circle, the ravens feast on the wide and empty eyes. Offerings to Odin,
the god of war.

When I sheathe the knife, I am in the Russian River Eagle again.
This is the life I would have led had I not been a homely adolescent and
thus forever handicapped with insecurity. This is the life I would have led
had I not developed such a root-bound passion for my native region, with
its blooming redbud and gold-green hills and detestable fundamentalists.
This is the heaven I have achieved like any warrior who slaughters many
foes before he himself is brought down in battle. The bartender is there,
and John, and—why not be greedy? It is, after all, Paradise—Little Gisli.
We're dancing together, all shirtless, hairy, and sweaty, and Wanda is in
the shadows, singing that anthem of fatalism, of acceptance: "Que sera
sera, whatever will be will be."

Now the walls of the bar shift, recongeal, and we four are in Cabin 7
of Paradise Cove. Wanda's invisible now, wandering out into the redwood
forest, singing, in the misty distance, Jackson Browne's "In the Shape of
a Heart." This is my heaven, so it's as kinky and fetish-full as I want it.
Little Gisli is tied to a chair: hands behind his back, thick thighs spread,
yards of white rope crisscrossing his beefy torso. His honey-blond hair
falls around his face. He's ball-gagged and groaning. Drool is dripping

from his goateed chin and pooling in the fur of his beer-belly. His long-lashed eyes are wide and eager. He's waiting his turn, watching John and me make love to the bartender.

Grettir—let's name the bartender after another Nordic outlaw, subject of another Icelandic saga. Grettir's hands are tied together, above his head, secured to the headboard. He's got a bandana knotted between his teeth and a wild look in his eyes. John lies between his widespread thighs, sucking his cock. I kiss Grettir's brow, lick his goatee. I run my fingers and my tongue over his hard nipples and then trace the chains tattooed into his torso and belly. He trembles and bucks and sighs.

John rises, nudges another log onto the fire. I take this opportunity to move between Grettir's legs, lube us up, and slide his legs over my shoulders. Behind me, the fire crackles. Grettir's eyes meet mine. He nods. Such a beautiful man, and all mine tonight. I push into him—slowly, gently. He nods again, I slip in another inch, and he groans.

Muffled by the knotted cloth, it's a long melancholy sound. It sounds like sadness, as if he's mourning the fact that our lovemaking cannot go on forever. But this is Valhalla in the redwoods, and so it can. His groan is gratitude, not grief. Grettir would thank me if he could, if I had not gagged him so tightly. But I understand. Words are archaic and unneeded in the afterlife, where consummation is continual, salvation is permanent, and union is complete.

I push in the last inch and start a slow rhythm. Grettir tugs at his bonds, slips his feet down my back, and locks his legs tightly around my waist. Here in Valhalla, we will gather all the ecstasy we ever deserved, all the ecstasy we were ever denied. We will take our time, John, Grettir, Gisli, and I, as the redwoods do in their long growth toward the sky.

COUNTRY BOYS, BUTCH QUEERS, AND
BROKEBACK MOUNTAIN

I.

Obsession feels like a great machine, a war-tank. I can feel it shifting and creaking inside, a rusty, cumbersome thing, with great wheels half-sunk in frozen mud, moving its focus from the last target to the latest, aiming the barrel of its gun, settling its inevitable sights on what must be loved, what must be possessed. Or a lens, focusing rays into a hot point that begins to smolder the surface of whatever it touches.

So I recognize the usual symptoms, and this time they are harmless enough. Certainly less harmful that the usual clumsy and destructive passions many men in mid-life entertain, the cliché of ill-advised love affairs. My latest obsession is *Brokeback Mountain*.

For a man who hasn't seen the film—which, as of this writing, mid-January 2006, just racked up several Golden Globe awards—I'm certainly a major *Brokeback* enthusiast. I have a long history of passionate obsessions, starting with childhood's rock collections, chemistry sets, and superhero comic books, and moving on to the Gothic soap opera *Dark Shadows*, the pagan religion of Wicca, and the guitar tunings of Joni Mitchell. Before I had the luck to meet my partner John eight and a half years ago, I'd collected a lengthy litany of futile and self-destructive romantic obsessions scattered over twenty years: Bob, Jack, Steve, Paul, and, most enduringly and most painfully, Thomas. Since John and I have been together, he's had to deal with my verbose passion for the *Lord of the Rings* films (in particular, Viggo Mortensen's portrayal of Aragorn), my interest in all things Celtic and Nordic (including dirks, swords, and kilts, as well as Welsh, Irish, and Icelandic sagas) and my half-tongue-in-cheek ardor for country-music star Tim McGraw (both the music and the man). Lately, I'm getting interested in another good-looking, goateed country-music singer, Chris Cagle, so John's preparing to hear all about Chris for a few months. The luckiest obsessives have abnormally patient spouses.

Still, despite my history of finely focused enthusiasms, *Brokeback* has seized me more abruptly than its predecessors. Lisa Norris, a colleague of mine who loves literature about the American West, mentioned Annie Proulx's short story to me years ago, but I never bothered to track it down. Then a student in my Fall 2005 gay/lesbian literature class, excited by the imminent release of the film, lent me *Close Range*, the short-fiction collection in which the story appears, and my haunting began. Soon after, "Brokeback Mountain," in conjunction with the film's release, was republished separately, complete with movie-poster cover image of actors Heath Ledger and Jake Gyllenhaal. Of course I had to have my own copy to reread and annotate.

The story's first scene depicts Ennis Del Mar, now a middle-aged man—about my age, I'd say—awaking from a dream about Jack Twist. Similarly, both the story and the movie images I've seen in magazines and online have leached into my subconscious. For weeks, on and off, I've dreamed of Ennis and Jack. Sometimes I'm traveling with them on horseback across the Wyoming landscape, a terrain I've seen only in films. Sometimes we travel together through my native mountains of Appalachia. Sometimes I *am* Ennis, feeling desire, fear, rage, and grief so intense that I disturb my partner with my groans and he has to shake me awake. Sometimes my dreams and sleep's-edge fantasies lean toward more erotic conjunctions. Insert here polite elision.

Other symptoms of this fascination? I've tracked down *Brokeback's* trailer on-line and gotten immediately wet-eyed. God help me when I see the actual movie. I'll no doubt be wrecked. Like most men, I'm reluctant to cry in public, but in this case I might make an exception, albeit silently and surreptitiously. I've listened to bits of the soundtrack on-line and have bought the CD, though I refuse to listen to it till I've seen the film. And I've bought a *Brokeback Mountain* movie poster for my Virginia Tech office, to join other icons—a little collection of Tim McGraw photos, a few magazines with cover pics of Colin Farrell and Viggo Mortensen. (I figure this nook of the Bible Belt needs some in-your-face queers just to keep the local conservatives from becoming too complacent.)

Brokeback has also influenced my latest reading material. The last several catalogs of the LGBT book club Insight Out have included Chris Packard's *Queer Cowboys*, an examination of "erotic male friendships in nineteenth-century American literature," so I began the year 2006 reading that. Packard's analysis of works by James Fenimore Cooper, Owen Wister, and Mark Twain appeals to what scholarly side I possess, and his discussion of male friendships in isolated natural settings of forest or prairie appeals to my long-trammeled wild side, the restless romantic that wearies of cozy hearth-side domesticity and yearns for passionate trouble and outlaw intensity in literal or metaphorical wilderness.

I'm also reading Richard Amory's *Song of the Loon,* an erotic classic I've coveted since my late teens. First published in 1966, *Loon* has been frustratingly out of print for decades. I stumbled upon a rare and thus expensive copy of one of its equally out-of-print sequels, *Listen, the Loon Sings,* in my late-seventies college days, and devoured it with horny relish. *Song of the Loon* was finally reprinted by Arsenal Pulp Press in early 2005, and so that book the young man hopelessly hankered after the middle-aged man at last possesses. It's only from the perspective of age forty-six, reading Amory's lyrical descriptions of gentle and seductive Indians making love to big, bearded, hairy trappers in wild Western landscapes, that I realize how much my youthful reading of Amory shaped my ideas of what was erotic, my expectations of what a gay man could be and where gay life could be lived. Certainly, *Loon* is pure erotic fantasy, but hope can't help but extrapolate, however likely it is that reality will disappoint.

Along with my on-going appreciation of *Loon,* which I'm savoring slowly, reluctant to finish it, I've also read an interview with Heath Ledger in *The Advocate,* an LGBT national news magazine, as well as many on-line reviews of the film, and I've collected a few magazines—*Out, Details*—with articles about Jake Gyllenhaal. In the way of an inveterate lecher, I've even searched the Internet for photos of Gyllenhaal bare-chested and have had some luck. Dark-haired men with face scruff, a little muscle, and chest hair are high on my list of aesthetic attractions, though Gyllenhaal's age—twenty-five—makes me just a little more conscious of the gray in my beard (as if someone had taken two handfuls of wood ash and playfully rubbed them into my cheeks).

Finally, in a self-shaping tradition of incorporating masculine looks I admire, I've bought two new cowboy hats from one of the three Western stores located in my area. This is hardly a radical style change for me. I spent my childhood eagerly watching TV Westerns, and during the back-road drives of my adulthood I have been kept company by many a cowboy-styled country-music singer's CD's. Since my college days in West Virginia University's forestry program, I've been wearing cowboy boots, common enough in my native hills of Appalachia, where most country boys sport the same. And I've been wearing a black straw cowboy hat on and off for about a year, influenced by my lust for Tim McGraw. (Yes, I admit, the usual consumer's silly hope: borrow the trappings, the style, and you'll somehow borrow the myth's erotic luster). For years I've dealt with male pattern baldness by shaving my head, and felt is a hell of a lot warmer on a hairless head than straw, so I've been meaning for a good while now to treat myself to a felt cowboy hat or two. *Brokeback* has given me an excuse. The brown hat's named Ennis, the black one's named Jack. By such seemingly adolescent enthusiasms, I add an ongoing vitality, an enriching variety to my life. I keep a streak of self young.

—⧖—

AS TRANSFIXED AS I AM by *Brokeback Mountain*, the film has been out for many weeks, and I still haven't seen it. It isn't coming to Pulaski, Virginia, the small Appalachian town where I moved six months ago; we don't even have a movie house here. It's playing an hour away in Roanoke, Virginia, at the Grandin, a small arts theater, but I doubt I'll make it up there. During the week I'm too busy teaching creative writing classes and attending committee meetings at Virginia Tech in Blacksburg, Virginia, and the weekends are bracketed by 2 1/2 hour drives to and from Charleston, West Virginia, where my partner John still lives. I hear that

Brokeback might make it to some cinema in Charleston. It's also likely that it will be shown at the Lyric, an historic little theater in Blacksburg, and it's in that liberal university environment that I would most prefer to see it. To be honest, I'm very reluctant to watch *Brokeback* in public. I'm afraid of my own rage, and—more pragmatic concern—I have no desire to go to jail. A prison term would not improve my chances of securing tenure at Virginia Tech.

—⁂—

MY FRIENDS IN THE OUTSIDE world—the cities of America I yearned for as a hopeful gay youth, the busy, noisy world I tried to join twenty years ago and, to my surprise, could not for long tolerate, too accustomed to the country to stand the crazy pace and the rude crowds—those friends let me know what's happening out there. No, Appalachia is not all that isolated these days—quite often I wish it were—but I'm somewhat of a media drop-out, preferring to read old adventure stories like *The Nibelungenlied* and to cook up some brown beans and cornbread rather than to watch the news or read a newspaper. Lately, those faraway friends have been telling me about the reception *Brokeback Mountain* is getting. Yes, in many settings the film has been met with lavish praise. But in other venues, in some cities and in some parts of rural and small-town America—my world, the world I am too stubborn, too ornery, too settled and resistant to change to leave—in those places my fears are sometimes being confirmed. As much as I want to see this film—and word is the DVD might not be available for home viewing till near the end of 2006, far longer than I'm willing to wait—I'm pretty convinced of the inadvisability of seeing it in a public setting.

A note from sweet cub Shane in Tallahassee, Florida: "*Brokeback Mountain* is finally here in Tally, and it's been doing well, according to a friend of mine who works at the local indie film theatre here. But he says that there have been a few people that have walked out of the theatre demanding their money back because of the gay content. I guess they thought it would be some run of the mill John Wayne-ish cowboy pic with gunfights and shit. They can't stand the idea of two cowboys making out. I think it's more the fact that they're cowboys than anything, because we see cowboys as being the man's man, but how the fuck do you define what a 'real man' is? People down here are stumping out of the movie like they didn't know what the movie is about. Even if the promo is shown ten zillion times a day, and there have been articles about it in papers and magazines, and it's only been nominated for 7 Golden Globes for fucksakes, they come out completely fucking clueless not knowing the content of the movie."

Cindy, my lesbian friend in Columbus, Ohio, tells me, "I'm not surprised about the response. Friends here tell me that some radio personality keeps insisting that they're not *cowboys* but gay *shepherds*, since there are no cows in sight. Guess that's a lot less threatening. As Gollum says, we hatessss them."

Cindy's known me since 1979. She knows better than anyone how I react to the world. Thus, she also warns, "BTW, I think your reluctance to see it in a theatre there (where you are, as opposed to in the big city) is probably smart. I'd hate for the showing to turn into a scene of mass murder (or perhaps worse, your removal from the theatre....). It's sure to be the case that teenagers and, yes, straight men will feel the need to shore up their heterosexual credentials (so fragile, so in need of shoring up) by loudly proclaiming how disgusted they are with the goings-on. Sigh. Our mothers—all our mothers—it's just what they do to protect us—would tell us to ignore them because they're just ignorant. And, of course, in this case they'd be right. Still....something to think about."

—⁓—

ANYONE WITH ANY SENSE MUST realize that we gay people are starved for literature, music, and films that reflect our experience. Surrounded by a frequently hostile majority, swamped by media that is infused with heterosexual images and values, we hanker like hell for affirming artistic mirrors of queer life. Lord knows John and I gobble up gay films all the time, courtesy of convenient mail-delivery Netflix, since such films are certainly not to be found in the local video stores in Charleston or Pulaski. These movies are frequently low budget and badly made, but an artistically inferior queer storyline is better than no queer story at all. Plus imbibing a martini or two along with the movie helps dull our critical faculties.

This need for gay narrative accounts for my initial interest in "Brokeback," but one of the more specific reasons that this country-dweller relates so much to Proulx's tale is obviously its setting. Unlike so much literature about gay life set in New York City, Fire Island, Los Angeles, and San Francisco, it reflects to some extent the world I know. No, I'm not a Westerner, and I'm not a cowboy. The horses my family owned in my boyhood were too frigging skittish for a child to ride, so, regretfully, horseback riding is not a skill I developed. But I have spent much of my life in mountainous, rural, or small-town settings, the Eastern equivalent of those in "Brokeback Mountain." (In fact, friends have recently been encouraging me to use "The *Brokeback* Angle" to promote *Loving Mountains, Loving Men,* my book about gay life in Appalachia. So far, little success on that score. America's always been more interested in fictional cowboys than real hillbillies.)

"Love is a force of nature," says the movie poster, setting Gyllenhaal's and Ledger's faces against a backdrop of snow-capped mountains, suggesting both the microcosmic natural wilderness within the human heart and the macrocosmic wilderness beyond it. Men loving men in isolated natural settings: it's the stuff of my *Loon*-influenced fantasy life. The tradition of the gay pastoral stretches back to Greek myth, to ancient writers like Theocritus and Virgil. Beefy, hairy, country boys grappling passionately in dim groves of white pine, in hay-lofts, in mountaintop red-spruce forests, in blooming rhododendron groves? Hell, yes. I certainly used to entertain such ithyphallic Arcadian fancies during my forestry-school days, tramping Cooper's Rock State Forest during dendrology field trips with my handsome, albeit sadly straight, classmates. So many of them were just my type, there were so many mossy woodland nooks just off the paths in which two lovers might hide. The greenwood, beyond society's disapproval, is, after all, where E.M. Forster sends his happily reunited lovers at the end of *Maurice.*

But Forster admits, in a "Terminal Note" to that novel, that these days there is no greenwood left to offer illicit lovers any escape. Certainly there's little to no greenwood wilderness left here in Appalachia, where

the saw-toothed greed of mountaintop removal mining is destroying the
landscape, the native folk culture is being eroded, and the outside world,
with all its technological busyness, is impinging on every side. All my
life, I have dreamed of retreating to a mountain cabin so isolated that the
abrading and homophobic world is left entirely behind, but such a retreat
I have never found. Those of us with such cravings must settle for the
occasional weekend at a rurally situated gay guesthouse.

For gay folks, even the shelter of a temporary escape into nature is
very problematic. As romantic as wilderness or woodland trysts might be,
in reality such spaces are double-edged, rife with polarized possibilities.
This occurred to me pretty vividly in the summer of 1991, when I was
having a secretive affair with another man's spouse. Thomas and I did
a lot of sneaking around to be together, hiding our passion from both
mainstream society and his suspicious husband. One afternoon, we took
a walk in some woods near Virginia Tech, and, isolated in thick summer
greenery, free of hostile eyes, I became affectionate. When Thomas
resisted for fear we might be seen, what I realized was that, to adapt Robert
Frost, there might be two roads of chance diverging in that emerald wood,
depending on whether our affections were observed and by whom. The
most likely event was what occurred: we kept our eyes and ears open, no
one else happened upon us, we held hands, I kissed and hugged on him a
little. The most extreme possibilities in that setting, we knew even then,
were idyllic ecstasy or violent death, the latter, perhaps, following closely
on the heels of the former. We could have taken the kind of crazy chance
that youth and lust are prone to, making love in that little patch of forest.
Inadvisable but tempting, the material of erotic what-could-be or, from
this distance, what-might-have-been. We could have been caught by the
wrong people in the midst of our intimacies and killed. Or, depending on
the size, strength, and number of our assailants, we could have killed in
order to survive.

My paranoia has good cause. In 1988, only a few years before that
woodland walk with Thomas, a lesbian couple was shot while camping on
the Appalachian Trail. One woman survived, one died. In 1996, another
lesbian couple was murdered in the Shenandoah National Forest. In the
Blacksburg queer community, I have heard stories about a young gay

man who was murdered on nearby Brush Mountain, a few years before I moved to the area in 1989. Word is his testicles were cut off. I don't know if that story is true, and I don't think I want to know.

Proulx is clearly aware of these extreme possibilities in "Brokeback." The pastoral mountainside where Ennis and Jack spend their summer making love is sufficiently removed from human habitation to allow them that freedom (unobserved save for one unfortunate exception). The same sort of isolation—a Texas highway in the middle of nowhere—in another part of the story allows for homophobic violence, the details of which I'll omit here so as not to ruin the story or film for those who haven't experienced them.

—m—

OTHER THAN MY TASTE FOR romantic tragedy—and what gives our puny human existence more breadth and depth?—the other reason that "Brokeback" appeals to me so grippingly is the fact that the heroes are masculine. They are the kind of man I am most often attracted to, the sort that, as a teenager looking for role models, I began patterning myself after, the start of decades of self-conscious self-shaping. Reading *Listen, the Loon Sings* in my late teens was helpful in this regard: the characters were manly without being insufferably macho. They were, in other words, men secure in their sexuality and their self-hood, rather than the insecure kind, the obnoxious, aggressive sort that makes the world difficult for everyone. Amory's trappers and Indians embodied the extremes of roughness and tenderness that form the basis of my version of Eros. The same can be said for other role models I found in the early novels of Patricia Nell Warren: *The Front Runner, The Fancy Dancer,* and *The Beauty Queen.* Strong gay characters like Harlan Brown, Billy Sive, Vidal Stump, and Danny Blackburn, fictions though they were, helped me realize early on that true masculinity encompasses gentleness as much as it does whatever violence might be necessary to protect one's self and one's kin.

Few gay characters in the Netflix films John and I have been watching lately are allowed to be manly. They can be delicate and confused adolescents, neurotic and amusing neighbors, witty and determined transsexuals and drag queens, or the urbane and helpless victims of gay-bashers. They can be kind but ineffective, beleaguered but sympathetic, successful but effeminate. These are characters I root for and admire but relate to only indirectly. The protagonists of "Brokeback" are a refreshing change of pace. I see myself in them more easily; the empathic leap is not as much of an effort.

One of the reasons Ennis and Jack got away with what they did as long as they did in rural Wyoming and Texas was their masculinity, which means their ability to pass for straight. (Whether they were indeed gay or simply bisexual I leave for others to wrangle over. They loved one another; that's all that matters.) Their sexual orientation might not have been the average man's, but their gender-role behavior was.

Pickup trucks, cowboy hats and boots, as I well know, can fool a lot of benighted folks who expect men-loving-men to sashay into a room clad in crinoline or crepe de Chine or other fancy fabrics I have heard tell of but would have problems identifying. Educated urban straights or fellow queers might pick me out in a minute as a queer leather-sex aficionado or a member of the gay bear subculture (hairy, beefy, usually butch guys who long for the same), but even in 2006, from what I can discern, many members of mainstream America unaccustomed to queers expect a gay man to be mincing, loud, garishly colorful, archly witty, and reeking with effeminacy's thick cologne. In other words, the variety one finds most often on TV and in movies. This expectation allows the rest of us to fuck around joyfully beneath the radar.

Like Jack and Ennis, what helps me survive in rural America is my ability to pass at least initially for straight. Having modeled myself on the images of Appalachian manhood I grew up around and the butch gay men I admired in Amory's and Warren's fiction, I'm a tolerably masculine guy. Yes, I love reading, music, and cooking, but so does my father, and thus my definitions of masculinity unapologetically include those activities. I suppose I've had the sense, thanks to my father's example, to sort through mainstream definitions of manhood, adopt what I've found valuable, and discard the rest. Tenderness, sexual passivity, assorted nurturing behaviors, all feel perfectly butch to me. I can cook up a pot of beef stew and bake some bread and not feel feminine. I can be the submissive partner in rough sex and still feel manly as hell. This maturity is one of the great gifts of aging: one's sense of self is less and less dictated by the narrow opinions of larger society.

Moving to Pulaski in the summer of 2005 highlighted for me how convenient it is, whatever one's private passions, to possess a conventionally masculine public persona in rural America. I've lived my last thirty years in the liberal and diverse shelter of university towns. Other than one abortive semester in Washington, DC in the fall of 1985, my adult years have been spent in rental apartments in Morgantown, West Virginia, from 1977 till 1989 and then in Blacksburg from 1989 till 2005. When John and I, tired of living apart for going on five years, decided to buy a house together near Virginia Tech, we quickly realized that we couldn't afford Blacksburg's ridiculously skyrocketing property values. However, a fine old Georgian-style house in Pulaski, thirty-five minutes away from Blacksburg, was a surprising steal, too great a deal to pass up.

Still, as I prepared to leave Blacksburg's diverse community, the thought of living in Pulaski, so much like Hinton, West Virginia, the small, economically depressed town where I grew up, was a source of some anxiety. E-mailing distant friends, I joked a lot—nervously—about the likelihood of crosses burning on the lawn and villagers armed with pitchforks, about how glad I was to own several swords. Secretly, I did expect, if not hostility, then some unfriendliness, since I had no intention, after all these years of honesty, of crawling back into the closet. Besides, I knew when John finally was able to sell his West Virginia house and move in with me, that anyone we met would realize what it was likely to mean, two middle-aged men living together.

It is in my nature to expect the worse. Thereby I hope to be prepared, to be strong enough to do what's necessary, when that worst of possibilities occurs. I have several unpleasant memories of growing up in Hinton as a bookish, timid teenager with obviously lesbian friends. There were shouted or snarled epithets, threatened or delivered-as-promised physical violence. Those events hit me (note the verb) at an impressionable age, so they have deeply colored my expectations.

But living in Pulaski for the last six months has pleasantly surprised me. It's also made me think about the ways in which conventional gender-role behavior, even when one is openly and honestly queer, encourages straight folks' acceptance. I am, admittedly, enough of my mother's son to care about such acceptance, and when, like me, one refuses to leave the rural world in which one was raised, acceptance, or at least tolerance, is crucial to comfortable survival. As I've often said, we queers can't all afford to live in New York City, Boston, Los Angeles, or San Francisco.

One of the first people I met in Pulaski was my next-door neighbor Robert. He's a local boy—well, man—about ten years older than me who grew up twenty minutes down the interstate from Pulaski in Wytheville, Virginia, a town with wide streets, handsome old buildings, and the legendary Skeeter's, a restaurant where friendly, elderly ladies call you "Honey" and serve you up exceptionally cheap and tasty hot dogs which, as far as this down-home gourmand is concerned, are another reason to remain in this area. Robert lives for the most part in the horrible maze of Northern Virginia, the suburbs of DC, but he and his wife plan to retire to their Pulaski home as soon as they can, and I don't blame them. He and I have gotten to know one another tolerably well, and we exchange meals, drinks, and coffee with regularity. On warm evenings, we sit out on Robert's patio under the stars, drink too much bourbon and tequila, and smoke too many cigars. Robert admires, envies and wants to possess my drover jacket, as well as several of my cowboy boots and hats, and I've promised to show him around the local Western stores some afternoon. For this reason, I tell my partner, tongue in cheek, that I am Pulaski's "Cowboy Fashion Plate," whose wardrobe is the envy of all local redneck boys, straight and gay, high and low.

I would call this cowboy look camouflage, and in casual public encounters—at the service station buying gas, in the municipal building paying the water bill—it is. My interactions with others in those situations are superficial and brief. But "camouflage" implies falseness, a convenient, self-protective lie, allowing a creature to survive by blending in and pretending to be what it is not. I am too convinced of the political necessity of coming out to lie.

Robert knows I'm gay. Within five minutes of meeting him, determined to start out on an honest foot, I mentioned my partner John. Yes, Robert's a Southern good old boy, but he sees enough of the same in me to have little problem accepting me. In fact, my interest in Wicca was initially more of a concern to him than my sexual orientation, before I explained the harmless nature of the religion. Were my gender-role behaviors unconventional—if he and I could not talk about pickup trucks, Harleys, cowboy boots, and other traditionally masculine interests—I wonder if we would get along as well as we do. As it is, he's been an ideal neighbor, and I look forward to sharing more bourbon-and-cigar evenings and exploring the region in his enviably humongous pickup truck. I also hope that the ways in which I do not fit the stereotype of the gay urban effeminate might shake up his and others' expectations, help them realize how complex and diverse the gay community can be. I remain hopeful that it's this kind of quiet grass-roots activism that can make a lot of political difference in the long run.

Mizz Donia, four houses up the street, who met me one evening at Robert's—she'd brought a pecan pie by for us to devour—during this last holiday season invited both John and me to her huge neighborhood Christmas party. "Hope you and your partner, whom I've not met, can stop in for a while. We look forward to seeing you," read her e-mail note. She knew exactly what sort of men we were, and so, I'm guessing, did several other people at that party, for word gets around fast in a small town. No one batted an eye, though I could feel polite curiosity—"Ah, so these are the gay guys we've heard tell of." One neighbor shook our hands warmly and said, "Welcome to Old Pulaski!" which felt like an official acceptance to the neighborhood. It's difficult to explain how cherished and welcome such kindness is when one moves to a new place, full of anxiety, fearing the worst, unsure of how minorities might be greeted. When I met the black couple that lives three houses down from us, I really began to relax.

I'm guessing several things have been working in John's and my favor. Part of the kindness we've encountered has been due to the natural Southern sweetness of our neighbors, and part of it has been the fact that I share with them many small-town/country/Appalachian/Southern values.

(John's a Yankee, but since he's with me, other Southerners assume he must be okay.) My neighbors find it easy to be good to me, because I am more similar to them than I am different. Certainly the ways in which John and I live up to conventional gender-role expectations are also an advantage. We are not the flamboyant gay stereotypes that the uninformed expect or fear. Such folks seem to find it easier to accept masculine men, whatever their sexual orientation.

In fact, sometimes I think what offends rabid homophobes the most is not queer fucking but effeminate behavior. I am very lucky, Proulx's Ennis and Jack were very lucky in this regard (though their story is evidence of how often luck runs out and camouflage has its limits). When I think about effeminate men anywhere, transsexuals and drag queens, when I meet them and hear their painful stories, I shudder at how difficult their lives have been, how much stronger and tougher they must be than I. Even straight men whose behavior is regarded as insufficiently manly are cruelly mocked, or even attacked by brutes not intelligent enough to distinguish gender-role behavior from sexual orientation. Recently I was told that a young straight man at Virginia Tech was beaten so badly he was taken to the hospital. His crime? His attacker thought his hat was "too gay," meaning, I guess, less than manly. Anyone who wore such headgear, the cretin assumed, must be queer.

Compared to these men's lives, my path, I know, has been an easy one. My relative masculinity minimizes my difference, thus making me less repulsive to those disturbed by difference. At the same time that my attraction to and emulation of traditional male signifiers and behaviors have been a blessing, for a long time I secretly thought that my own manliness, because it has been so carefully constructed, so deliberately modeled after others, was therefore false. Then I stumbled upon queer theory and its concept of gender as performance. What this idea made me realize was that all men are performing some version of gender, that my version is no less authentic for being more self-conscious. Most other men simply don't realize they're performing.

—∭—

So, MASCULINITY IN GAY MEN makes them more palatable to heterosexuals? Most of the time, I'm guessing. But not always.

To repeat part of my friend Shane's e-mail comment about negative audience reaction to *Brokeback Mountain*: "They can't stand the idea of two cowboys making out. I think it's more the fact that they're cowboys than anything, because we see cowboys as being the man's man, but how the fuck do you define what a 'real man' is?" When I reported this to my partner, he told me that some conservatives somewhere were up in arms about the movie because they claimed that little boys admire cowboys as male ideals, and seeing two gay cowboys would encourage those children to turn queer. Here gay masculinity is regarded as dangerously appealing. As usual, the Religious Right's rhetoric suggests that homosexuality is so headily intoxicating that any child, given half a chance, will succumb to the sinister siren of sodomy and start vigorously sucking cock in public restrooms or—to use a pastoral image more appropriate to this essay— within the nearest grove of trees.

What we see here is the butch queer as more frightening and more dangerous than the queen. From this viewpoint, as long as gay men are silly mincing faggots, they're contemptible but dismissible; they are exactly what's expected. One can "spot them from a mile away," and take sufficient precaution. But if they're butch—monsters that blend in, that appear normal, monsters whose unnatural appetites are not at first discernible—that makes them dangerous. Plus their masculinity means power, and power means threat.

I was pleased to see an eloquent affirmation of my suspicions in the November 22, 2005 issue of *The Advocate*. Richard Goldstein, in his fine essay "Fear of Phallic Queers," points out that queer characters, male and female, are not allowed in films "the virtuous aggression [which is] the signifier of heroism in our culture. This is a myth of valor we are denied." He complains, "I've yet to see a genre movie in which a gay man plays a paladin protecting the innocent." "Why are there no queer top-gunners?" he asks. "Why do we never get to mow down the enemies of freedom?

Why are we not even shown walking large dogs? Because of heteros' fear
of the phallic queer, the homo who can love *and* fight."

—ɯ—

TRYING TO UNDERSTAND MY RECENT obsession with "Brokeback Mountain"
and reading Goldstein's essay have helped me make sense of many of
my odd enthusiasms mentioned earlier in this essay. What they have in
common might be obvious to any intelligent and interested outsider, but
sometimes we are the last to comprehend the consistency of our own
obsessions. I grew up reading Arthurian romances, *The Iliad* and *The
Odyssey*. As an adolescent, I was always bugging my father to stop by
Butler's Pharmacy so I could pick up the latest issues of Marvel Comics
like *The Avengers*, *The Fantastic Four*, or *Thor*. In the last three or four
years, I've been excited and delighted by the movie version of Tolkien's
trilogy, as well as the *X-Men* films, *Gladiator*, *Alexander*, and *Troy*. I've
read Celtic and Nordic literature, relishing Irish tales about the warrior
Cuchulain and Icelandic sagas full of swordplay and Viking adventure.
Just recently I've bought Seamus Heaney's new translation of *Beowulf*
and am sure to savor it.

The common thread is heroism. Which is to say, turning one's energy
toward smashing injustice and protecting what one loves. It's not an
unusual male preoccupation. There was much talk of the concept in the
days after 9/11. It is perhaps an unusual preoccupation for a gay man, a
poet, an English professor. But heroism is feeling more and more needed
here in Bush's America, with the Religious Right in a position of power it
has never enjoyed before; in Appalachia, where the ubiquitous presence
of intolerant Christian fundamentalism makes it difficult to be gay or
lesbian; and in Virginia, where legislators have passed one of the most
virulent laws in the nation against same-sex marriage. They have also
tried, so far without success, to pass laws against gay/straight alliances
in high schools and against gay and lesbian adoptions. Less than a week
ago, ironically on Martin Luther King Day, the members of the General
Assembly were busy trying to pass a constitutional amendment that
would further outlaw same-sex marriage. As of this writing, it looks as if

the issue will now be voted on by the citizens of Virginia. [December 29, 2008—This amendment was passed in November 2006.]

These homophobic measures arouse in me a rage I find it difficult to express; a rage I find it harder and harder to turn to positive use; a rage that, when it ferments and rots without constructive outlet, so often metamorphoses into despair. For years I have defended my native regions, Appalachia and the South, from their detractors, trying to convince people of the richness of our culture, arguing that we are not backward rednecks. I'm tired of expending my energy on that defense. I feel betrayed by my own homeland, fearful of what the future might bring the LGBT community.

More and more, it is clear that My Queer Clan is under mounting attack. Though I have not personally faced direct expressions of hatred for many years, other than a few hostile e-mail messages, it exists very close to home, or, rather, close to work, for antigay behavior is on the rise at Virginia Tech, despite the many attempts of administrators and committees to squelch it. Queer students come to me with reports of mockery and abuse that madden me. I have little in the way of parental instincts—children generally get on my nerves—but in this case, I feel as if these LGBT kids are children of mine who are in danger and whom I cannot adequately protect.

And so it is that a fascination with warriors and with heroism, with masculinity and with strength, is my quirky response to this state of siege. Living in America these days feels like war for many queer men and women, and war requires courage, sometimes physical, more likely emotional, spiritual, and political. Jack and Ennis, the heroes of "Brokeback Mountain," were emotionally heroic enough to continue their dangerous and passionate connection, strong enough to take the chances they took. In some settings, feeling anything radically unconventional and acting upon those feelings is heroic. The tragedy of their particular story is that Ennis was not brave enough, and he paid for that with the greatest loss and the greatest regret.

Watching Aragorn sword-slice orcs in *The Fellowship of the Ring* and reading Sigurd's exploits in *The Saga of the Volsungs*, I am on some level preparing to protect myself and those I care for against what feels like an increasingly hostile world. The battles I fight, like most conflicts in the early twenty-first century, are not physical. My several swords are decorative. They, and I, may lust for blood, but law, order, and the complexities of conscience prevent us from slaking that thirst. My weapons are honest speech, as I teach, as I publish. I have little to no experience as a brawler or street fighter. However, I suppose there is the small, unlikely possibility that, as open as I am in Southwest Virginia, I might be ambushed by a passel of homophobic bastards some night, too many for me to handle, big and angry as I am, and in some spot too far from habitation to summon help. There are worse ways to die, far more painfully drawn out, pointless, and trivial. I hope that, inspired by the heroic literature and films I've cherished, I will conquer fear. With luck, I'll drive my assailants off. At the very least, I'll take a few of the motherfuckers down with me. Certainly I pray that I am able to hold them off long enough for anyone who is with me to escape. And, at any rate, unlike Ennis Del Mar, I have lived my loves to the fullest and so, however I leave this world, I will not have to suffer his terrible regret.

—∭—

IT WAS IN A FICTION workshop I was teaching a few years back that I was first able to articulate my greatest fear. In response to a suggestion in our textbook, I asked the students to write an in-class paragraph about what they most dreaded. As they wrote, I thought. When they were finished, in order to encourage honest responses, I went first.

Only the week before, I had seen the film *Troy* and had waxed lustfully ecstatic over Eric Bana's black-bearded portrayal of Hector, so that story and that actor were on my mind. As a gay man, I naturally should have sided with Achilles and Patroclus (though their erotic relationship was carefully excised from that film). But it was Hector I sympathized with, partially because I was so enamored of Bana, partially because Hector's fate is my greatest fear. He knows that all that stands between his land, his city, his family, his kind and total destruction is his strength and valor. He "wields weapons righteously," to use Goldstein's phrase from the "Phallic Queers" essay. But Hector's heroism is not enough. Though he has done his best, he has failed, and, because of that failure—I can see the fact in his amazingly handsome face as he drops to his knees, pierced through by Achilles' sword—as he dies he knows that all he loves will soon be destroyed. It seems to me one of the most agonizing ways to perish, with such a realization as one's last conscious thought. This is, I think, the fate I am trying to circumvent as I scrutinize heroes' exploits on the screen and the page. Surely, if I make myself as hard and as brave and as strong as possible, my efforts to defend what I believe in and whom I care for will be more effective, less futile. I will be never be as hard and strong and brave as Hector—I am a husky, middle-aged, slightly muscular university professor—but I must do what I can with what I have and hope I am luckier.

—⁕—

TODAY, ACCORDING TO THE VIRGINIA Tech LGBT Faculty/Staff Caucus listserv, *Brokeback Mountain* will begin playing at a theater in Christiansburg, just down Route 460 from Blacksburg. A group of local queers might go together. That would be the best option: safety in numbers. What bitter irony, to worry about homophobic audience reaction while watching a film that depicts how fear of homophobic violence thwarts love and starves hearts. I so well remember when *Making Love*, one of the first mainstream films to deal with gay subject matter, made it to Morgantown in 1982. How delighted my friends and I were finally to see gay life reflected in film. That exuberance was short-lived. When the male leads got intimate, the primarily straight audience exploded with disgust. "Oh, fuck! Sick! I'm gonna puke!" Much younger, much smaller, much more timid than I am now, I sat there frightened, seething with hatred, afraid to say anything, praying that they'd shut up. I was not strong; they were too many. I despised my own fear as much as or more than I despised them. Sometimes it seems to me that everything I have ever done or said has been a way of dealing with my own fear, passivity, and cowardice.

—ᴍ—

I'VE BEEN BROODING ON A few quotations while I wait to see if or when LGBT Caucus members decide to attend *Brokeback Mountain* en masse.

Shane says, "That's one thing about our community, we can be so fucking passive while heteros get to stomp our fucking nuts both physically and politically. I mean, shit, there's a breaking point."

In a recent e-mail note from Equality Virginia, an LGBT political organization trying to create positive change in our embarrassingly conservative state, I read a quotation from Martin Luther King: "Our lives begin to end the day we become silent about things that matter."

Richard Goldstein says, "In enlightened movies we're allowed to be complicated—but not valiant. . . We pay a price for this omission. It reinforces the belief that we can't defend ourselves. When we internalize that message, we become the fairies we are meant to be. Straight men can rest easy; the phallic queer remains repressed."

"Brokeback Mountain" ends with this wonderful line: "If you can't fix it you've got to stand it." True enough. That's the sort of countryside stoicism and fatalism most Appalachians grow up on. But sometimes you *can* fix it, or, at the very least, try. That's what courage is about: taking risks in order to fix things. When I finally make it to *Brokeback Mountain*, I will be wearing shit-kicker boots just in case. I don't know if the contemptuous jeers and snickers I'm dreading will begin when Jack and Ennis make love. But if they do, I am confident of one thing: I will not be silent.

II.

THE BOOTS ARE ROUGH, DARK brown leather, with steel toes. In fact, it even says "STEEL TOE" in small bright yellow letters on the side of each boot. Not the kind to wear through airport security—they take too long to unlace. Yet security was on my mind when I wore them at Park Place Stadium Cinemas in Charleston, West Virginia, the day my partner John and I finally saw *Brokeback Mountain*.

On February 2, 2006, a teenager attacked patrons of a gay bar in New Bedford, Massachusetts. On February 4, 2006, I sat in the cinema dark, wearing not the cowboy boots I usually wear, the kind most appropriate to the film, but the heaviest work boots I own, the sort I always wore on those evenings in the late '70's when I attended meetings of the gay and lesbian student group at WVU, hoping to be prepared if any frat guys showed up with baseball bats.

I sat against the back wall, waiting for the film to begin, nervously chewing on handfuls of John's popcorn. We were, from what I could tell, the only gay couple in the place, and the audience was far larger than I would have preferred. Every man who entered the room I sized up as a possible opponent. (I don't always expect the worst but I'm always trying to prepare for it.) The audience at that 3 pm showing, I noted with cautious optimism, was composed for the most part of the middle-aged and elderly. No young men twice my size who might throw me against the wall, if push literally came to shove.

John, bless him, though he knew exactly what I was thinking and fearing, seemed as calm as ever. (How does one set up house on the rim of a volcano? Ask him.) He hadn't read the story as I had, but surely he could gauge when Jack and Ennis were about to grow intimate, because those were the spots where I sat on the edge of my seat and tensed up, waiting for the snickers or the jeers to begin, ready to leap from my seat and pick a fight.

My country brothers made love in their high-mountain tent. They kissed violently after four years apart. They sprawled naked in a motel bed together, delighting in their reunion. And that Charleston audience was absolutely silent.

When the film ended, I was of course quietly wrecked. *Brokeback Mountain* embodies almost all of my issues and most of my fears. But, as weak as I was with relief—no fisticuffs necessary, no jail term for me as yet—I was also welling with gratitude. As John drove us home to martinis (that evening required several) and slow-cooked Hungarian goulash, I was more thankful than ever to have him beside me and to live and work in places where we are for the most part accepted. Whatever the future brings us, we have escaped the bleak fates, the half-lived lives of Jack and Ennis.

And I was thankful for the respectful silence of that audience. Perhaps the world has changed for the better since those contemptuous shouts met *Making Love.* Perhaps it was simple luck to share that particular showing of the film with those who were my age or older and thus less likely to behave badly in public. Perhaps Charleston is more a bastion of liberals than I imagined. Perhaps the past has warped me so badly that I can't believe in human goodness when it takes my hand.

I'm not ready to make any of those generalizations. I only know that *Brokeback Mountain* is one of the great movies of my life, and that I will always remember that, the first time I saw it (for you can be sure I will soon own the DVD and in future years will watch it again and again), those with whom I experienced that story recognized love and tragedy and met those eternals, those immensities, with the silence witness they deserve. That other immensity, hate, which so shapes the fears I share with Jack and Ennis, was not among us in that darkened room, on that winter afternoon.

"TILL THE DUCTILE ANCHOR HOLD":
AN APPRECIATION OF APPALACHIAN FOLK CULTURE

(for Elizabeth Fine)

WHITMAN'S SPIDER

I'm reading Walt Whitman. It's August of 1982: very hot in the second floor apartment of 715 Willey Street. Franny and I are both students, and neither of us can afford an air-conditioner. I sit by the kitchen table in cut-off denim shorts and drink cheap beer, leafing through *Leaves of Grass*, preparing for the grad classes to come.

> A noiseless, patient spider,
> I mark'd where on a little promontory it stood isolated,
> Mark'd how to explore the vacant vast surrounding,
> It launch'd forth filament, filament, filament, out of itself.
> Ever unreeling them, ever tirelessly speeding them.

"A Noiseless, Patient Spider" is one of my favorite poems, the one my present sense of isolation most directly relates to, along with some of the more hopelessly yearning pieces in "Calamus." I've spent the summer chasing a charming, red-moustached bartender whose beauty's been shared with half of Morgantown and who, after a few moist nights together—hosta lilies opening beneath the bedroom window, the wood thrush calling in morning fog—has little further interest in me. I'm about to begin graduate school in English at West Virginia University—a desperate attempt to translate at least some of my interests into eventual employment—and I'm dreaming of moving to Washington, DC once the degree is won. There, perhaps, I will belong better. I am twenty-three, and the wider world calls me—big cities, foreign countries, cultural and romantic opportunities. I cannot be fully myself around my family or in Hinton, my small West Virginia hometown. Perhaps in the DC gay community of Dupont Circle, I will lose this loneliness, the loneliness of Whitman's spider, seeking ceaselessly for something to connect to, for something to confirm identity, to locate home.

—◊◊—

ALL THROUGH MY CHILDHOOD I have loved the sound of trains. A sweet sound to fall asleep to, like rain on the roof, or the rushing white water of the New River, just below my parents' house. This particular twilight, however, I am on a train as it skirts that same river, among slate-gray, December-bare trees. After just over three months of teaching part-time at George Washington University in DC, I have returned to Hinton. My colleagues at the university were cold and rude, the city traffic was annoying, good manners rare, good barbeque not to be found. My shy Southern ways allowed me less love-luck in the city than they did in Morgantown. I stood in the corners of bars, watching beauty pass but completely lacking the aggressive confidence to approach it. The entire autumn of 1985, I missed the mountains and my family—ironic fact, considering all the effort I'd mustered to escape them. What I'd found in the city was not a home, but the "vacant vast surrounding" of Whitman's poem. What Amtrak was returning me to was Appalachia, a place in which I, with my particular passions, would never entirely belong. Nevertheless, it was a place I would have to make my peace with, a culture I would have to reconnect to. Otherwise, I would belong nowhere. I would wither, like a weed uprooted and tossed onto asphalt.

—◊◊—

IN THE SECOND AND FINAL stanza of "A Noiseless, Patient Spider," Whitman's extended metaphor comes clear:

And you O my soul where you stand,
Surrounded, detached, in measureless oceans of space,
Ceaselessly musing, venturing, throwing, seeking the spheres
    to connect them.
Till the bridge you will need be form'd, till the ductile anchor hold,
Till the gossamer thread you fling catch somewhere, O my soul.

A gay man in the nineteenth century, Whitman would inevitably ponder the "measureless oceans of space," silence and secrecy that detached him from mainstream society. A gay man in twenty-first-century Appalachia, I sometimes muse on the same. More often, however, the filaments, the ductile anchors that keep me alive, relatively content, and still living in this region are the aspects of an abundant folk culture that remains in the mountains. My approach to this folklore is, for the most part, personal, passionate, emotional, not primarily intellectual, since, as a poet, I focus on feeling—the learning of the heart, not the head. Folk culture allows me to connect my own experience and history with that of my family, of the region, and eventually—a sense of relevance widening like the rings inside trees—with other places and even other times.

YOKING THE HORSES

Spring 1995. After several years of teaching at Virginia Tech, I am assigned, thanks to a colleague, Elizabeth Fine, my first section of Introduction to Appalachian Studies. My gratitude is great, for each section of Appalachian Studies allows me to escape an onerous section of freshman composition. As the semester progresses, as the duties of teaching encourage me to examine my region intellectually, I only appreciate Appalachia more, just as, in forestry classes at West Virginia University, I loved woodland more with each new tree I could identify. The head and heart, so frequently foes, in educational endeavors are often yoked together, the white horse and the black horse of Plato's *Phaedrus* friendly, complementary for once.

Then one day it arrives in my office mail, the desk copy of a book I never ordered, I never asked for. I've heard of Jan Harold Brunvand before; I've browsed a few books of his on urban legends, books with memorable titles like *The Choking Doberman, The Mexican Pet,* and *The Vanishing Hitchhiker.* This one's *The Study of American Folklore: An Introduction.* Browsing it brings a forceful realization: what I love most about the region, other than the literature, is the folk culture. And odd to see, in Brunvand, details of daily living I'd grown up with and taken for granted as nothing special, now preserved, honored, and analyzed in a book. Odd to see the foods, the sayings, the songs, the tales, neatly categorized into oral, customary, and material folklore, then connected to lore from other eras and other lands.

SLICKY SLIDES AND CORN SONGS

Oral folk culture, Brunvand starts with. Mentifacts, a highfalutin word indeed. And speaking of the expression "highfalutin," Brunvand has a lot to say about folk speech. When you spend your entire life in the same region, with only the occasional vacation into the outside world, you forget that the way you talk is not found everywhere. When you meet outsiders, the fun starts. Or the mockery.

"Juberous" is a word my great-grandmother used and one I have since adopted as a colorful substitute for "dubious." My Aunt Doris used to say "boosh" and "feesh." An undergraduate friend used to beg me to say "can't," which comes out of me as "cain't (and if it's good enough for Tim McGraw and Brooks and Dunn, it's good enough for me). Then there's "slicky slide," which my students howl over. "Pen" versus "pin" (pronounced the same, of course). And the dead giveaway, the sound I make which convinces the more stereotype-bound of my Northern students that I've got to be a incestuous racist: that vowel sound in "my," "eye," and "pie." The accent comes and goes, softening in more formal social settings, deepening when I'm excited, angry or amorous. Or when I'm around folks who sound the same. So often, meeting other mountaineers or Southerners, up North, out West, or overseas, I hear those accents and feel an immediate bond. I relax, my usually aloof demeanor warms, and my native accent waxes anew. Whether speaking in Piccadilly Circus, on the Acropolis, or on a Swiss mountainside, our words wrap aural wisps of home around us.

—⟋⟍—

THE GREATEST POEM, I'VE ALWAYS said, is the cycle of the seasons. The majesty of this eternally recurring epic is one of the reasons I'm dedicated to Wicca, a faith greatly focused on seeing the divine in the natural world and in the changes that flicker over the planet as one season grades into another. So much of folklore is seasonal, and knowledge of that folklore encourages us to pay attention to the present, to the beauty of the seasons, rather than ignoring that beauty in favor of increasing our efficiency or brooding on the past and the future. In this respect, I think of Ralph Waldo Emerson in "Self-Reliance": "These roses under my window make no reference to former roses or to better ones; they are for what they are; they exist with God to-day. There is no time to them."

—⟋⟍—

"YOU SHOULD PLANT CORN WHEN the white oak leaves are as big as squirrels' ears," my father says. It's been a while since I've gotten close enough to a squirrel to carefully study the size of its ears, but this week the new gray-green leaves of the oak seem to be about right. Daddy has plowed a straight furrow (yes, I'm an adult who calls his father "Daddy"—it's a Southern tendency), and now we drop in the seeds, three or four at a time.

Years later, I run across Louise McNeill's poem "Mountain Corn Song," and there it all is. " Oak leaves are big as a gray squirrel's ear / And the dogwood bloom is white . . ./ Four bright grains to each sandy hill / With, *'One for the beetle and one for the bee / One for the devil and one for me.'*" The shard of folklore that McNeill echoes is a well-known planting rhyme, according to Brunvand: "One for the blackbird / One for the crow," reminding me of the constant fight with wildlife every countryside gardener wages.

We Appalachian writers are wise to incorporate folk culture into our works: all that richness to be borrowed from the public domain with no paying for permission. Readers from the region immediately identify with such work. Why such folklore-imbued literature is not more often taught in Appalachian schools, I don't know. What other writing would feel more relevant to mountain kids? For the most part, it is that very inclusion of folklore that makes it relevant, that allows students to "connect the spheres" (using Whitman's phrase), to link the literature they're reading and the lives they're leading. What all readers yearn for, consciously or unconsciously: to see their experience mirrored in literature and thus affirmed.

DEEPENING THE DAILY

I STILL HAVE A DOG-EARED paperback of Edith Hamilton's *Mythology*. It was one of my favorite books in childhood, as were *The Iliad* and *The Odyssey* and other collections of Greek myth. These days, along with poetry by Virgil, Hesiod, and Ovid, I'm avidly reading Celtic and Nordic myths, those descended from the various blood lines I've inherited, ancestries common in Appalachia: English, German, Scottish, Irish. I've spent the last year poring over tales about the Tuatha De Danann, Thor, Odin, and Loki. Strange parallels occasionally crop up. For instance, the theme of "The Unquiet Grave," an Appalachian folk song, is perfectly embodied in "The Second Lay of Helgi the Hunding-Slayer," a poem found in *The Poetic Edda*.

Reading myths shifts one's perspective, opens one's eyes to natural phenomena one might otherwise ungratefully take for granted. This summer, after browsing Ovid, when I walk through my father's corn patch, enjoy his corn on the cob, or pour sorghum onto a slice of his cornbread, I can't help but think of Demeter, the Greek goddess of agriculture, and the search for her lost daughter Persephone, a tale which seeks to explain the seasons, the eternal shifts from fruitfulness to barrenness and back again. I also think of myths closer to home, having heard a few Cherokee stories about Selu the Corn Mother, from whose side kernels of grain fell forth to feed her family, from whose dead body crops of corn sprang up.

The greatest gift of myth is the depth it adds to the daily, the sense of mystery, of divine immanence, it evokes. Under the gaze of a mind imbued with mythology, the prosaic solids of the world smolder at the edges with a sense of the sacred. When I see the moon rise over the line of pines behind my house, I think of the Roman Diana, the Welsh goddess Cerridwen. When a summer storm rolls in, I put on my Thor's cross, a miniature hammer meant to represent Mjolnir, the Nordic thunder god's weapon. When I drink a beer, I think of John Barleycorn, subject of a British folksong, descendant of any number of sacrificed vegetation gods. When I sip wine, I remember Dionysus, Greek god of intoxication and ecstasy. When I lift weights or take a shower, I study the tribal tattoo on my left shoulder, the bearded face and antlered forehead of Cernunnos, Celtic god of forests and male energy. When I admire a statue or a painting of Christ, I remember the dying Adonis or the murdered Osiris. When I see a handsome muscular man, I think of the Greek hero Hercules, or the ithyphallic chalk carving of the Giant of Cerne Abbas in Dorsetshire, England. Spirit is always there, waiting to be sensed and honored, flickering just beneath the surface of things.

THE LADY OF THE LAKE

EARLY MORNING, BROAD DAYLIGHT, BUT the ghost taps my guest bed nevertheless. I'm visiting some friends in Roanoke, and we're all sleeping late after a Friday night out. I wake to the tapping, the odd nudging beneath the bed. An occult enthusiast but skeptical nevertheless, I get up to peek beneath the mattress, expecting one of Keith and Tony's pets to be responsible. No such explanation. Over breakfast, Keith explains that his old friend Rick, who died of AIDS several years ago, haunts the house, turning on lights, patting guests' shoulders, tapping on furniture. "He's completely harmless," Keith promises, spooning me up some grits.

We love ghost stories because we enjoy the adrenaline that intense feelings like fright can summon, because we want to believe that the world is more than it seems, because, in a universe whose details are so often accounted for by science, we long for a sense of mystery. In a world full of flux, memento mori, we cling to the comforting idea of an afterlife. When I read about the ghost in Abingdon's Martha Washington Inn, or the avenging ghost of Zona Heaster Shue, when I attend ghost tours in New

Orleans, Williamsburg, and Charleston, South Carolina, I can't help but connect those tales to my own weird experiences: that tapping under the bed in Roanoke, that sighing that disturbed Franny and me at 715 Willey Street the summer of 1982, or the weird incubus-like weight I've felt on my chest after midnight at intervals throughout the last decade.

Every locale has its own ghost. My home county of Summers has the Lady of the Lake (with apologies to Arthurian legend). Teenagers, smoking pot down by the Bluestone Reservoir, used to tell the tale till their heads spun with paranoia. It happened in the forties, so the story goes. The Bluestone Dam was built, the water backed up, but she refused to leave her land, despite official attempts to recompense or remove her. She sat on her front porch, rocking in her rocking chair, shotgun still in hand, as the water rose up around her ankles, her shoulders, and so on up to swallow the house. To this day, it is said, she can be seen emerging from the water, lantern in hand, interrupting the marijuana hazes and heavy-petting sessions along the lakeshore.

GIVE ME A BOAT

I HAVE COME BY IT indirectly, my love for ballads and the more mournful Appalachian folksongs. Oddly, it was mainstream sources like albums and textbooks that introduced me to this music, not true folk transmission, which is oral. In the mid-seventies I fell in love with the music of Joni Mitchell, and, as a consequence, taught myself to play piano, guitar, and lap dulcimer. It took me a while to realize that the reason Joni played dulcimer was because the folk singer Jean Ritchie had popularized that native Appalachian instrument in the mid-sixties. Now, along with Joni classics like "A Case of You," I strum a decent dulcimer version of "Poor Wayfaring Stranger," complete with Joni-style percussive slaps, as well as "Amazing Grace," the song my grandmother used to play with gnarled hands on her piano.

Then there's "Pretty Polly," a lugubrious song by Judy Collins, which I've come to discover is what folklorists call a murder ballad. And "Barbara Allen," which turns out to be a British import that Samuel Pepys listened to in London in 1666, I discovered while listening to an album by Joan

Baez. "Edward," sung by Jean Ritchie, I read in my first undergraduate British literature class. "The Water is Wide," one of my specialties on the guitar, I first heard in a Morgantown coffeehouse, later on a Karla Bonoff album, still later in a Scottish pub, and finally found printed in a collection of folk songs.

> The water is wide, I cannot cross o'er,
> And neither have I wings to fly.
> Give me a boat to carry two,
> And both shall row, my love and I.

I cherish this music for the same reasons past generations have. Like good poetry, such songs reduce our isolation. They give us a context in which to understand our own rapture, loss, hatred, and heartbreak. They give us boats to cross the wide water between Self and Other.

JEWELWEED SALVE AND WOOLY WORMS

THE SECOND CATEGORY OF FOLK culture Brunvand describes as sociofacts—customary behavior. I flip through his chapter on superstitions and folk cures, or examine such classics of West Virginia folklore as *Witches, Ghosts, and Signs* by Patrick Gainer, and the words of many loved ones, living and dead, come back to me.

We're driving from Hinton to Lewisburg down a back road lined with pastures when my sister points out the local livestock and predicts the weather. "Before noon, and the cows are lying down. That means it'll rain today." By the time we settle into a restaurant for lunch, the downpour begins.

My father and I are raking leaves when we find a wooly worm slowly making its way across the grass. These caterpillars are usually black and brown, but this one is entirely black. "Bad winter coming," my father opines.

My boyfriend and I are hiking around Long Branch Lake at Pipestem State Park when he brushes poison ivy, a plant I know by sight after a countryside childhood, but which he, a native of Daytona Beach, has problems recognizing. Jewelweed, my aunt had advised. Fortuitously, it's growing nearby with its orange-red flower spangles. I crush the leaves and spread the juice on his skin.

I don't have cable these days. What I miss most, other than *The Simpsons*, is the Weather Channel. But I well remember my grandmother reciting that well-known piece of weather folklore about "red sky in morning, sailor take warning." Today, the English teacher takes warning as he peers out the bathroom window at a crimson sunrise and decides to take a sweater and an umbrella. It's a saying that most often is accurate.

Folk medicines and omens—whether involving good luck, bad luck, or weather conditions—appeal to our craving for control, obviously. In a universe in which little can be either controlled or predicted, these superstitions assure us that order can be found, causal connections can be detected. Such folk beliefs are comforting, encouraging us to believe that misfortune can be prepared for or even averted, that knowledge really can be power.

Folk religion is another matter. As a sexual nonconformist growing up in rural West Virginia, I've developed a rabid detestation for most versions of fundamentalist Christianity, regarding such people with the same distrust, contempt, and downright hatred that they level at me. But as a former forestry major, I love the religion-tinged folklore that has grown up around some species of Appalachian flora. The redbud, for instance, known in this region as the Judas tree, its flowers stained red by Judas' guilt and Jesus' blood. The notches in the creamy bracts of the flowering dogwood, red-brown like dried blood, said to symbolize the wounds of Christ. In such botanical folklore lies a gentle poetry I think Christ would have approved of, but which so many of his hillside followers sorely lack.

HIGHLANDERS, ANCIENT AND MODERN

THE NAMES OF APPALACHIA'S FOLK festivals would make a list poem all by themselves. Pumpkin Festival, Maple Syrup Festival. Dogwood Festival, Black Walnut Festival. Railroad Days, Apple Butter Weekend. Strawberry Festival, Honey Festival, Feast of the Ramson. Several festivals commemorate ancestry or historical events, but many emphasize agriculture, the spinning wheel of the seasons, logical focus for a primarily rural culture. These events echo in spirit the pagan harvest festivals of pre-Christian America and Europe, focusing on the gifts the earth gives us, and finding in those gifts reason to celebrate.

—⁂—

AT AGE TWENTY, I'VE GOT a hell of an appetite. It's late September 1979, full of goldenrod, morning glories, and red maples just beginning to turn color up on Chestnut Ridge. Karen, Mona, and I are strolling through the Buckwheat Festival in Kingwood, West Virginia. I've been eating little all day, preparing for the feast to come. In the fire hall, long tables are set up, crowded with locals. We're seated, and soon the servers come by. My idea of Glutton's Paradise: as many buckwheat cakes and sausage patties as you want! I consume fifteen syrup-topped pancakes and six pieces of sausage before waddling out, wishing I had the mountain equivalent of a rickshaw boy to push me around in a wheelbarrow. Afterwards, we admire displays of garden produce—I'm a farmer's son, so I can appreciate huge tomatoes, sweet potatoes, and pumpkins—as well as bushels of the odd, angular seeds of the buckwheat plant. Then we take to the carnival rides. After only three minutes on the whirling Octopus, my stomach lurches and I begin wishing that I hadn't been such a pancake pig.

—⁂—

TOO HOT FOR A KILT, I'd say, so I've left mine at home. My mother's family is a sept of the Clan Maclaine of Lochbuie, from the Isle of Mull, and our tartan—a mixture of red, blue, and black—is quite handsome, unlike some of the orange and muddy yellow monstrosities other clans are sadly stuck with. When the weather is cool, I wear my kilt sometimes and think of my Highland ancestors, whose hardscrabble life must have been not unlike many lives in Appalachia.

But the muggy Kanawha Valley heat hasn't stopped many other men from wearing woolen highland garb at West Virginia's Highland Games and Celtic Festival, held this August 2001 in South Charleston. There are all sorts of athletes competing on the field—big muscled men with tight tank tops, kilts, and work boots who are hefting cabers with great weight-lifters' grunts. My partner John and I mutter "Woof" a lot, a folk expression used by bears, another subculture I belong to. At my request, John takes photos of one beauty in particular, with a black goatee, big chest, and thick brown arms adorned with tribal tattoos. When, after some lecherous peering, we realize that the athletes are not wearing kilts in the traditional manner but instead are wearing modest Spandex shorts beneath their tartans, we lose interest and head for the food court, where the pleasures of sausage rolls and shortbread can be enjoyed without complex wheedlings for consent.

—m—

IN MY FORTIES NOW, AND I'm still all about appetite, albeit with frequent trips to the gym and not entirely successful diets. Labor Day Weekend in Clarksburg, West Virginia, and it's my first visit to the Italian Festival. My heritage is entirely Northern European: the Taylors from England, the Manns from Germany, the McCormicks from Scotland, and the Ferrells from Ireland. But that chilly legacy doesn't stop me from appreciating an event where you can swig wine on the street. My partner John and I do so, with as much abandon as our age allows, before digging into a plate of meatballs over pasta and a few cannoli. Then an indigenous West Virginia treat invented by Italian miners over a century ago as an easy-to-carry lunch: pepperoni rolls, the biggest and most profound we've ever found. Later, at Jim and Phyllis Moore's, our kind Clarksburg hosts, I will sit out on the screened-in porch, sip sweet iced tea with lemon, smell the perfume of the white-blooming virgin's bower, gobble another pepperoni roll, this one with Oliverio's Hot Peppers on top, and I will try to imagine those Italians who came to West Virginia so long ago, hoping for and finding work in the coal mines. What richness they've left. I wish there were a way for them to see how their descendants flourish. I wish there were a way to thank them for coming.

—ᵐᵐ—

HOLIDAYS: ANOTHER CATEGORY OF CUSTOM. John and I are spending Christmas and New Year's in Charleston, West Virginia, where he's moved for employment. Driving annoyedly up and down the Kanawha Valley in search of a grocery store that hasn't sold out of oysters, I point out the big signs at Foodland and Kroger advertising cabbage. My Aunt Sadie, I explain, always served fried cabbage on New Year's Day. One had to eat carefully, however, for she always included a scalded penny in the cabbage. Whoever got the penny (hopefully avoiding dental damage) would get luck for the coming year. Like serving black-eyed peas on New Year's Day in South Carolina, John points out, remembering his undergrad years in Columbia.

We serve both on New Year's Day, a pleasant compromise. Afterwards, hopeless pedant, I pull out an Irish cookbook and point out the recipe for barmbrack, a fruit bread in which a coin or ring is baked, served on Halloween. The same superstition prevails: whoever finds the token gets the luck. John doesn't understand the complete parallel until I explain that Halloween is a modern version of Samhain, the Celtic New Year.

AUNT DORIS'S QUILTS

IN APPALACHIA, IF YOU'RE LUCKY, material folk culture, the kind you can touch or taste, surrounds you. When my father taught me during my high-school years how to split wood with a chisel and a maul, the maul was a store-bought sledge hammer, but propped up in my bedroom still is the wooden maul my great-grandfather Allen Mann carved in one piece from a hickory tree.

On my office bookcase is a wooden spile, another tool become memento. Daddy cut it from an elderberry twig and used it as a homemade spigot for collecting sap in our maple-syrup-making endeavors during the early 1970's. Hard work, but good inspiration, in later years, for poetry. Odd how an artifact can serve as shorthand, can bring an entire era of personal history back:

. . . those mornings split between winter and spring,
when sun against the maple flanks conjures up
the sap's ascent. All that charcoal-gray silence
in the sugar grove, a flicker rapping remotely.
About me the tiny plink plink plink.
Siphoned up roots from the mountains' rocky flesh,
the rain and ground water some alchemy in maples
makes sweet. Dripping from spiles of elderberry
in summer broken and carved, freed of pith. Each drop
ignited by early sun trembling pendant on the spile-
lip before the silver shudder and fall. Zinc buckets
propped on sandstone stoops my great-grandfather set,
the bark pocked with vague scars he drilled
in the Februaries of another century.

—⟋⟍—

THE DEAD KEEP ME WARM. Aunt Sadie's wedding-ring quilts, heavily tattered
from thirty-some years of "everyday use" (to borrow Alice Walker's
phrase), which lie on my bed here in Blacksburg. Aunt Doris's bear-claw
quilt, the one she gave me as a Christmas present in the last years of her
life, which lies on the bed in Hinton, the bed I used as a boy, the bed I
use now during frequent visits home. I lie beneath the heavy legacy of
blankets, watch frost paint maidenhair ferns on the windowpanes, and
imagine those women bent over needle, quilt rack, or machine, hour
after hour, providing for someone else's future. It would be good to leave
behind something more substantial than words.

CREECY GREENS AND OTHER PERQUISITES

TEACHING APPALACHIAN STUDIES HAS HAD many edible advantages. Perhaps
it's because I encourage mountain students proudly to retain their
regional culture, to resist complete assimilation, to jeer back at those
who mock their accents. Perhaps it's because they sense that, despite my
peculiarities, I am one of them, someone who will cherish what gifts they
have to offer. Perhaps it's just that many of them were brought up—thank

God for what's left of good child-rearing and good manners!—to be kind, generous, and appreciative, as I was. Whatever the reason, every semester students in my Appalachian Studies classes have given me homegrown gifts. Deer jerky. Kudzu jelly (and a relief that anything worthwhile can be made of that creeping green morass). Paper bags full of creecy greens, which I spent hours meticulously rinsing to remove the grit before setting them on to simmer with chunks of fatback. Glad Bags crammed with ramps, the infamous wild onion, about which many feeds and festivals revolve, earth-scented delicacies that I fry up with eggs in bacon grease. And, occasionally, presented carefully *after* class, jars of clear liquid which taste like the surface of the sun, which have already been tested for purity: if it burns blue, it's safe to drink.

—⁓—

IF MY FATHER HAS A patron deity, it's Demeter, Greek goddess of agriculture. As soon as he can, he leaves the law office to my sister Amy, a recent graduate of West Virginia University's Law School, and heads up to his garden. The man's grown just about every vegetable I've ever heard of, even oddities like kohlrabi and Jerusalem artichokes. He returns this August weekend with buckets of banana peppers, corn, and tomatoes. The kitchen is redolent of the sugar/vinegar scent of pickling. When I take a break from *Grettir's Saga* and some class preparation, he proudly shows me his summer-stash, jar after jar after jar of canned tomatoes, pickled beets, green beans, and chowchow. It's not as if he can't afford to go to Kroger. It's a matter of getting your hands in the earth, collaborating with nature, doing for yourself just as his grandparents did.

In previous summers, Daddy and Amy had covered table after table with the vegetables they'd put up. This year, they've filled empty bookcases with the jars, even pushed a few jars of spaghetti sauce and hot peppers up against novels by Trollope and satires by Twain. Today he gives me a jar of corn relish, an unusual lavender color. "Added the red cabbage I grew this year," he explains. He hands me jars of homegrown, home-canned food the way he used to hand me books. Gifts that encourage health, that encourage growth. We give what nourishment we can, we give what we are able.

—ɯ—

LEGACY: WHAT DOES IT MATTER when we are young, light and whimsical as the airborne seeds of the dandelion, the silver seeds of the milkweed? Later, we grow heavier, like the heads of sunflowers drooping in late summer, facing the earth. Then it gains importance, where our blood came from.

Many of my travels have been toward the source of my bloodlines, attempts to see the landscapes my forebears saw in centuries past. A boat ride along the Rhine, where our branch of the Manns came from. A few days swilling Guinness and walking the pastures in Longford, Ireland. A hazardous wrong-side-of-the-road drive through the Isle of Mull to see Castle Moy, the clan seat of the Maclaines of Lochbuie. When I come home to Appalachia, after these brief and expensive sojourns, I have just a little more than memories and photo albums. Son of a fine cook, I also have cookbooks.

There is something comforting about discovering heritage in a recipe. Heritage is a concept. Concepts rarely comfort. But recipes are real in the way the body is real, and if you can comfort the body, you are well on your way to consoling the mind. I had relished many of my father's pot pies before I finally got to England, where I discovered, to my delight, that meat pies are the norm. I had many times watched my sister make wilted lettuce—a hot dressing of bacon grease, sugar, and vinegar—before discovering the same recipe in a German cookbook. I had heaped many a spoonful of chowchow or corn relish atop brown beans, forked out many a bowl of pickled beets, before a Pennsylvania Dutch cookbook informed me of the German passion for vivid combinations of sweet and sour. And, enjoying Scotland's infamous national dish at last—haggis, made from the minced heart, liver, and lungs of a sheep—how could I not remember my father, that great hater of waste, boasting that in West Virginia we use every part of the pig but the squeal?

Much of Appalachian eating is about harvesting the wilderness. Paw paws. Black walnuts. Serviceberries. Pokeweed greens, which my father taught me to harvest early, before the new green takes on a reddish blush, warning of poison. It's a small miracle we ignore in our search for greater ones, a miracle the pagan mind pondered over and celebrated in tale after tale. Season after season, the earth sustains us, with gifts of garden and of forest, gifts both coaxed from the soil and utterly unasked for, plucked from bush or tree like grace.

THE FERRELL FAMILY CEMETERY

"FILAMENTS, FILAMENTS, FILAMENTS," SAYS WHITMAN. Folk culture, family, and the sparsely populated beauty of the landscape—these hold me here, in the Appalachian Mountains, despite their pockets of poverty, their frothy-mouthed fundamentalists convinced of my damnation. Filaments: like spider webs, yes. Like blood vessels connecting the body with itself. Like the rope that attaches ship to anchor. Like roots and root hairs pushing down instinctively into soil, roots taking up the rainwater that maples transform into sweetness.

Roots of the spruce tree towering over the Ferrell family graveyard, and one set of Brunvand's categories I've left out: death customs. I want a big black granite obelisk over my grave, I joke with my sister Amy, so that literary pilgrims who track me down posthumously might be suitably impressed. There will only be a handful, I know (if any), those few inspired by writing that oddly combines gay and Appalachian concerns. But they deserve some sort of spectacle, I argue, trying to unnerve Amy with humor the way big brothers often do to little sisters.

She rolls her eyes. We waste nothing in our family, especially not money. "You'd better start saving for it now," she drawls, returning to her bowl of half-runners in need of stringing.

Well, obelisk or not, I'll be buried facing east. Or rather, whatever tombstone I get will face east, since I intend to "end up on the cookie sheet" in a crematorium, to use my mother's phrase. So she did. So shall I.

Once a sweet little cat of mine—named Hecate, the Greek goddess of witchcraft—died suddenly. It took years for us finally to figure out that she must have lapped spilled car-radiator fluid, and I still hope that the owner of that car has ended up in a ditch, "flies buzzing around his eyes," to adapt a Bob Dylan phrase. I took her up to the Ferrell family cemetery the dawn after she died and buried her beneath a cedar, where she wasn't likely to be disturbed by the addition of future occupants. I had her half-buried when I realized that she wasn't facing east. Tears in my beard, dew on my knees, I dug her up and repositioned her, determined to do it right.

I will be buried near Hecate, between her spot beneath the cedar and my grandmother's grave. Pauline Ferrell White was the one who loved me not as a parent—those tangled relationships of ambivalence, power struggles, conflict, and complexity—but with the warm simplicity and fidelity of a grandparent. She was the only one able to ignore my multifarious flaws. When she died, I knew I would never again be loved simply for myself: love that does not seek to change or control.

Cicadas shake their sistrums this time of year. The fireflies are almost gone, those misty pasture-flickers that wink like eyes, like constellations too restless to stay still, unlike those fixed and patient stars above, beginning to appear in the late-summer arch of indigo over Forest Hill, West Virginia. I sit in the grass above the spot that will hold my urn, if all goes well, and I think of what I've been taught—stories, recipes, songs, sayings—how to split red oak, how to simmer maple syrup. I look at the headstones about me, and beyond those, the fields the Ferrells used to farm, and, beyond that, the hills of Summers County. It is a great comfort—one of the greatest, in fact—to know that such knowledge will continue, such beauty will survive me.

HERE AND QUEER

John and I are having a few rooms in our house painted, here in Pulaski, Virginia. For several days now, two young guys have been showing up every morning, working on the basement, then the living room, now the bedroom. They're friendly, fast, and efficient; I can tell from their good manners and their accents that they're Southwest Virginia natives like me. They're both handsome. I enjoy looking at them: burly, bearded, tattooed Jim and lean, buff, clean-shaven Mike. I assume that they understand what kind of household this is, two men in their forties sharing a home, sharing a master bedroom. "We're really, really sorry we have to leave you guys' bedroom in such a mess," Jim said yesterday, at day's end. We explained that it was no problem, that we'd just use the guest bedroom. Thus it's clear to me that it's clear to them that John and I sleep together. And I haven't exactly bent over backward to hide incriminating material. My latest reading material, *Gay Warrior*, by F. Jim Fickey and Gary S. Grimm, is in full view on the coffee table. *Growing Up Gay in the South, Gay Spirit, Love Between Men,* and *Betty and Pansy's Severe Queer Review of San Francisco* sit on the bookshelves our sexy painters pass every time they leave the house for more supplies. All that, plus there's a Tim McGraw calendar hanging in the sunroom. This month, June 2008, Tim's showing off quite a bit of tasty chest hair via his half-unbuttoned shirt.

Are they surprised to find two gay men living together in this small Appalachian town? Many folks would. Lesbian/Gay/Bisexual/Transgender people have rarely been considered in discussions of Appalachian life. No one really knows what percentage of Americans are LGBT; the numbers

vary according to the researcher. 3%? 6%? 10%? Go with the lowest
estimate: 3%. What's the population of the Appalachian region? About 23
million people, according to the Appalachian Regional Commission. 3%
of 23 million is 690,000. That's a lot of queers.

Yes, quite a few gays and lesbians leave the mountains. Conservative
attitudes and religious intolerance encourage LGBT out-migration in the
same way that economic hardships drive folks of all sexual orientations
from the region. For instance, most of the gay and lesbian friends I made
during my college days at West Virginia University now live in big cities
beyond Appalachia—Baltimore, Maryland; Cincinnati, Ohio; Berkeley,
California; and Washington, DC—all places where gay life is more open
and active. But many of us remain, or leave and then return, making up
the fabric of Appalachian cities and small towns.

Hill-queers are as Appalachian as any other mountain-bred
individuals. I'm a representative example. When I first read Loyal
Jones' well-known essay "Appalachian Values," that litany of regional
characteristics, all I could say was, "Yep, yep, yep…," recognizing such
traits in myself and in my upbringing (though I do have a problem with
"Religion," since fundamentalist Christianity is responsible for much of
American homophobia, and "Modesty," since we writers tend toward the
egotistical). Like most hill-folks, when I leave the mountains, I miss them.
Like most hill-folks, I pride myself on my manners, self-reliance, and
hospitality. My students at Virginia Tech have gently pointed out the way
I fit certain Appalachian stereotypes: I have a passion for pickup trucks,
I wear cowboy boots and baseball caps, I love country music. (Less
conventional, admittedly, is my infatuation with Tim McGraw). When
I am stressed, I put on a pot of pinto beans, open a can of chowchow,
heat up the cast iron skillet, plop in a few tablespoons of bacon grease
(carefully hoarded in a tin), and mix up cornbread batter.

I am many other things, true. My country/mountain side is only one
of several facets. In this context, I think of the late Rita Riddle, who said,
in *Her Words: Diverse Voices in Contemporary Appalachian Women's
Poetry* (Ed. Felicia Mitchell. Knoxville: University of Tennessee Press,
2002), "there is no such thing as 'or.' Everything in the world, so far as
I know, is 'and, and, and'" (240). In other words, I can read Ovid *and*

quietly admire the handsome painters *and* play the mountain dulcimer *and* publish gay erotica *and* make piecrust *and* study Wicca *and* lift weights. Rita Riddle again: "I don't want to cull anything, cast out anything. I don't want to reduce Appalachia to a narrow little alley that doesn't allow me the depth and breadth of everything else that I am" (240). This seems to me a very intelligent approach. Why should I diminish my natural complexity in order to fit society's expectations, regional stereotypes, and simplistic pigeonholes? The same man who detests the modern abomination of mountaintop removal relishes goateed, hairy country boys in worn jeans and scuffed boots. The same man who hankers regularly for mountain tidbits like fried apple pies and ramps watches *Queer as Folk* DVDs at day's end and is going on a gay cruise of the Mediterranean in less than a month. The same man who relishes violent action movies (especially those involving bearded, half-naked warriors swinging swords) admires the delicate wordplay of Emily Dickinson's poetry.

"We are everywhere" is a slogan often used by the gay rights movement. It is accurate. I have lived my entire life in Appalachia, and I have never suffered for want of queer company. (Here's hoping this statement about LGBT pervasiveness makes Christian fundamentalists very, very nervous.) I had several supportive lesbian friends during my high school days in my hometown, Hinton. I had many, many gay and lesbian friends during my undergrad and grad years at West Virginia University. Now I have a goodly number of queer compatriots at Virginia Tech.

Despite this lucky history, I was a little anxious moving in July 2005 from liberal and culturally diverse Blacksburg to Pulaski, a small mountain town a good bit like Hinton. John joined me there in April 2006, putting his house in Charleston on the market. We wondered if we'd run into any gay folks in Pulaski. John and I are so busy and we so cherish our quiet time that we don't do much socializing. Like many settled couples, our idea of a good evening is a few drinks, a home-cooked meal, and a Netflix DVD. (How's that for a sinister gay agenda?) But we did hope there would be a few other LGBT folks around, just so we wouldn't feel entirely out of place and isolated. We shouldn't have worried. We've met and socialized with four other male couples, and there are others we've heard of and haven't met. Some are open, some aren't. All are from this area and have no intentions of leaving. Like John and me, they enjoy the quiet atmosphere, friendliness, slow pace, and gorgeous countryside of Appalachian Virginia.

When it comes to small-town or rural living, it helps to be coupled and of an age when one's identity is solid, one's libido is no longer raging, and gay nightlife is no longer appealing. My guess is that queer youths in the mountains are as restless for entertainment options as their straight counterparts. At least they have the Internet, an option lacking in my lonely single years, to help them feel less alone.

We LGBT Appalachians who remain in our native region do so despite the hostility we often find here. Life is still miserable for many queer high-school kids, who have few defenses and fewer protectors. In the Mountain South—and, indeed, all over America—homophobic behavior ranging from verbal to violent occurs all the time, aimed most especially at the young and slight. (Most homophobes have the sense to leave alone burly, hot-tempered bears like me.) Such nastiness isn't limited to small, isolated towns. It even appears at liberal Virginia Tech. One of my favorite gay students transferred to Virginia Commonwealth University in Richmond because he was tired of being called "Faggot!" every time he walked through the student union.

Again and again, the Bible is invoked to excuse prejudice and encourage hate. After living all these years in Appalachia and hearing Leviticus and Romans regularly thrown around, I've come to respond to Christian imagery the way Black folks are likely to respond to pointy white hoods. When I grab lunch at the little diner down the hill from us in Pulaski, I do so despite all the crocheted crosses and framed Bible verses on the walls. The servers are super-friendly, the food is cheap, tasty, down-home…but part of me is very nervous, as if in the presence of foes. I *know* many Christians are kind, compassionate people, but it seems to me they are in the minority when it comes to the battle over LGBT rights. I *know* that equating Christianity with homophobia is a paranoid generalization, an irrational prejudice. Still, the frightened little queer kid in me is always relieved to leave that restaurant. If he had his druthers (and a lot more money), he'd move back to Blacksburg. There are too many churches in Pulaski, too many fundamentalist bumper stickers and what I call "Jesus fish." We even have a bright pink "Prayer Infirmary." The ubiquitous presence of Christianity sometimes makes me feel as if I have stupidly chosen to pitch camp behind enemy lines, in a dangerous foreign country.

On a wider level, homophobia, institutionalized, infuses national and regional politics. In November 2006, Virginia passed a particularly virulent constitutional amendment banning same-sex marriage. Thus my partner John and I have no legal status as a couple, despite our eleven years together. I have no real interest in marriage as an institution, but the tax and insurance benefits would be damned nice. If I were in a serious accident, John might be denied access to my hospital room. We are not, after all, relatives. I will never forget Charlotte, a lesbian I knew who used to sell her leatherwork at Pipestem State Park in the 1970's. One night her car was hit head-on by a drunk driver. Medical personnel wouldn't allow her lover of many years to see her. She died alone.

This unwelcoming atmosphere has caused some gay and lesbian folks to flee. Not me. This is my home. I'm as much a part of these mountains as the pious and the narrow-minded. The scared child inside me might want to run away. Not the prideful adult. I'm not leaving, and neither are most other gay and lesbian Appalachians. We mountaineers are notoriously devoted to our homeland; leaving goes against our nature. Plus many of us have inherited Scottish and Irish blood, and supposedly that Celtic disposition makes us prone to fight. Why live in a cozy gay ghetto in a faraway city when our native region needs changing for the better? The days of queer self-hatred and passivity are fading fast.

I'll miss the painters when they leave, at the same time that I'll be glad to get the house in order again after weeks of remodeling chaos. I've enjoyed looking at them, because I'm a gay man. I've enjoyed shooting the breeze with them, on topics ranging from tattoos (turns out Jim and I share the same tattoo artist) to down-home cooking (Mike's mother makes a good red velvet cake with cream cheese icing), because I'm an aging country boy who enjoys the easy camaraderie of other country boys. Here's hoping the painters leave with a somewhat expanded sense of what gay men can be like, if they didn't already possess that knowledge. The more open LGBT people are, the more everyone else will realize how much we share with the heterosexual majority. Like straight people, most of us make good friends, coworkers, and neighbors.

To adapt another oft-used gay rights slogan, "We're here, we're queers, we're mountaineers, get used to it." If you've read this far, I'm guessing you're already used to it. Perhaps you have an LGBT sibling or relative or acquaintance; perhaps you're gay yourself. If you're not used to it, you'd better try to be. We *are* everywhere, we're tired of being treated like second-class citizens, in Appalachia and across the country, and we will have our rights. See how far we've come since the 1969 Stonewall Riots, where the movement for gay liberation was born? Now imagine how far we'll go in the next forty years.

SOUTHERN (LGBT) LIVING

For a few years in the early to mid-'80s I was a fan of *Southern Living* magazine. I was single, poor, and hadn't traveled much, so the articles, recipes, and slick photos gave me exciting glimpses into a larger world I had yet to experience. At one point, the Southern lesbian friend who'd introduced me to the magazine even got me a gift subscription to it. I read eagerly about glamorous Southern cities like New Orleans, Savannah, and Charleston and dreamed of being there. I smacked my lips over pictures of fried chicken, scalloped oysters, coconut cake, and mint juleps and wished I had a handsome lover with whom I could share such Southern delights. For a few Christmases, my mother even bought me the recipe collections that the magazine annually published in book form.

Southern Living was a good way to remind myself of what pleasures the South had to offer, since, as a gay man who'd spent almost all of his life in relatively small towns in Appalachia, I was more than aware of what nastiness my native region contained. Homophobia and Christian fundamentalism were ubiquitous, gay life was sparse. The same love for tradition that I'd inherited from the South also encouraged, in many of my fellow Southerners, reactionary attitudes, prejudice, and a surly suspicion toward anything different. Like Quentin Compson in William Faulkner's novel *Absalom, Absalom!*, I used to mutter, "I don't hate the South! I don't!" in an attempt to convince myself. Browsing through *Southern Living* was one way to come to terms with my problematically complex identity as a Southern gay man. Staying in the closet was another. My sense of self wasn't sufficiently solid to allow regular coming out till graduate school.

Only a few months of living in the very crowded, noisy, and frantic Washington, DC metropolitan area in 1985 convinced me that, as ambivalent as I felt about the small-town and rural South, I liked it a hell of a lot more than a big city, so I returned home and have lived in West Virginia and Virginia ever since. I realized I was gay in 1976, I'm 48 years old, so that means I've been balancing my Southern identity and my gay identity and coming out to people in the South for a little over thirty years. At this age, *Southern Living*, the magazine, has little to teach me. I've been to New Orleans, Savannah, Charleston, and many other Southern cities and tourist attractions; I know how to cook all sorts of tasty Southern food for my partner and friends. But Southern living as an openly gay man, that remains interesting, as challenges always are. It's an ongoing education. As a teacher, I know that examining one's own learning process often confirms and affirms that learning, so let me examine this Southern education and share here some of the things I've discovered.

—ɯ—

I CAN'T REMEMBER WHETHER IT was Vince Gill, Billy Ray Cyrus, or Travis Tritt. Some male country-music star. (I know it wasn't Tim McGraw. I would have remembered that, since I've been desperately in love with him for many years.). I do, however, remember who my fellow concert goers were that evening at the Roanoke Civic Center and what the pre-concert dinner conversation was like, for it was one of the first times I came out after being hired in 1989 as an English instructor at Virginia Tech.

Tammy and Lori were members of the English Department staff, Tammy the administrative assistant, Lori the bookkeeper. Both were country-bred like me. Their Virginia home county, Giles, borders my West Virginia home county, Summers, at the state line. Though Virginia Tech is set solidly in the Appalachian South, most of my colleagues in the department were far from Southern, and so Tammy's and Lori's mountain accents made me feel at home. We shared the same values, loved the same landscapes, grew up on the same food. And we enjoyed country music, often attending concerts together.

Over down-home Southern food in Roanoke's K&W Cafeteria— let's say country-fried steak, peppery milk gravy, mashed potatoes, green beans, corn, and coconut cream pie, since that's what I tend to order at such spots—I came out to them. It was one of those pre-emptive self-revelations, where a straight person you honestly like starts talking about gays and, in order to save her or him from future embarrassment—since uninformed straight people often say stupid things about gays—you come out. Lori started a sentence about gay men—this many years later, I don't remember the content, but it must have seemed to me potentially negative—so I interrupted, telling Lori and Tammy I was gay. They might have been mildly surprised, but neither seemed truly shocked. There was a second or two of awkwardness, they both said that was fine with them, and off we went to the concert. A few days later, Lori even asked me a few simple questions about what gay life is like.

Lori left the department a year or so after that, but Tammy remains. Over the years, we've discussed relationships, shared occasional lunches, talked about departmental politics, *Will and Grace, Brokeback Mountain,* country music, motorcycle runs, homophobia, and Southern cooking. She was one of my major comforters and supporters during my eventually successful bid for tenure, a process made unsettling by the very queer and often erotic nature of my publications. One winter day when I wrecked my pickup truck in a sudden snowstorm, her husband Lee, a good-looking country-boy trucker, fetched me in his huge four-wheel-drive and they put me up for the night. I made biscuits, Tammy cooked up home-canned beef, we had a good meal and a few drinks and watched the mountain snows come down. Their hospitality, like most Southerners, was superb.

What have I learned from this? One, Southerners tend to like Southerners, in the same way that most of us are soothed by sameness and made somewhat uncomfortable by difference. I think that my Southern qualities make my gayness easier for other Southerners to accept. The fact that I'm friendly, not critical, mannerly, not abrupt and blunt, helps. Tammy and Lori, neither of whom had experienced gay people up close before, already knew and liked me, so they were predisposed to continue

liking me even after my homosexuality was disclosed. What they did
share with me allowed them to accept what we didn't share. (Well, we
don't share heterosexuality, but we do share an appreciation for men.
Tammy and I still compare lustful notes about various sexy country music
and film stars.)

I was also reminded of the importance of coming out. Since that
evening at the K&W Cafeteria, I've been pretty much out to everyone
in my department, and by now—I've taught at Virginia Tech for almost
twenty years and published lots of openly queer material during that
time—I'm well known as the Appalachian/gay writer, "the Mountaineer
Queer," as I half-jokingly describe myself. One of the many reasons I've
insisted on being so open has to do with stories Tammy's told me since
I came out to her: she's sternly scolded a long series of homophobes
about their attitudes, defending me in particular or My Queer Kind in
general. Influenced by this liberal attitude, her daughter Nicole even took
a persecuted gay kid under her wing during high school. I suspect that
Tammy is naturally understanding and kind to begin with, but I like to
think that knowing me has made her even more likely to spread the word
that gay people are just fine the way they are. My guess is that such grass-
roots one-on-one interactions are more effective as political activism than
any marches or rallies. The conservative Highland South needs as many
folks like Tammy as it can get.

—w—

I DO IT IN SEVERAL ways. I used to make a big production about coming
out to my classes, informing students that this personal disclosure was
meant to contribute to their education in ways that specific course
materials could not. Now I do it casually, simply because many of my
students, master web-surfers that they are, already know I'm gay. I have a
webpage, they check out websites that rate teachers, so my homosexuality
is likely known to a goodly number of them on that first day of class in
Intro to Creative Writing or poetry workshop. Now, instead of a grand
announcement, I frequently mention "my partner John," during the little
anecdotes I use to start the class or to provide illustrations for various

points I want to make. (We Southerners are, after all, supposed to be good storytellers, and students have told me in the past that my illustrative tale telling is one of my best teaching techniques.) I mention meals John and I have made, movies we've watched, trips we've taken together. I use our commitment ring as an example when I talk about symbols, and I manage to get in a few caustic words about anti-gay-marriage laws while I'm at it. When I talk about dialect and other distinguishing features of subcultures, I use not only Southern examples—I say "cain't," not "can't"—but gay examples—"Woof!" is what a randy bear says in response to a sexy man. I joke about my crushes on assorted country music stars and actors and even wear my several Tim McGraw T-shirts to class when the weather's warm. I confess that the movie *300* must have been made for me, between the classical setting, the half-naked men, the swordplay, and Gerard Butler's black beard. I have no discipline problems (being a burly male is, I know, helpful in this regard), my classes generally go very well, most students seem to be relaxed and to enjoy themselves, and I receive high student evaluations of my teaching, enough so to have netted me a coveted Certificate of Teaching Excellence from Virginia Tech recently.

What have I learned from this? True, it's a liberal environment, the university. True, most of my students are somewhat worldly young people from the Northern Virginia suburbs. True, I am in charge, so they are less likely to be publicly homophobic. But I think my manner helps. Except for the most virulent queer-hating cases, good will goes a long way. I treat my pupils with respect, I don't put them on the spot, I'm helpful and kind, I'm relaxed, honest, and humorous, and I'm truly concerned about the quality of their classroom experience. Here too, I am deliberately out because I want them to know a gay person. I want, with my relatively masculine and fairly Appalachian behavior, dress, and looks, with my bushy beard, bear-brawn, faded jeans, and cowboy boots, to challenge whatever stereotypes and preconceptions they might have about gay men as perpetually effeminate, urbane, delicate, over-refined sophisticates. After a semester with me, I'm hoping that any homophobia they might have possessed will have dwindled a bit, as well as any biases they might have entertained about dumb hillbillies.

—⚏—

PEOPLE SURPRISE YOU. SOME YOU might imagine to be intolerant turn out to be accepting; some you expect to be accepting turn out to be intolerant.

I call her Mizz Mayberry. (As a Southerner, I was not brought up to call my elders by their first names). She's my next-door neighbor. She's ninety-one years old, very frail but sharp, funny, and smart. No one brings out the well-mannered Southern gentleman in me like Mizz Mayberry.

When I first moved in, I took Mr. and Mrs. Mayberry a basket of blueberries I'd picked at a friend's farm, hoping that the gesture might win them over and manufacture some good will I might need in future. When Mizz Mayberry asked me what church I attended, I started worrying. When I found out that they didn't allow alcohol in the house, I worried more. I assumed that, as old as they were, their attitudes would be rigid, traditionalist, religious, and, well, homophobic. I assumed that they didn't understand the full import of the phrase, "My partner John will be moving in soon." "Partner" means "business partner" to folks of the Mayberrys' generation, I thought. They're going to have a shock when they realize homosexuals live next door, I thought. I prepared myself for chillier interactions once the truth was out. I liked them very much, and I dreaded their judgment and disapproval.

In February of 2006, the *Roanoke Times* ran an article about me, "The Brokeback Professor," discussing my book *Loving Mountains, Loving Men* and the elements it shared with *Brokeback Mountain*. A big color photo of me accompanied the article. My residence was listed as Pulaski. In other words, I was suddenly even more identifiably queer than before (and indeed, I received, along with many friendly e-mails from fellow LGBT folks, at least one virulent note telling me to "get medical help"). At the same time that I was a bit anxious about coming out in such a public way, the writer in me basked in the ego-food and attention, and the activist in me figured becoming more widely known as the Appalachian gay writer might help other Appalachian queers feel less alone.

I picked up that issue of the *Roanoke Times* early that morning at a nearby gas station, then read over the article at a local coffee shop before returning home. I felt a little exposed, true, but I knew that, one, no one would pay the article much attention, writers being the sort of public figures that few people find interesting, and, two, my usual baseball cap and dark glasses were likely to disguise me from the roving bands of well-armed gay-bashers I was suddenly sure stalked the Pulaski streets.

Mizz Mayberry called me at 10 am. When I recognized her voice, I steeled myself for the worst. Instead of expressing horror, disgust, or pious shock, she asked me, in her sweet, quavering voice, if I wanted her to save her copy of the newspaper so I might keep it for my files. She also congratulated me on the publication of my book and expressed a desire to read it. Since then she has remained a warm and welcoming neighbor. We have reciprocated her kindness, fixing her fence, taking her baked goods, picking up candies for her amidst our travels to appease her chocolate craving. She owns a signed copy of *Loving Mountains, Loving Men*. One summer day she even hosted a little poetry reading on her porch. Several neighbors attended, cookies and lemonade were served, I read some of my poems (admittedly avoiding the man-loving-man verse and focusing on the poems about Appalachian living) and played the mountain dulcimer. When her ninety-three-year-old husband passed away, John and I were two of a very select few invited to the funeral home for a private service. As I write this, February 2008, snowdrops are springing up like tiny ivory bells beneath her oak tree. Paradoxically, their evidence of new life in a new year makes me worry about her health and advancing age. I pray that she lives many more years yet to admire in late winter the snowdrops beneath the oak, then in spring the daffodils on the wooded slope behind her house, then in summer the huge lemony blooms of the magnolia tree in her side yard.

—⋙—

THEN THERE ARE THE UNPLEASANT surprises. John says they were simply drunk, not harassing me deliberately. It could have been anyone's mailbox, he says. I don't know. What I do know is that the closest I've gotten to killing someone occurred not in a small, conservative town like Pulaski but in Blacksburg, the liberal university town where Virginia Tech is located, where I lived for fifteen years.

A group of young people lived across Airport Road from the old house I rented for my last eight years in Blacksburg. They might have been graduate students; I don't know how many actually lived there and how many were friends who came and went. I like my quiet and privacy, so we had had few interactions before the night of the stoning, and those interactions hadn't been particularly pleasant. On two or three occasions I'd gone over to tell them, politely but sternly, that their middle-of-the-night party music and conversation were disturbing my sleep. The young woman who seemed to be the spokesperson always apologized, but it sometimes took two visits in the same night for them to get the fact that I meant business.

It was a night in mid-May 2005, one of the last times I slept in that house. My lease was soon up, I was soon to move into the Pulaski house John and I had just bought. John was in Charleston, West Virginia, that night. We owned a house there we were planning to sell, so he continued to work there and we got together on weekends. Thus I was alone when the noises woke me, a series of dull thumps from somewhere outside. I checked the bedside clock: a little after midnight. I raised a blind and peered out.

Another party was going on across the street. It was a warm evening, so many people were drinking outside on the front porch, celebrating the semester's end. I had to watch them for a while before I figured out what was causing the intermittent thumping that had woken me. A young man was pelting my mailbox. He stood on the opposite side of Airport Road with a beer in one hand. With the other he picked up rocks and threw them across the street. He had a good arm. He struck the mailbox often.

One of the greatest and most nightmarish fears of many LGBT people is to face or be chased by a violent, hostile heterosexual mob. We move, occasionally invisible, occasionally not, among such people all the time. We wonder how they might hate us if they knew what we were; we wonder how cruelly they might treat us if they had that knowledge and the power to implement their disgust. This is no doubt why I always relate to the persecuted monster in horror films: Dr. Frankenstein's creation fleeing the torch-wielding villagers, the vampire hiding from his hunters. This is no doubt why, despite my oft-professed title as "The Only Gay Man in North America Indifferent to Broadway," I loved *Wicked* when John dragged me to a performance during our last trip to New York City: it's all about being a harassed, detested, maltreated, maligned outsider. Being LGBT anywhere except the most liberal setting is bound to create in us a siege mentality, a paranoia that is sometimes reasonable, sometimes not.

I don't know if my response was reasonable. It was more instinctual, I think: the instinct of a threatened animal. I should have called the police; a postal service employee friend of mine has said that I could have gotten them in serious trouble for defacing a mailbox. But I'm nothing if not prideful. I have a Southern sense of masculine honor that insists that I defend myself rather than involve legal authorities. So I pulled on my jeans, cowboy boots, sweatshirt, cowboy duster, and baseball cap: my usual attire, but, in that context, I was well aware that such butch clothing would help make me more intimidating. Still, one man, however big and angry, isn't much of a match for a crowd, and there was indeed a small crowd of people on that front porch and on that lawn across the street. So I took my own equalizer, albeit one more archaic and romantic than the solid practicality of the firearms many country boys might have toted in similar circumstances.

I grew up on King Arthur's exploits and other heroic epics. More recently, I've relished films like *Gladiator*, *The Lord of the Rings* trilogy, and *300*, as much for the sword-swinging action as the sexy bearded men. In other words, I own several knives and swords. It took me a minute or two to choose. Aragorn's ranger sword was far too long to conceal in the pocket of my duster. My Scottish dirk was too long and straight to fit. But Aragorn's elven hunting knife, when removed from its wall plaque, was just right. Its scimitar curve allowed me to slip it into my duster pocket, and it, like all the other blades, was sharp enough to do damage.

My father and sister are both attorneys. I know about the laws prohibiting concealed weapons. I didn't care. I was not going out there unarmed. Again, I don't know whether this move was unreasonable or wise. I do know that, if ever faced with the same situation, I'd do the same thing.

The confrontation didn't last long. Shaking with adrenaline, I strode to the front of my lawn, the top of a small slope overlooking the street, a high point that, I realized, gave me a tactical advantage. With my habitual sarcasm I asked the young man if he were enjoying his target practice. Between the rage and the fear, my voice wasn't as steady as I wished it had been. I accused him of stoning my mailbox, he denied that he'd been stoning my mailbox, I quipped that I must then be having vision problems since I'd clearly seen him do it, and the young woman I'd dealt with before apologized, promised me that no one meant me any harm, and swore that the party was dispersing. That was it. Not much of a story, I must admit.

The story's in what might have happened. When I turned away from that crowd and stalked back toward my house with a deliberate slowness that I hoped might project the fearlessness I did not feel, I expected one of those stones to hit me between the shoulder blades. If it had, if one of those no-doubt-drunk guys had gotten his dander up and followed me with violence on his mind, I would have pulled that knife. I would never have carried it out there if I hadn't been truly prepared to use it. At the very worst, I would have killed someone. Less terrible possibilities were wounding someone or being arrested for carrying a concealed weapon.

Instead, I sat on my porch in the dark, pulled the knife from my coat and stroked it as the gathering across the street broke up, people drove away, and lights in the Party House finally went off. The weight and sharpness of the scimitar were a comfort. When everyone was gone, I walked around the property, checking the perimeters, making sure no one had decided to outflank me by sneaking around the back of the house. I was, at this point, operating more like an alert animal or novice soldier than a writer and professor. I stood in the darkness and sniffed the blooming bush honeysuckle. I walked down to the mailbox, touched its dented sides, and examined the scattered rocks on the ground around it. Then I returned to my house. I pulled off my boots and turned off the light. I slept still clothed, with Aragorn's elven hunting knife unsheathed on the floor by my bed.

For a long time I wondered, if the mailbox stoning were truly a malicious anti-gay gesture, how those partygoers knew I was gay. As I've said above, I look like just another country boy. I lived there alone. John was only one of a number of people, male and female, who visited me. It was only months later that I pieced together facts that helped all this make sense. Living next door to the Party House was a woman who briefly dated a colleague of mine. She told him that she and her friends in the Party House called me "Spooky Guy" because I lived in an old ramshackle house, wore black occasionally, and kept to myself. She was later to write me a letter telling me how much she enjoyed reading my books of poetry. I can only guess that the homoerotic nature of many of those poems was something she shared with her neighbors. Whether those stones were lobbed at a conveniently close mailbox, at the world in general, at my previous complaints about their noise, or at my homosexuality, I won't ever know. But I do know now that some if not all of the drunken folks at the Party House were aware that I was gay.

—m—

THAT TRAUMATIC EVENING HAS BEEN the exception, not the rule. Being Southern, butch, and brawny has made my life in the South much, much easier, I know, than the lives of many LGBT folks. Having patterned myself on the kind of beefy, bearded country boys I desired in my youth, on the surface I have assimilated. No one seeing me drive my pickup truck down the country roads between Virginia Tech and Pulaski or interacting with me superficially at the grocery store or local restaurant would ever guess that I'm a professor of creative writing who occasionally teaches gay and lesbian literature, as well as a Wiccan, a leather bear, a poet, a bondage enthusiast, a writer of erotic sadomasochistic fiction, a member of Phi Beta Kappa, a lover of ethnic cuisine, international travel, Greek and Roman literature, Nordic sagas, and Celtic culture. My differences are, in other words, complex, deep, radical, and myriad but not visually apparent. I look and occasionally act like a Southern redneck, and this saves me from many a conflict, allowing me to conserve my energy for activities more fruitful than regular fisticuffs with homophobes. This is not true for many of my queer kin, and I can only imagine what sort of daily stresses, humiliations, and difficulties they must experience if they remain in the small-town or rural South. I've had enough students tell me stories of name-calling and abuse on the Virginia Tech campus to guess at how hard it is to be discernibly gay. Kids suspected of being queer at the local Pulaski High School are made miserable, or so I've heard, just as they were made miserable in the high school I attended so long ago in Hinton.

As relatively easy as I've had it, I don't know how many of my own "Southern Living" experiences might be helpful or relevant to other LGBT Southerners. Certainly my early interest in those glossy photos and articles in *Southern Living* magazine was no preparation for dealing with hostile preachers, Bad Good Ole Boys, rock-wielding drunks, or my own fear and rage. But that magazine did help confirm in me a lifelong love of the American South, despite its flaws, and that love has helped me remain here. I love the mountains, the pastures, the accents, the good manners, the friendliness and hospitality, the folk culture and deep sense of history. On most days, that love is greater than my hate for my native region's weaknesses. (On bad days, such as when Virginia passed its law against same-sex marriage, the love beats out the hate just barely). And don't most of us, gay or straight, Southern or Yankee, both love and hate where we're from?

For some queer folks, the hate they face in the South causes them to hate in return, and what they learn to love is life in the Castro, in Silver Lake, in Chelsea, in Dupont Circle, those gay communities elsewhere. I wish them luck and wish them better lives, queerer lives, in those faraway places far too busy, crowded, and costly for my taste. For those of us from the South who choose to remain, who have some sense of how horrible an ache homesickness is, I wish us bourbon, barbeque, and biscuits, determined queer comrades and devoted lovers. I wish us the strength that allows life on the front lines, where the battle is fiercest and its outcome unsure, where courage counts for everything, where the greatest changes can be forged.

BONDAGE TAPE IN BUDAPEST

The pastry's good at Gerbeaud, a legendary confectionary on *Vörösmarty Tér* in the heart of Budapest. John and I sit here on the sunny patio, delighted to be in Hungary at last. We watch the activity in the busy square and take our time savoring slices of Dobos torte, a complex cake flavored with butter, chocolate, and caramel, something we've sampled in American cities but never in its country of origin. It's rich, intense, and decadent; it's sure to contribute to the furry belly I relish on other men but am not too fond of on myself. Oh well, I *am* a bear. With luck we'll burn a few calories off this afternoon while we climb Castle Hill, walk along the Danube, or visit St. Stephen's Basilica to see the saint's mummified hand. Tonight, we'll hit Fatál, the restaurant Tibor suggested, and afterwards we'll tie Tibor up. He's bringing his bondage tape and a ball-gag. I'm bringing my long experience as a bondage Top who passionately believes that every handsome man is even more beautiful restrained.

—⁓—

AS FOND AS I'VE BECOME of my native region of Appalachia, I need to escape it occasionally. I need to immerse myself in other cultures, other worlds, though I always return home with an even stronger conviction that the Southern Highlands are indeed where I belong. When I travel, I prefer super-queer places like Key West or Provincetown, where I can get my "gay fix." Spending almost my entire life in Southwest Virginia and West Virginia, where LGBT culture is relatively invisible, besieged, or nonexistent, has made me queer-starved. Or, finances permitting, I

97

head for Europe, so as to indulge my intellectual interests in European history, language, literature, and culture, and my hedonistic enthusiasms for European food, drink, and men.

Devouring Dobos torte is somewhat of a symbolic act. I am a variety and intensity addict, a lover of all things new and extreme, an unabashed sensualist dedicated to harvesting bodily pleasure, a poet with a sharp sense of aging and mortality who has subscribed to *Carpe diem* from adolescence on. All this makes me restless, promiscuous, perpetually dissatisfied, and polymorphously perverse, sort of a hillbilly Byron. And so my quiet life as a university professor in the Mountain South has been punctuated by infrequent but colorful overseas adventures. I have devoured cuttlefish and admired black chest hair in Greece; have swilled Guinness and shagged a furry auburn-bearded Irishman in Cork; have sampled *smørrebrød* and a St. Andrew's cross in Copenhagen; have groped strangers in a gay steam room in Berlin. Since 1997, my remarkably patient partner John has been my traveling companion, and this summer of 2004, he and I are visiting Prague, Vienna, Budapest, and Salzburg, clutching our guidebooks, our Czech, Hungarian, and German dictionaries, eager to sample the local pleasures. Not only have I learned many food and drink words in those languages, but I've also set us up a date here in Budapest via an online leather site.

Where was the Internet when I was single and lonely and living in various towns in Appalachia hungry as hell for affection, sex, a simple date, eager to meet other bears or leathermen but not at all sure how to do that? I discovered the World Wide Web about the time I met John, so for a while my only online interests were learning more about Joni Mitchell's guitar tunings and trying to find photos of my favorite country-music stars shirtless. But then, about the time I began to accept the fact that I was not naturally monogamous, a buddy introduced me to a couple of leather and Bear sites. My online flirtations and resultant extramarital adventures in search of the BDSM I wasn't getting at home worried John a lot, until he figured out that I was playing safe and I wasn't planning to leave him. Pretty soon, chatting with good-looking men in foreign countries became just another kind of research, along with learning pleasantries in the native language and finding the locations of the best restaurants. Why not set up a little frolic? Might as well taste all that a country has to offer.

Tibor's photos caught my eye fast. Handsome thirty-year-old guy with pierced nipples and big muscles. Interested in trying kink. Wanted to be tied up. Needed someone trustworthy. Uhhhhfff! A few desultory months of chat back and forth, and he was convinced I'd treat him right. What is it about me that persuades the inexperienced that I'm a nice guy, won't hurt them, can be trusted absolutely? I don't know. But I'm thankful. I've initiated a goodly number of neophytes into the dark arts of BDSM, and, to a man, they've all left happy. (We Leos are prone to boasting.)

—◊◊◊—

BUDAPEST IS EVERYTHING I IMAGINED. There are the wide Danube with its many bridges; the monumental Royal Palace, Matthias Church, and the white-towered Fishermen's Bastion atop Castle Hill; the huge neo-Gothic Parliament building; and, on the summit of Gellért Hill, the Liberation Monument. After touring around all day, we're ready for some substantial nourishment, so it's a pleasure to discover that Tibor was right about Fatál: they have superb down-home Magyar cooking. Hungarian food's got the density and heft of Middle European cuisine, but it's spicy, not bland, thanks to the ubiquitous use of that Ultimate Hungarian Ingredient, paprika. I swill a good bit of Dreher beer in this cavernous cellar restaurant, eye the sexy goateed waiter, and consume to the last morsel a local version of the German *Schlachtplatte*: several wursts, ribs, red cabbage, potatoes, and a huge dumpling. Got to have a lot of energy for tonight's topping.

John's out picking up some more beer when Tibor knocks on the door of our little rental apartment right off *Váci utca*. He's on time; I like that. I like his looks even more: far sexier than the photos he'd sent via e-mail. At six foot four, taller than me by several inches, he's a Magyar giant, right out of some Middle European adventure tale. I take in delicious details: the very short prematurely gray hair, the blue eyes like burning moonshine, the endearing silvery chin-scruff. His shoulders are broad, his arms are intimidatingly thick, his pecs push out the front of his T-shirt. I'm a pretty big guy—the moderate bear belly is balanced by a decently solid set of pecs and arms, due to years of regular if not-too-strenuous weightlifting—and so not many men make me feel small. But Tibor does. He would have done some major damage against the invading Turks a few hundred years ago. I can only pray that he finds me half as hot as I find him.

Tibor sits beside me on the couch and pulls out his backpack stash: bondage tape, lots of blue rope, a ball-gag. My captive-to-be and I chat for a while to make sure he's ready. He will, after all, soon be bound for the first time, powerless and in a relative stranger's hands. But we've gotten to know one another well enough online for him to be relaxed, the chemistry feels right, and I assure him that he'll be safe, that I'll release him immediately if it all gets to be too much. (He's also had the sense to leave my name and address with a friend, just in case I turn out to be a psychopath.) By the time John returns with the beer, I've pulled off my T-shirt, and Tibor's down to nothing but briefs. We're leaving the delicious vulnerability of his complete nakedness for later, once he's been tied.

He is, of course, even more manly and beautiful stripped down. I'm a body-fur fan, and Tibor's torso is just about hairless, but the sculpted curves of his chest more than make up for that lack. Plus I'm crazy about pierced nipples, and there they hang, two steel rings just waiting to be tugged. Even without stripping him completely, I can tell Tibor's proportionate in the dick department—big man, big cock—because of the immoderate bulge in his briefs. His erection's pushing out and curving up against the cloth like the sinuous neck of a water bird, like the stalk of a desert succulent growing toward sun. It makes such a prominent profile that John takes a digital picture of it. (Note to travelers: a trip to a Turkish bath in Budapest will convince anyone that Hungarian men are all unnaturally and enviably hung.)

"Ready?" I ask.

Tibor nods, closes his eyes, and hangs his head submissively: the proper position for a bottom about to be bound.

"Hands behind your back," I say, gripping his elbows gently.

He obeys. "Stay there," I order, and reach for the soft black leather straps I have brought all the way from Virginia for this moment. John sits back and sighs, sips a beer, and watches me go to work. He's seen this light in my eyes, he's seen all this before. Vanilla boy that he is, he knows, and no doubt regrets, that this is erotic fifth-gear for me. This is my only sacrament. This is how I fly.

Tibor takes a deep breath as I cross his wrists and begin to tie his hands behind his back. For a minute, I expect second thoughts, more than mock resistance, backing out, but he doesn't fail me. He keeps still until I'm done knotting the straps.

I step back and grin. "Feel all right?"

Tibor nods, his head still bent in submission.

"Not too tight?"

"No," Tibor mutters. His huge shoulders strain a bit—he's testing his bonds—then slump. He can tell he can't get loose without a struggle, and that makes us both happy.

God, is there anything more beautiful than this, a finely built, bare-chested, masculine man with his eyes on the floor and his hands tied behind him? I know, I know—it's an odd aesthetic. Every time I bind or am bound, I wonder why helplessness, strength in restraint, so moves me, on all levels, genital on up. Every time, I decide I don't really care from whence this rare passion springs. Why question the silence in a shrine, the mystery?

I cup the soft silvery bristles of Tibor's chin and lift his gaze to mine. Blue, like pale morning glories that used to bloom on my grandmother's porch in September. I smile, he smiles, and I kiss him. He kisses back, hard. I chew his lower lip, gently bite his scruffy chin. Soon enough I have his beefy tits in my hands and am kneading them, feeling the welcome density of muscle—as if marble were malleable. I'm sucking his pierced nipples, lapping the hard points of flesh, the harder rings of steel, and he's groaning. I'm tugging on the rings and listening to his groans grade into a sweet baritone growl, much like the deep, gruff bear-grumble I make when I bottom. I'm pushing him to his knees, unzipping my jeans, and shoving my cock into the tight sword-sheath of his mouth.

Out of the corner of my eyes, I see John take a few more snapshots, some with Tibor's camera, some with ours, before settling back on the couch, sipping his beer, and watching us impassively. I suspect he's feeling left out, a bit bored, or, worse, threatened by my passion for this beautiful stranger, but I'm so het up, to use a mountain expression, touching and tasting this helpless Hungarian giant that I don't care. My appetites—their breadth, depth, and focus—are my greatest strength. They are also my greatest weakness. Appetite often leads to selfishness. It's hard to be considerate of others when your cock is in a captive's skillfully working mouth.

And so my husband's listlessness distracts me only briefly from the pleasures at hand. "Time you were taped up, buddy," I say, helping Tibor to his feet and reaching for the perverse stash he's left on the sofa. Who could have guessed that you could find bondage tape in Hungary? Let's hear it for the insidious creep of Western decadence.

Still, as a connoisseur of kink, I'm mildly disappointed: this tape isn't the kind I like. It sticks only to itself, not to skin, so it doesn't bind a prisoner half as securely as the PVC tape with adhesive I'm fond of using on bottoms and occasionally submitting to myself. As used as I am to binding hairy men who do a lot of wincing when tape comes off (a pain that I, as a fairly furry part-time bottom, know intimately, a pain that does not translate easily into pleasure), I want to take full advantage of Tibor's smooth chest by taping him up with The Real Thing. Well, I'll have to make do with what's available, and besides, the ball-gag Tibor brought is just right, the sort of sweet boy-silencer I'm used to: a fat black rubber ball with leather straps and buckle.

By the time I have the shiny black tape wrapped around Tibor's meaty chest and arms, John's deep into his second beer and a visible pout. He moves from the couch to the bed, stretches out, and stares at the ceiling. He's making me feel guilty, and that interferes with my fun, and that pisses me off. I should involve him, ask him to help, but instead I concentrate on the way the taut tape accentuates the bulges of Tibor's chest. Another tit-munching feast—no finer food than a hard nipple atop a hard pec—then I push Tibor to his knees, gently lower him onto the floor and over onto his belly. With a few more leather straps, I bind his ankles together and finally cinch wrists and ankles together in a tasty, tight hog-tie.

Tibor moans, rolls onto his side, tugs at his bonds, moans some more. As tall, young, and muscular as he is, he no doubt takes his strength and power for granted. He's probably never been this helpless. And oh, it feels so good. I can tell by that look of blank bliss in his blue eyes.

So sweet to give up control, to lay down all that masculine force, its weighty responsibility. And, for me, so sweet to see such brawn entirely vulnerable. Each man's masculinity is reasserted, his in giving up power, mine in taking it.

Finally it's time for his cock. I peel his briefs down to his knees and take his hard shaft in my hand. He's uncut, which pleases me inordinately. I almost never get to play with an uncircumcised cock, and when I do, I'm like a bright-eyed child with a new toy. His foreskin is so tight I have to slide it down off the head, which is glistening with precum. Tibor bucks and sighs; his flesh throbs in my fist.

"This next part may be my favorite," I whisper. Taking the ball-gag in hand, I lie on the floor beside Tibor. I kiss him, then push the ball into his mouth and buckle the straps behind his head. We lie there for a second, staring into one another's eyes, the captor and the captive, then I kiss him again. Fuck, I love kissing a gagged man. He works the ball around in his mouth till the dull black rubber turns shiny with spit. I lick the ball, lick his chin-scruff, press my mouth over his, over the gag wedged between his teeth. I've taken away the freedom of his limbs and his power of speech, and all that remains is to take away his sight, but the look of rapturous submission in his eyes is too delicious to miss for a minute. The Danube should be the hue of this captive warrior's gaze.

I must be grinning like a fool. I lick his gag-stretched lips, tenderly nip his nose, and ask, "Happy?" Tibor manages a distorted grin, rolls his eyes, and nods vigorously. "Uhhhh uhh! Uhhhhhh uh!" he grunts. I wrap one arm around him, brush my hand over his cropped, soft hair, and press his face to my torso. I know from heady experience that a ball-gag inevitably inspires drool, and I want to feel Tibor's drool matting my chest hair.

With that, the camel's back breaks, and John begins to dress. I prop myself on one elbow, ask him where he's going. No response. Within about a minute and a half, he's slammed the front door and headed out into the night.

Tibor looks up at me with consternation, cocking one eyebrow.

"Well, fuck," I snarl. "Time we had a beer."

I can feel guilty later. Right now I have the Hungarian Hercules to torment. Hell, I haven't even gotten to his ass.

—⚏—

TIBOR MAKES A FINE FOOTSTOOL. He lies contentedly hog-tied on the floor; I sit back in a chair and rest my boot on his hip. "God's in his heaven, all's right with the world," I mutter, swilling Stella Artois and wondering how a small-town boy from West Virginia got here, how the cute little kid in those childhood photographs grew into the complex erotic monster I've become.

When Tibor starts to get sore, I free him just long enough for him to stretch and step out of his briefs. Then I use the long yards of blue rope he's brought to tie his hands in front of him, to wrap around his torso, belly, and thighs. When his jaw starts hurting, I replace the ball-gag with a sock-gag. Our time together is running out, and I want to see this hot, hot man bound and gagged in as many ways as possible.

Now he's on his elbows and knees on the bed, and that hard, shapely ass is propped up for use. I grease him up, give him a lengthy finger-fucking, nudging his prostate and delighting in the muffled, ecstatic sounds he makes into his gag. We've met only hours ago, yet here I am, privy to his most vulnerable and secret place, the tight, slick heat wrapped pulsing about my knuckles. What a privilege. What a blessing. Tibor groans and rocks himself back onto my hand, clenching his flesh around mine. I really, really want to push my cock inside him and ride him till he sobs, but that would violate one limit he's set, and any trustworthy Top always respects a boy's limits.

When I think he's had enough, I bite each ass-cheek hard enough to inspire yelps, wipe off my fingers, and pull the sock-gag out of his dry mouth. He's allowed a few welcome sips of Stella before it's time for a different gag. I wrap several layers of bondage tape between his teeth and around his head, then prop us up on pillows against the wall and hold him in my arms, stroking him tenderly, soothing my prisoner.

Soon enough, though, the sadist in me starts roughly fingering his pierced tits again. (Note to future captives: it's almost impossible for me to keep my hands and mouth off a bound-up man's nipples.) Tibor begins breathing deeply and whimpering with hurt. He leans his head back against mine, shudders, closes his eyes, and takes it like the big man he is. The tape over his mouth and the pain etching his brow make him even more desirable. When the song of his suffering gets too loud, I clamp one hand over his lips, grip his jaw, and tug and twist his nipples even harder.

"Good boy," I whisper in his ear. "I want you very sore for several days. I want your pecs to throb when you pull a shirt over them tomorrow morning. I want you to wince and grin and think of me."

Tibor nods beneath my hand, gives me a muffled "Yes, Sir," squirms a little in my grasp, then takes the pain a good while more before finally begging me to stop.

With my pocketknife I carefully cut the tape off his face. Tibor's thirsty after his torture; I lift the bottle to his lips again and again before taking my turn. We gulp heartily, like blood brothers celebrating in a medieval mead-hall. Helping a bound man eat and drink is a great pleasure, as are any acts that emphasize his helplessness and dependence. When the bottle's done, Tibor settles his cheek against my hip, swallows my cock, and sucks me with a gentleness surprising in such a butch guy. I lie back, torn between rapture and anxiety. Where the hell has John gone? I'm going to pay for all this tomorrow.

I'm getting close, so I pull Tibor off. "Could we have another beer?" he asks. "And I think I'd like to be freed now. My arms are getting pretty stiff."

For a novice, he took a pretty lengthy bout of bondage. I untie him, pop another Stella, and turn off the bedside light. We lie side by side for a few minutes, passing the beer back and forth in silence till it's gone. I grip his still-hard dick, he runs his fingers through my graying chest hair.

"Uhhh…I really love being gagged. Would you tape my mouth again, please?" Tibor says, with a sheepish meekness made even more exquisite by his superior might. Now that he's unbound, he could probably pick me up and throw me through a wall, yet instead he's continuing to surrender to me. How I love men strong enough to give up strength, honest enough to ask for what they want, brave enough to crave powerlessness.

"Damn, man, I'd be glad to gag you," I reply. As soon as his mouth's taped up, he surprises me by pulling me roughly into his arms and working my tits with his fingers. I couldn't resist him if I tried—he's much, much stronger—but resistance is the last thing on my mind, since I'm a sucker for forceful tit-work. When it starts to hurt and I start to groan, he reaches for the sock-gag on the bedside table. He holds it up in front of my face and looks at me quizzically.

"Hell, why not?" I say. I'm a voracious versatile; turn-about is fair play. And the best thing about fighting for top is that no one really loses. Tibor stuffs the gag into my grinning mouth, knots it behind my head, and starts into tugging my nipples again. I bite down on the cloth, already wet with his saliva, slip my fingers into his tit-rings and twist till he's hissing against the tape. Talk about hurting good. A little brotherly cock-work on top of pec-torment, and in about two minutes we're done, two big gagged men panting in one another's arms, nipples on fire, bellies smeared with semen, heartbeats slowing, drowsing together in the dark.

—⟋⟍—

WELL, YES, I PAID. I would've liked to have kept Tibor bound and gagged in bed beside me and held him all night long, but I ushered him out near midnight, afraid of John's reaction if Tibor were still there when he returned. At it was, John didn't get in till 2 am, having miserably walked the streets after drinking a beer or two in a nearby gay club. We slept back to back, we had one of those Big Talks in the morning, the kind I used to initiate with past lovers and now dread as scab-picking that doesn't do much good for anybody. After another day in Budapest, we left that apartment, its tiny trashcan full to overflowing with beer bottles and bondage tape, and took the train to Salzburg. We found another man there, Thomas, in a bar beside the Salzach River, one who preferred John to me, or so I perceived it, for my insecurity is boundless. We drank a lot of absinthe, we took Thomas to bed. From mutual resentment, John and I eased slowly back into comfort. Things even out. Time and habit help.

—⟋⟍—

OCCASIONALLY I E-MAIL TIBOR. He has a lover now; they sound happy together. I wonder if his lover ties him up. If so, I hope Tibor thinks of me sometimes as he flexes those amazing muscles against his bonds.

Every so often I cook Hungarian food—*gulyás*, *pörkölt*, chicken *paprikás*, Transylvanian cabbage. When I taste the combination of rich sour cream and spicy paprika, and later pour out some of Hungary's famed dessert wine *tokaji* to accompany Dobos torte, I wonder how Tibor is doing, how we might have gotten along if personal and geographical circumstances had allowed us more time together. It's highly unlikely that we will ever meet again, and that is strange to know considering the intimacies we shared, albeit for only a few hours years ago. He's one of many men I wish I'd had more of, wish I could move from past to present.

When I look at the digital photos John took of Tibor bound and gagged, I'm only reminded of photography's greatest irony. Such art is meant to preserve the subject but only highlights its absence, reminding us, like a chemical equivalent of memory, of what's missing. Is that why I long to bind desirable men? Is that the reason for this Top-man ache? Some childish, subconscious delusion, some futile hope that tying them up might somehow force them to stay, might detain them and delay their inevitable departures? With what unsettling velocity so many beauties, and the passions they inspire, move into, through, and out of our lives. Isn't this every lover's greatest regret? Art is the only way I know how to slow it all down. And that method is—let's face it—almost completely inadequate. Photographs, poetry, this essay? So paltry compared to the brief, warm, hard physical facts they try to memorialize. Sometimes I think that, rather than write, I might as well strip, sip some *tokaji*, knot in a sock-gag, close my eyes, try to picture past lovers, and simply jack off. And so I might. But I must finish this sentence first.

UNRECONSTRUCTED QUEER

FOREST HILL, WEST VIRGINIA

Great-great-grandfather Carden was almost ninety when my father, only ten, had lunch with him one autumn afternoon. His knotted hands shook with palsy as he tried to cut the pie. Old age wasn't too bad, he claimed, trying to make conversation with the shy child across the table, but it had become difficult making water.

This is my only (obviously borrowed) memory of my Confederate ancestor. When I visit the Ferrell family graveyard to put my own struggles in perspective, I always visit his grave plaque: Isaac G. Carden West Virginia Pvt Lowry's Btry VA Lt Arty Confederate States Army Aug 10 1841 Feb 28 1932. What did he endure, I wonder, in which battles did he fight? Would I have had the strength to survive what he and his comrades did? From his epitaph I brush away fallen leaves.

BLACKSBURG, VIRGINIA

THE CELLAR DOWNSTAIRS IS ALWAYS smoky and loud. Jane, Jim, Charlotte, and I are splitting a pitcher of cheap beer after grading midterms all day. These colleagues think they know me. I am a liberal Democrat, an English instructor at Virginia Tech, a poet, an openly gay man. Yet, when they roll their eyes over the Confederate flag controversy, dismiss the Stars and Bars as the emblem of racists and rednecks, I put down my mug of beer and pull my key fob from my jeans pocket. On the small strip

of metal are inscribed three letters: CSA. They look at me as if I have
suddenly slipped off a mask and revealed the thorny face of a gargoyle.
The argument commences.

HINTON, WEST VIRGINIA

"I CAN'T BELIEVE YOU HAVE something in common with Jesse Helms," my
sister says accusingly. This convergence of opinion is indeed amazing,
and true proof of the world's complexity, or perhaps simply of my own
arcane and neurotic contradictions. For many years I've realized, with a
perverse streak of pride, that I have too many internal divisions for anyone
but family to begin to grasp. As a gay man, I despise Jesse Helms. I took
true delight when, a few years ago, an AIDS activist group stretched a
huge condom over his house. Commiserating with other Southern gays, I
loudly ask "*When* will he die?!" and construct fantasies in which he and
his ilk are fed piecemeal to wild dogs. Yet on the issue of the Confederate
flag, this execrable man and I agree.

One absorbs regional loyalties from the water and air, I sometimes
think. I cannot trace my passionate defense of the Confederacy to any
particular person. My mother raised me to be an old-fashioned Southern
gentleman and thus, in this vulgar world of contemporary culture, I
am an anachronism (another point of pride). My father, who attended
the University of Virginia and Washington and Lee, brought me up to
admire Robert E. Lee but speaks of the Civil War not with the partisan
rage I sometimes feel but with sadness and regret. Nevertheless, when I
stand before the Confederate statue in my hometown, I curse those who
would remove the Stars and Bars from any public setting, as if the flag
my forebears fought for were a shameful thing, an American swastika.
I know that they would raze this statue, had they the chance. These are
affronts I will not forgive. They might as well take chisels to the stone-
etched epitaphs of my ancestors.

RICHMOND, VIRGINIA

MY BOYFRIEND AND I ARE visiting friends in this summer city. Though I have not made it to Richmond very often in my forty years, I have a few memories of what was once the capital of the Lost Cause. 1990, touring the Museum and White House of the Confederacy, strolling the Capitol grounds. 1992, a gay rooftop party near VCU, admiring a few bearded men and looking over the city at midnight. The lights of banks and office buildings tinged the low clouds red. Red as disaster: the Fall of Richmond, the fires in Shockoe Slip, the explosions and screams, the invasion of the victorious Yankee army.

This summer, 2000, John and I drive down Monument Avenue. The crepe myrtle is blooming, pink and fragrant. There, atop pedestals, are the statues of my heroes, Lee and Jackson. But there is another statue here now, one I do not want to see, and so we turn off the avenue and into the Fan District to track down a pub. Something honoring Arthur Ashe makes sense to me, for I too am a member of minorities: Appalachian and gay. I am not, despite my Confederate sympathies, a racist. I have some sense of the importance of role models for youth in any subculture. But Ashe's statue should not be on Monument Avenue. Locating that statue here is a deliberate affront, as if, unable to tear the statues of Confederate heroes down, black leaders will simply co-opt the avenue. And somehow, the juxtaposition of war and tennis seems to me absurd.

Another insult has occurred since I last visited Richmond, I suddenly remember as John and I gratefully sip our beers, frothy cool relief from the Tidewater heat. A newspaper article passed around the Virginia Tech English Department office, details I blocked out, for, when it concerns this topic, I am angry enough. Something about a wall in Richmond, a public celebration, the figures of historically significant Virginians painted or draped on that wall. In the face of rabble outcry, the image of Robert E. Lee was taken down. Skimming that article, furious—this the man that, I often joke, sits on the right hand of the Father—I simply cannot understand how other residents of Richmond, many the descendants of Lee's army, could have allowed this to happen.

HINTON, WEST VIRGINIA

MY FATHER, MOTHER, AND I are sitting around the breakfast table, plates
sopped clean of biscuits and gravy. Always trying to impress my father
with my accomplishments, I preen: an ex-colleague has invited me to give
a poetry reading at Fredericksburg, Virginia. Site of an important Civil
War battle, my father explains. "Get the Catton upstairs," he requests, and
soon, *This Hallowed Ground* in hand, he begins to read the historian's
description. Looking over the opposing army as sun burns off the morning
mist, Lee says, "It is well that we know how terrible war really is, else we
would grow too fond of it." After several paragraphs, my father's voice
cracks and he stops. He cannot continue. I take the book from his hand
and begin to read where he left off. Now my voice grows husky with
suppressed tears and I too must stop. My mother looks at us as if we are
both insane.

FREDERICKSBURG, VIRGINIA

JANE AND I HAVE AGREED to disagree. She is a Midwesterner, a huge fan of
Lincoln. This afternoon, a few hours before our poetry readings at Mary
Washington College, we tour Fredericksburg Battlefield, slowly strolling
over the park. Where once the Confederates won a great victory, now
carefree tourists walk through burnt-orange maple leaves, which drift
defeated, wild embers, along October's breeze. Touching the stones of the
Sunken Wall, behind which the Southern troops took shelter, I can feel,
oh-so-vaguely, the cold of that December morning, can watch the blood
oozing into half-frozen mud. I can see the young rebel soldier Richard
Kirkland, "The Angel of Marye's Heights," leaping over this wall to give
dying enemies a few sips of water from his canteen. Kirkland, who would
die at Chickamauga, age 20.

    Stopping to locate bullet holes in cabin walls, I try to explain to Jane
how deeply I feel those conflicts and loyalties that raged almost a hundred
years before I was born. Lincoln's cause was not that of abolition but
federal control. Witness the late date of the Emancipation Proclamation,
as carefully aimed as more tangible Union fusillades. Yes, slavery was

wrong, but that was the South's business, and an institution the South would have abolished on its own. Imagine being forced to belong to a country, a religion, a relationship which one wants only to escape. "No, you can't leave." The effrontery of it. Like any individualist, I want to live my life as I choose, I want to be left alone, free to do what my nature dictates. Lincoln's insistence that the Southern states remain in the Union reminds me of how straight society insists that we all join up, conform, be normal, or pay the price. "Reconstruction" takes on new meaning.

Jane will have none of this. But later that night, as we relax over a bottle of burgundy in the campus guesthouse, she admits, "I was surprised to see how solemn you were on the battlefield. It was a big victory for the South. I figured you'd be jubilant." I think of Kirkland, those men gasping their last in his arms, courage ending with a bullet in its brain. I shake my head, take a swallow of wine, head off to my comfortable bed.

BERKELEY PLANTATION, VIRGINIA

DOWN TO THE JAMES RIVER the green lawns slope, terraced expanses of clipped box-hedges and flowering crepe myrtle I pull to my face and nuzzle, breathing deep the scent. I am enamoured of plantations, the romanticized details of antebellum life, and I resent the plebeian indignities of the twentieth century, I resent missing the opportunity to live in such a place. Like all the beautiful buildings of the world, Berkeley's elegance was allowed by surplus wealth, which in turn was allowed by social inequities, social injustices like slavery. But aesthetics have always been more interesting to me than ethics. I am grateful for any beauty, despite its origins. Today morality seems secondary.

A path leads away from the plantation house toward the cemetery, and I follow it. There beneath great trees rest a few headstones, the blue blossoms of vinca. I sit in the grass nearby, lean against a tree trunk and close my eyes, free of the irritating presence of other tourists. For some reason, perhaps because death reminds me of its antithesis, passion, my daydream is erotic.

It is dusk, the summer of 1861, one of the war's hopeful early years. Birds roost noisily in boughs above the James, and, as darkness deepens, fall silent. This tryst has been carefully prearranged. Beneath the trees, amidst the graves, they meet once night is complete. They do not understand this need, this damnation, but they are here nonetheless, at great risk, two men in gray wool, each with frantic fingers peeling off the other's sweat-stained uniform. Their bearded mouths press together— taste of bourbon and tobacco. One runs his fingers through the other's chest hair, then drops to his knees. What they do together feels like the gravest sin and, simultaneously, the greatest reason to endure.

CHANCELLORSVILLE, VIRGINIA

I FOLLOW THE SIGNS PAST the last snowy puffs of serviceberry, spring's earliest bloom. Here stand a large inscribed monument to Stonewall Jackson, and, down another short path, a low crude stone, the original marker placed at the spot where he fell, accidentally and mortally wounded by one of his own men. He was a mountaineer like me; he would have recognized the serviceberry, its guarantee of new life. His arm, amputated in vain, was buried first, his body interred elsewhere. Why do my eyes mist over? Grief is comprehensive: tears for Stonewall, for the South, for my grandmother's death, for the loss of a lover I could not convince to remain. "Sorrow's springs are the same," said the English poet Gerard Manley Hopkins. "Let us cross over the river, and rest under the shade of the trees," were Stonewall's last words. Beneath those trees, he is spared the bitter vagaries of history, to see the flag he fought for misused by the vicious and pulled down by the righteous as an emblem not of homeland but of hatred.

BLACKSBURG, VIRGINIA

I HAVE A NEW COLLEAGUE, and, in an attempt to make him feel welcome, I have invited him over to dinner. My martinis are profound, I've promised, and my pasta puttanesca deeply meaningful. He is black, which only encourages me to take him under my wing, for, as a gay man, I rapidly relate to minorities of any sort. However, in my campus office he's noticed the Stars and Bars shot glass on my bookshelf, which, in his eyes, is probably a disturbing sign, so before he arrives for dinner, I do a little apartmental rearranging. For the same reasons that I rarely wear my "Rebel" or my "Heritage, Not Hate" T-shirts in public, today I take down the huge Confederate flag draped over my guestroom door. The same Southern upbringing that has encouraged my respect for the Stars and Bars has bred me to be hospitable, to avoid confrontations or giving offense. As a host, it is my duty to make my guest comfortable. My one compromise, which serves to illustrate the odd contraries that compose me: a small Confederate-flag refrigerator magnet, which secures against the fridge a magazine-cover photo of Andre Agassi, sexy as hell with shaved head, goatee, earrings, cocky grin, and beautifully hairy bare chest. If my guest notices the magnet, I will sigh and begin the usual explanation—"I'm a very complex person. . ."—before pouring him more wine. Odd, in these politically correct times, to apologize for Confederate sympathies rather than for homosexuality.

WASHINGTON, DC

MY BOYFRIEND IS WELL EMPLOYED, not an academic, and I cherish the occasional luxuries allowed a corporate spouse, accustomed as I am to the insultingly small salary and pathetically sparse travel funds allotted me as an English instructor at Virginia Tech. This weekend we have met in DC and are staying at the Hay-Adams, one of Washington's fanciest hotels, built at the spot where Henry Adams' house used to stand. I relish such accommodations, the aristocratic elegance that I, in my openly elitist and entitled way, have always believed I was born to, but, bitterly, have rarely been able to afford. As I stand in the window overlooking Lafayette Square and the White House, I can't help but think of Henry Adams, who felt that his education had prepared him for living in a century already past.

While my partner is in meetings, I walk fast about the streets of Washington, trying to work off all the German, Spanish, Mexican, and Chinese food we've been devouring during our few days here. The Mall is sunny, the elm leaves are drifting down, jagged tears of topaz, a few shirtless joggers lope by, deepening the scenery. In the distance, the

Lincoln Monument whitely asserts itself. I love this city's grandeur (as much as a country boy can love a city), but my patriotism, like the rest of me, is conflicted, far from simple, bristling with ambivalence. Not only do I regard Lincoln's shrine with a mixture of admiration and resentment, but, looking across the Potomac to Arlington Cemetery, a national monument for most, I cannot forget that it was once the estate of Robert E. Lee, taken from him during the Civil War and made into a cemetery by his Union opponents. When I head back to the hotel, near the White House I pass an equestrian statue high on a granite pedestal. Sherman. Over a century after his merciless and destructive swath through the Deep South, I curse him, hoping by now he's well charbroiled in hell.

CHARLESTON, SOUTH CAROLINA

THIS IS WHERE THE FIRST battle broke loose, beginning the conflict that for so many Southerners lives still. On the tour boat to Fort Sumter, my partner and I have christened a fellow tourist "Tommyknockers," inspired by the way his gym-molded chest swells beneath a boastfully tight T-shirt. When we disembark, our admiration shifts to the sunlit flags high above, whipping in this heavy wind which surges off the sea. We wander through brick arches, past long-unused cannons. There is something peculiarly bereft in places which once hosted actions of great significance and now simply host the curious, the placid, the unheroic. Corpse-like, a husk from which spirit has passed. Something about the contrast between legendary past and quotidian present is chafing, abrasive. I simply cannot imagine this small island as anything but what it is today.

Back in Charleston, we walk down to the Battery, where live oak leaves pile up in brittle drifts and azaleas flower, pink, white, and luminous as youth's skin. Near the peninsula's very tip, the Confederate monument looms, a naked warrior before which John and I stand in awe: the shoulders, torso, biceps, thighs of the ideal male body. It's as if the sculptor had somehow convinced a god to be his model. Behind the statue, beneath the oaks, the Stars and Bars flutter here and there. A crowd has gathered to protest the latest attempts to remove the Confederate flag from public display. I move forward eagerly, grinning, but the sense of camaraderie is adulterated. "They're the sort of people who'd probably like to kill you," I remember my mother warning me once as together we watched a televised march in support of the flag. What do I share with these folk, other than love for this flag, this pride in my Southern heritage?

Today, as I move through the crowd, I wonder how many are homophobes, how many of these scruffy strangers, if they knew what sort of man I was, would, given the opportunity, despite our common sympathies, bludgeon me into a heap. Some, perhaps, are racists, whose use of the Stars and Bars in the last several decades has helped sully its reputation so badly that most Southern intellectuals and liberals feel obliged to renounce the flag rather than be accused of racism themselves. Inadvertently, these espousers of racial hatred have only contributed to the South's lingering defeat. When the last Confederate flag is relegated, like an artifact of shame, to a museum, the North will have completed that victory begun at Appomattox. Conquering not only those young men who laid down their arms in 1865 but all the generations to come, convincing the descendants of those suffering soldiers that Lee's armies struggled in support of evil—these are the last vicious acts of Reconstruction.

PLANTATION FANTASIES
OR,
ONE HILLBILLY'S JOURNEY TO THE TIDEWATER AND BACK

(for Cindy Burack)

The Old White, they used to call it, when Robert E. Lee and other Southern aristocrats, fleeing the Tidewater summer heat, used to visit the mountain resort. Torn down in 1922, rebuilt in the late twenties, it is now called the Greenbrier, still a luxurious resort for those who can afford it. For most of my life, I have wanted to spend the night there, but considering the cost of the rooms—$228 per night is the cheapest rate I can find on their web page—I doubt that I will ever fulfill that particular dream.

Those mountains once were Virginia; since 1863, they have been part of West Virginia. In particular, Greenbrier County, which is just east of Summers, the county where I spent my adolescence. I remember the first time I entered the Greenbrier, when I was a shapeless preteen visiting relatives there. My mother's sister, Aunt Jane, had married well, a Chrysler executive whose company treated him to occasional visits to the resort. I walked into the lobby, admired its high ceilings, its expensive furniture and wallpaper, its air of gentility, and proclaimed, "Ah, the elegance I was born for!"

At that point in my life, I had yet to realize that I was gay, but on some level I certainly knew I was different. During my first ten years, in my mother's hometown of Covington, Virginia, my peculiarities were not all that remarkable. I played with the other neighborhood children, attended grade schools, tinkered with my rock collection and my chemistry set, watched *Batman*, and passionately collected comic books. My only salient oddity was an interest in the occult.

After age ten, however, when my family moved from Covington into the mountains of West Virginia, my father's original stomping grounds, and, after a few years, I entered junior high in Hinton, it became clear to everyone that I did not fit in. Along with the continuing enthusiasm for witchcraft and magic, which horrified the local devout Christians, I was not interested in sports, I was not interested in band (which all the popular kids joined), and I was a straight-A student in a region only beginning to value education. This led to a bit of name-calling: the word "queer" was lobbed at me well before my sex drive began to take shape and long before I realized that the admiration I felt for some boys and many men was sexual.

I responded to such hostility with one haughty conviction: my intellect made me superior to my persecutors, made me an aristocrat amid peasants. It was this self-defensive belief, I suppose, that led me, a descendant of Appalachians and all my life a denizen of small towns in the Highland South, to identify with European royalty and the antebellum aristocracy of the Tidewater South. Thus my sense of entitlement, of coming home to luxury and expensive grandeur, when I entered the lobby of the Greenbrier.

Though none of my ancestors or my immediate family had possessed anything even approaching the finances appropriate to an upper class, I quickly learned the phrase "genteel poverty" and soon set about emphasizing my genteel differences. If I could not have the money (and no future career that caught my adolescent interest would provide more than a decent wage), I could possess the other attributes of nobility: a wide-ranging education, fine manners, a well-developed aesthetic sense, an enthusiasm for things cosmopolitan.

These "highfalutin'" interests of mine my parents more than approved of. Though both came from modest backgrounds, neither were typical Appalachians of that time period, the 1960's. They possessed many of the traits I yearned for, and they encouraged my intellectual development. My father, the grandson of mountain farmers, was the first on the Mann side of the family to earn several degrees. He taught English and French in high schools and colleges and then later became a lawyer. As soon as I learned to read, he pointed me in the direction of serious literature and music. He bought me comic-book versions of classic novels and an entire set of encyclopedias, read me stories from King Arthur's exploits and from Greek mythology, taught me bits of French, and played me records of Puccini, Beethoven, and Brahms.

My mother, daughter of a nurse and a machinist, had dropped out of Longwood College to get married but continued to read novels of depth and shared my father's passion for classical music. In one major respect, however, she differed from Daddy. He had traveled a good bit as a soldier in the Second World War and had had more than enough of the outside world. He was content never to leave the mountains again. She, on the other hand, though immured most of her life in two uneventful little towns—Covington, then Hinton—yearned for international travel and passed that yearning on to me. Luckily, her sister Jane lived far from Appalachia, in interesting cities like Chicago, then Detroit, then San Diego, so that gave my mother an excuse to escape the monotony of the mountains, to take her children—my younger sister Amy and me—into the outside world and expose us to classes and cultures not our own.

Along with my parents' relatively genteel tastes, then, another factor that encouraged my longing for elegance was my Aunt Jane and her well-off lifestyle. Her husband, Uncle Garm, the Chrysler executive, had scads of money (at least compared to my father, who as a schoolteacher made little and as a novice lawyer made not much more). In Chicago, they lived in Deerfield, one of the more affluent suburbs. In Detroit, they lived in Bloomfield Hills, with the other well off. In California, they lived in La Mesa, a wealthy suburb of San Diego. What a treat it was to visit them, to get on the train in Hinton, to see the mountains diminish, the flat lands and the cities begin, and, at journey's end, to be whisked from the rail station to their home. Always a living room reserved for special occasions, with furniture too expensive for children to touch. Always exotic foods: lobster and cheese broiled on English muffins, shrimp cocktails, crab enchiladas, avocado salad, and the adults' fancy cocktails from which I occasionally got a tiny sip. In Detroit, a huge boat on which to explore the Great Lakes, big enough to spend the night on, rising to chipped beef on toast in the mornings. In La Mesa, a pool surrounded by rustling palm trees and birds-of-paradise.

These were my first tastes of the life of the rich and the wide world beyond Appalachia. After glamorous and novelty-filled weeks with Aunt Jane and Uncle Garm, it was always a letdown to return to Hinton —the shift from colorful otherworldly adventure to black-and-white home that so many have noted in *The Wizard of Oz*. My father rarely went with us on these visits, having, as I've said, lost any interest in travel, and he always seemed to resent my aunt. It was clear to me even then that he regarded her values as trivial, materialistic, and shallow. It's only now, from the perspective of a 45-year-old, that I realize he must have feared that she might kindle hungers in me equally shallow, desires that his means and my region would never be able to satisfy.

A few other elements of my youth were to sharpen this hunger for wealth, privilege, and my fascination with aristocracy, whether in the form of American mansions or European royalty. Those stories my father read me as a child—how clearly I can remember lying with him on the chaise longue on my grandmother's back porch, the Howard Pyle edition of King Arthur's exploits held between us, the wonderful illustrations of Merlin, Lancelot, and Vivian. Here, and in Edith Hamilton's *Mythology*, another early favorite, were castles, kings, warriors, fortresses, magic, and heroism. This is the sort of fare that both fertilizes the imagination of a bright child and also, for many of us, makes quotidian reality forever inadequate. When I finally got to junior high and had access to the library, the first two books I checked out were big photo collections of European castles and cathedrals, grand edifices very, very far away from Hinton, West Virginia.

The third book was *Dracula*. *Dark Shadows*, the Gothic soap opera that ran from 1966 to 1971, would also prove to be a huge influence. Already fascinated with the occult, I took to its stories of witches, vampires, ghosts, and werewolves with avid interest. And there it was, an American castle, Collinwood, the huge family estate on which most of the storylines centered. Baronial fireplaces, ancestral portraits, grand staircases, looming turrets, romantic terraces and gazebos...

and American royalty, the wealthy members of the Collins family, who lounged about in formal clothes and sipped sherry (or brandy, when they needed resuscitation after the latest supernatural shock). How I hankered for the vampire Barnabas' characteristic Inverness cape, onyx ring, and silver-wolf's-head-handled cane (all souvenirs I have since, as an adult, acquired). Such props might not only add dash to my appearance—and as a pudgy, insecure, bespectacled bookworm, I needed all the dash I could get—they might also invite adventure into my life or distinguish me from my inferiors. They might reveal to the world my inner aristocratic nature, so far quite efficiently buried within a doughy, asexual body and quiet mountain towns.

—⁂—

NEEDLESS TO SAY, THIS INTEREST in things grand and aristocratic made me look down on my own culture, that of Appalachia, with contempt. What had I in common with hicks and farmers, railroad workers and miners? I recall one particular expression of this contempt. One autumn night when I was about fifteen, I went out to dinner with the playwright Maryat Lee and her partner at the Oak Supper Club near Pipestem, West Virginia. Maryat, a family friend, occasionally invited me off on jaunts without my parents in tow, perhaps sensing my potential as a writer, or, more likely, as a budding queer. What a sense of arrival: a fancy restaurant with candles and silver, a menu on which brown beans and cornbread did not appear. I ordered duck, my first. The fact that it turned out to be all dark meat, and dry at that, didn't matter. It was the sort of entrée I imagined might be enjoyed at Collinwood, or some Tidewater plantation. When a family of locals sat at a nearby table and began talking, I quietly mocked their accents as indicators of ignorance. Maryat smiled, but gently told me not to make fun of them, admitting that she liked this region's dialect. I smiled back, rolled my eyes at the table of "hillbillies," and began contemplating the cheesecake menu.

When I tell this story now to my Appalachian Studies classes, I use it as an example of cultural hegemony: how mass media prod us into assimilating into mainstream culture and encourage us to deride and reject our regional or ethnic legacies. Where did a high-school kid who had spent almost his entire life in the Highland South get the idea that mountain accents revealed stupidity? What Appalachians on television or film are depicted as anything other than provincial laughing stocks? There are exceptions, but they are few. For both "queers" and "hillbillies," mass media often spread the seeds of self-hatred.

But these were realizations I was far from achieving that evening in the Oak Supper Club. I did not belong in my native mountains, I felt sure. I belonged elsewhere, in a faraway world of privilege from which only an accident of birth had exiled me. Somewhere, a turreted house or massive plantation awaited me, with, perhaps, a passel of servants. After all, the Ferrells, the Irish side of my father's family, were descended from royalty, a fact my grandmother was fond of pointing out, a fact I clung to in order to make sense of my pervading and inescapable sense of displacement.

Soon after, when I turned sixteen and, through the help of lesbian friends, realized I was gay, that sense of displacement grew, and my attitude toward Appalachia grew more fraught. Now I had another reason to seek the outside world: not only might there be some aristocratic life awaiting me, there were, I knew from my furtive reading of gay novels borrowed from my lesbian friends, places Out There where gay people could live openly and safely. I knew that, in my hometown, to live as an open queer would invite pariah status, verbal abuse, and violence.

My rapidly developing sexual tastes added a sharp complication, however. I found myself attracted to the country boys I'd grown up around, the same "peasants" I feared and looked down upon, the intolerant straights from whom I did my best to hide my desires. This was thoroughly confusing: how could a would-be aristocrat yearn for rough mountain men? Shouldn't I be turned on by men like those I wanted to become, gentlemen in suits, men with the visible attributes of the upper class? Hopelessly ambivalent, I wanted both to flee the culturally backward country for big cities and gay ghettos and to stay in Appalachia and sleep with its men.

This lust for the locals, by necessity, I never acted upon, and I knew that as long as I remained in Hinton my desires were irrelevant, condemned to suspended animation. Nothing could change till I finally made it to college, where I could cultivate my gentility in the rarefied halls of Higher Learning. In high school, I already had a reputation as a bookworm that was inescapable. (I was declared "Biggest Bookworm" and "Most Polite" in my senior yearbook.) Hanging around discernible lesbians didn't help my reputation any: I "associated with known ducks" and was thus tarred with the same brush. After my lesbian friends graduated a year ahead of me, I kept to myself, concentrated on my studies, and survived as best I could during that slow and painful time between the realization of my sexual identity in early 1976 and my escape to West Virginia University in August 1977. I was meticulously nondescript, except for the rebellion of shaggy hair. Striding around blue-collar Hinton looking like Barnabas Collins or an elegant Southern gentleman or any other upper-class ideal would only have encouraged catcalling and jeers.

Once I made it to Morgantown and WVU, where few folks knew me, where I had no reputation and could be someone new, I took that opportunity to transform myself. And it is here that my lust for Appalachian men took an interesting twist. Despite my aristocratic pretensions, I had to face facts: men in suits did not appeal to me. Scruffy mountain men did. An erotic syllogism: country boys are sexy, I want to be sexy, so looking like a country boy will make me sexy. Plus blending in would be a way to stay safe. I used mimicry, not unlike the Viceroy butterfly, whose coloration imitates the foul-tasting Monarch so as to dissuade the hungry interest of birds. I took up the very signifiers of masculinity that I admired in local men: jeans, work boots, flannel shirt, beard. Queer novels I discovered in Morgantown's bookstores mentioned the leather community, my fantasies about tying and gagging handsome men were thus given a context that helped them make sense, and so I bought my first leather jacket. As I strode around Morgantown's bars with my lesbian buddy Bill, two self-conscious butches in search of a good time, my fascination with a far-away and long-ago aristocracy faded a bit, and when I decided to major in Forestry as well as English and began hanging around with other booted, bearded country boys, my yearning for a world of sherry-sipping, fashionable, courtly, plantation-owning gentlemen began to wane.

Other factors have eroded that early passion for Tidewater elegance, those antebellum dreams. When I moved to DC to teach in the fall of

1985, I did not take to the city at all, and, in fact, realized how much of a small-town Southerner and hillbilly I really was. Yes, my mother's careful training had given me sufficient manners to get along at fancy parties in fancy queer townhouses—in fact, for a West Virginia boy who'd never had money, I felt fairly secure in such settings—and yes, there I was, at last surrounded by what I had come to call "piss-elegant" furnishings, the same wood-paneling and the very crystal decanters displayed at Collinwood. But the sense of arrival I'd felt as I first entered the lobby of the Greenbrier as a preteen, that was not there. Instead, I missed the mountains, I missed the down-home cooking, the slower pace, my family. The few folks with Southern or mountain accents whom I met in DC I immediately took a liking to: they sounded like home.

At the end of that semester, I returned to West Virginia. I had had enough of city noise, Beltway traffic, and too many people. Somehow the yearning for a plantation house, a Newport mansion, or a crenellated Irish castle had transformed into a desire for an isolated plot of land in the mountains, with a vegetable garden and a big farmhouse.

—⁓—

TEACHING APPALACHIAN STUDIES AND APPALACHIAN Literature at Virginia Tech has completed my fondness for my native region and further dwindled my Tidewater-plantation aspirations. How fond I am, how protective, of local kids in my classes, kids from West Virginia or Southwest Virginia, bright well-mannered kids who tell me shocking stories of being mocked—by other students, even by some of their professors—for their accents, their backgrounds, whatever makes them discernibly Appalachian. As I have learned about the history of Southern Appalachia—the exploitation of the natural resources by outside interests, the consequent environmental destruction, the courageous battles of coal-miners to form a union, the economic declines and out-migrations—I have been moved and saddened and angered, and my allegiance to my region has immeasurably deepened. Encountering the fiction of Harriette Arnow, Lee Smith, James Still, and Denise Giardina, or the poetry of Louise McNeill, Irene McKinney, and Maggie Anderson, I have come to feel more and more respect for the struggles of the mountain working class, and I have learned to take pride in being the descendant of country farmers.

In my identification with Appalachia I have achieved, I suppose, an awareness of class issues and class conflicts, a recognition effectively obscured for most of my life by my haughty craving for aristocratic privilege, my "identity envy." And recently, race issues have also tarnished my Tidewater fantasies.

To the shock and disapproval of many, I respect the Confederate flag. That flag means to me, as it does to many Southerners, "Heritage, not Hate," to use a T-shirt slogan. However, this is an opinion I keep pretty much to myself so as not to offend the many people for whom the Stars and Bars are a symbol of racism. My in-laws are black, as are several of my favorite colleagues. A double minority myself—Appalachian and gay—I immediately gravitate to minorities. And in the company of several African-American colleagues, I have been given gentle reminders of their perspectives on the antebellum elegance I've admired.

Brilliant, deliciously acerbic Grant, joking, as we entered a faculty reception held in the grand mansion in which the president of Virginia Tech lives: "Well, my kind are traditionally asked to enter edifices of this sort through the back door." My snort, mingling contempt and camaraderie: "Hahh! Well, you can be damn sure if they asked you to enter there, I'd be right by your side."

Lucinda, the chair of my department, one of the most exceptional human beings I've ever known, who, during my first year as an openly queer assistant professor worried about achieving tenure in conservative Virginia, passionately defended me from a homophobe who sent around a vicious e-mail note to alumni about my web site and the gay-themed publications listed there…Lucinda, as we entered a fancy restaurant in New Orleans with other colleagues attending a national creative writing conference, "Hmmm, so this part used to be the slave quarters, according to the waitress. Well, Larry," addressing her husband, "I guess this is where you and I would have ended up."

—⚄—

MY ARISTOCRATIC PRETENSIONS AND CRAVINGS are far from dead, I freely admit. Much of my travel revolves around visiting the remnants of empire in one form or another, the monuments left by an opulent past. In Richmond, I have toured the White House of the Confederacy, then driven down to the James River to quietly drool during tours of Berkeley Plantation and Shirley Plantation. Like any Southerner with an historic sense, I have toured Mount Vernon and Monticello. In Charleston and Savannah, amidst azaleas and Spanish moss, I have swelled with envy over the great white-columned homes there. Near New Orleans, I have sipped a mint julep on the back porch of Oak Alley Plantation and wished I could own it (with, preferably, a stable of beefy, hairy, perpetually shirtless, black-goateed young men to keep the property up for me while I write and read).

My jaunts in search of aristocratic relics have, over the years, ranged farther and farther from home. One Spring Break I dragged John to Newport, Rhode Island, to see Seaview Terrace, the great mansion that served as Collinwood in the original *Dark Shadows*. When I make it to Europe, I have to push my way into Prague Castle, Neuschwanstein, Edinburgh Castle, and the Hofburg with all the other slavering tourists. Obviously, I still have a fondness for royalty. The lives of the Windsors interest me to some extent, and the thought of a United Kingdom without a queen or king disturbs me. The fate of the Russian Romanovs is so painful to me that for years I have carefully avoided learning the details of their deaths, and visiting their tomb in St. Petersburg, I was wet-eyed. I have eagerly read biographies of homosexual royalty like Edward the Second of England and Ludwig II of Bavaria, and I have visited their tombs to pay my respects. If I ever make it back to Vienna, I will not only snap up assorted pastries but also revisit the Hapsburgs' imperial burial vault.

When I finally got to Ireland in 1994 and visited Longford, home of the once-royal Ferrell clan whose blood has, diluted, descended to me, I discovered that the ancestral castle I would gladly have claimed as my rightful inheritance had long ago been razed. In its place was a parking lot. Once I realized that there was no royal edifice left to lust for, what seized my sympathies in Ireland was the many ways in which it is like Appalachia: small towns and rural dwellers; crumbling, abandoned homes and other signs of out-migration; high unemployment and poverty in a scenic landscape. I stroked the green leaves of huge potato plants, admired the colorful cottages with their plumes of peat smoke, listened to old ladies planning another round of gooseberry-jam-canning, sat in pubs sipping stout with sexy Celtic country boys and watching televised soccer, and felt pretty much at home, with farmers and livestock herders, with people who have never known money and who make do, as we do in Appalachia, as best we can.

—◦—

I AM NOW, AND PROBABLY always will be, a hive of hopeless contradictions. The refined and cosmopolitan traits that as an adolescent I dreamed of acquiring I have to a great extent achieved. In my home, there are crystal decanters like those in Collinwood, sherry and brandy snifters, a rack of good wines. My cookbooks range from Ireland to Germany to Greece—in fact, most of the countries of Europe. My travel-photo albums are numerous: I have been to just about every European country that interests me, though Iceland, Norway, Spain, Italy, Poland, and Romania are still on the Yet-To-Be-Ravished list. With a little practice, I am competent in French and German, and I can speak a little bit—a very little bit—of Greek, Hungarian, Czech, and Dutch. I know a great deal about certain aspects of literature and mythology, a smattering of history and philosophy, and a good chunk of botany. I listen occasionally to Puccini, Beethoven, and Brahms, as my father still does. Right now I am enjoying Ovid's *The Metamorphoses*. Next summer, I hope to return to Greece and show John the delights of Mykonos and Santorini. Unlike many of my fellow mountaineers, especially those caught in the economic crisis of the coalfields, I am obviously not poor, though I am certainly not well off. English professors rarely are.

However, beside the Inverness coat I bought in Edinburgh, the coat almost identical to my aristocratic role model's, *Dark Shadow's* vampire Barnabas, there hang the coats I wear more often: the scruffy brown duster John's sexy straight ex-roommate left me, the new biker jacket John bought me for my birthday in a San Francisco cycle shop, or the worn black-leather jacket with a patch on the chest depicting the Celtic god Cernunnos. Kept in the same guest room are my boots: lumberjack boots, cowboy boots, harness-strap boots. In them conveniently converge two worlds, often mutually exclusive, that live side by side in me: the world of the Appalachian countryside, the world of gay leather bars.

On the dresser, beside the elegant onyx ring I sometimes sport, à la Barnabas, are the black-leather cock rings I often wear as wristbands. In the front hall is my collection of "redneck caps." For baseball caps, mine are, I must admit, a mite unusual. One is from Lost River, a gay guesthouse in West Virginia, one celebrates Joni Mitchell's CD *Both Sides Now*, one commemorates *Dark Shadows'* 30th anniversary, one displays a black-and-blue leather-flag, and one bears the logo of Mr. S, a leather store in San Francisco.

Odd how a regional identity I so wanted to escape as a younger man I have almost entirely come to terms with in my middle age. These days I drive an extended-cab 4x4 Toyota Tacoma pickup truck I bought off my father, and I am so delighted with the way my "Macho Mountain-Man Mobile" climbs steep dirt roads and maneuvers in the snow that I have sworn never to live without four-wheel-drive again. The country music I so loathed in my adolescence is, other than my continuing passion for folk-rock stars like Joni Mitchell and Carly Simon, my primary musical enthusiasm. There is little I love more than driving the back roads of West Virginia and Southwest Virginia in my truck, watching the woodlands and meadows shift colors with the seasons, and listening to Kathy Mattea, Mary Chapin Carpenter, Toby Keith, or Brooks and Dunn in my CD player.

Then there is my favorite country-music star, Tim McGraw, with whom I am so infatuated that his handsome goateed image appears on my fridge, on my bedroom wall, and even in a bookcase nook in my office. Listening to his new CD *Live Like You Were Dying* on my way to Charleston, West Virginia, or Washington, DC to give poetry readings has been a real delight this autumn of 2004, and John and I will be attending McGraw's Charleston concert in a few weeks. With any luck, John's rational grasp will prevent me from rushing the stage like a lust-addled thirteen-year-old girl.

All this is surface detail, obviously—clothes, truck, CD collection. But these details accurately reflect a deep change in attitude. Yesterday I gave a talk on Appalachian poetry and fiction and played my mountain dulcimer for an Elderhostel group at Mountain Lake, Virginia. Last night I read poems at a rally against the massive environmental destruction caused by mountaintop removal mining, an invention of Satan if there ever was one. In a few days I will be speaking on a panel focused on Language Diversity and will discuss how Appalachians are often mistreated due to the ways in which their pronunciation and usage are perceived as ignorant. Later this autumn, at a symposium on mountain music, I will be reading a series of poems I composed about the dulcimer, and next spring I will be moderating a panel of West Virginia poets as part of the Appalachian Studies Conference. My career as a writer and a scholar is, obviously, pervaded thoroughly by my Appalachian identity.

Despite the homophobia and religious fundamentalism of this region, pestilences common in Southern Appalachia but certainly not exclusive to it, I intend to stay here, albeit in the sheltered environment of a university town, where I can be openly queer without having to engage in street-brawls every day. Someone needs to stay—not to flee to New York City, DC or San Francisco—to stay here and continue the fight. I intend to, and to fight on two fronts: for Appalachians and for LGBT people. I have, after all, inherited from my hardscrabble ancestors an innate orneriness and a taste for battle. Despite my cherished sword and dagger collection, despite my hot temper, I know that, in the twenty-first century, the pen (or, rather, the laptop) is a handier weapon than a honed blade and more likely to be free of uncomfortable legal consequences. I intend to use this keyboard with pugnacious regularity—as claymore, mace, dirk, or battle-axe—to attack conservative stupidity, as well as using it—as lyre, dulcimer, banjo, or guitar—to praise mountain and queer cultures and to tell the truth about my life as an Appalachian gay man. Beneath my earlier yearning for a Tidewater plantation and a life of privilege I have found an inescapable fondness for underdogs, for the persecuted and the marginalized.

—〰—

TODAY I AM TAKING JOHN to lunch at the Greenbrier. The main dining room and the Sunday brunch are far too expensive to be worth it, but luckily there is a small, reasonably priced restaurant in the basement of the hotel, surrounded by shops selling garish golf clothes and jewelry. After a rainy stroll around the autumnal grounds under John's huge umbrella, we settle into a table and examine the menus. It takes me only a few minutes to realize that all the other diners are palpably well off and Not From Around Here, and all the water-servers and waitresses are locals who speak like I do. Yes, their accents are deeper than mine, more prominent. Education often smoothes the edges of dialect, and it has mine, though my accent deepens considerably when I am angry, drunk, amorous, or around others of my region. Nevertheless, I feel that immediate kinship that common language can create.

This afternoon I respond to the restaurant staff the way I usually do when courteous people are waiting on me. I have enough empathic imagination to guess how hard their jobs are—much harder than mine— and I do my best to return their friendliness and to be appreciative of their efforts (though I will be the first to admit that unfriendly service brings out in me the supercilious aristocrat faster than anything, except, perhaps, waiting in line). The fact that they sound like fellow mountain folks only makes me friendlier. I have lived long enough to realize that the differences between their education and mine, their salaries and mine, are nothing I could take credit for, but are, rather, caused by chance, luck, fate, or accident.

As John and I sip our sweet iced tea and wait for our meals, I watch the overworked staff dash back and forth while I sit comfortably in my chair. I think about class differences and regional identities, the luxury of free time that allows my reading, writing, and contemplation. I think about the gentry I once wanted to be and will never become. Being waited on makes me feel uncomfortable and apologetic, I realize, as it did when I was a child at my grandmother's, where the woman would cook for hours, and after dinner the men would retire to the living room to watch TV while the women cleaned up. As much as I like dining in the fancy atmosphere of the Greenbrier, I would not have made a very good Southern aristocrat. In fact, considering my penchant for underdogs, I would probably have done a lot better as a member of the Underground Railroad than as a plantation owner.

Social injustice, class differences, and unequal distributions of wealth have created so much of the beauty I love: the castles of Europe, the plantation houses along the Mississippi and the James, the mansions of Newport. Always driven more by aesthetics than ethics, I cherish that beauty despite its origin, as I am today relishing the opulent surroundings of the Greenbrier. It is a world I love to visit.

But I know in which world I belong, if I belong anywhere. What I want to share with John one day is not a plantation but a cabin or a farmhouse with a big porch, in the countryside or in some liberal small town. A wood-burning fireplace would be nice, and an orchard, and a small garden, and a wood-lot for chopping kindling and splitting chestnut oak…though, admittedly, I am so immersed in reading and writing that those elements might work better in fantasy than in fact.

Our chicken-salad croissants arrive, and our spinach/English walnut/ mandarin orange salads, and as I thank the waitress and hear my home in her inflections, as I not-so-elegantly dig into my food, I remember a phrase I often use with my best friend Cindy.

My People. It started at one of the big gay marches in Washington, DC when I was much younger. A kid used to the homogeneity of small towns, I studied with dubious fascination what I regarded as a cavalcade of shockingly colorful queers—some of them, to my inexperienced eyes, extreme and ridiculous freaks. I rolled my eyes with scorn—as I did years before at the Oak Supper Club, when I mocked those Summers County accents. I sighed resignedly, then said to Cindy, "These are….. my people?!"

My sense of irony is as sharp as many a gay man's, but there is little irony left in that phrase now. When I think of the drag queens, the Radical Fairies, the transgendered, when I think of the coal-miners, the truck-drivers, the railroad workers who live along Cabin Creek, down in Logan or up in the Potomac Highlands, I am certainly aware of our differences, but now, in the face of a world hostile to both hillbillies and queers, I am more interested in our outsider commonalities. I know them for who they are, and I know who I am. Today in the Greenbrier, amid aristocratic elegance I was not born for, as I smile at my partner and order my pecan pie, I am grateful at last to know my own people.

HOW TO BE A COUNTRY LEATHER BEAR

Everyone thinks of us as a city species, we leather bears. But you know better, you small-town gay men sporting beards, body hair, and brawn, you country-dwelling devotees of BDSM and rough man-on-man sex. Perhaps you live in a rural area because you grew up there to begin with and had little desire to leave, even after you realized you were queer. Perhaps you stayed in or near your hometown to be close to family or friends. Perhaps you left the city for financial reasons, to take advantage of the lower cost of living in the provinces. Perhaps you once tasted city life and recoiled, decided that living the urban gay lifestyle wasn't worth the noise and traffic, the crowds and expense, and so returned to your roots, determined to stay. Whatever the reasons for your rustic existence, know that being a country leather bear is easier than the city-loving twink might imagine.

Yes, country folks tend more toward homophobia and conservatism than frequently liberal urbanites. Most small towns sport churches on every other corner, crammed on Sundays with frothing fundamentalists convinced that men-loving-men are satanic monsters. But you, as a leather bear, are likely to deal with such unfriendly surroundings better than many of your queer brethren. There are two reasons for this. One, the outfits of the typical leather bear are identical to those of most straight country boys. In winter, both kinds of men wear work boots, cowboy boots, thermal undershirts, sweatshirts, faded jeans, leather jackets, denim jackets, and cowboy hats. In summer, they sport baseball caps, cargo shorts, camo pants, A-shirts, muscle shirts, tank tops, and T-shirts. (The proof of this is Larry the Cable Guy, the blue-collar comedian. Step into any bear bar, and four out of every five men there will resemble him.) Thus, if you choose not to be openly gay, you're well camouflaged. If you wear the typical leather-bear ensemble, you'll look like any other redneck and will more easily be able to go about your life without having to tolerate public harassment as many of our more effeminate compatriots must. (Here's the downside: if you, like many bears, are attracted to men who look like you, you're often going to be seething with frustrated lust, surrounded by all those sexy straight men who look like leather bears but aren't.)

The second reason why living around rural conservatives is easier for leather bears is purely physical. We're not young, slender boys weak from constant dieting. We're big—bulk being part of the definition of being a bear—and our furry faces and bodies make us look manly and menacing. The intolerant are simply less likely to pick a fight with men like us. Hit the gym, buddy. Work some heft into your chest and arms. Sport a few intimidating butch tattoos. While you're at it, boxing and the martial arts are fine hobbies to adopt.

This protective coloration said and done, I'd recommend that you come out to as many of your neighbors as possible, unless they're obviously pious swine, gun collectors, or twice your size. People need to know that queers are all around them and that we come in many sizes and shapes. Diffusing ignorance diffuses hatred. Plus it's simply easier to be honest about who you are.

So, made relatively safe by your brawn and your apparent similarity to other rural men, what you must figure out is how to lead a fulfilling life so far from Queer Central. Since you live in the countryside or a small town, spend some time exploring what pleasures these settings provide. Visit the local restaurant, doing your best to ignore the Jesus paraphernalia on the wall, and take advantage of down-home cooking at low prices that would cause city folk to faint with disbelief. Respond in kind to the servers' small-town friendliness and good country manners. Order sausage biscuits, grits, soup beans, chicken and dumplings, sweet iced tea, coconut cream pie. Attend seasonal celebrations that occur annually in your neck of the woods: the county fair, the Maple Syrup Festival, Railroad Days. For God's sake, get outdoors as often as possible. Take advantage of the natural world that city and suburban dwellers rarely get to appreciate save on vacation. Hike up to Dragon's Tooth Knob, bike the New River Trail, walk along Claytor Lake. On weekends, visit nearby state parks and national forests. Keep an eye out for hawks, butterflies, muskrats, white-tailed deer. Luxuriate in the silence, the dark country nights that city folks are denied. If you have the land, grow a garden. Pick fresh tomatoes, peppers, corn, basil, oregano, mint.

Many urban queers hanker after occasional escapes from metropolitan ruckus. Fulfilling this need is a fine way to enjoy small-town living and queer companionship at the same time. All you need is a guestroom…and a talent for cooking. Learn to mix drinks, make pasta, cook up stews, bake biscuits and pies. You're a bear, after all: you love to eat and drink. Your gay and lesbian friends eager for a change of pace from DC, San Francisco, and New York City will be grateful for a weekend in the country: quiet evenings by the fireplace, playing some guitar, sipping some bourbon, savoring some chili and cornbread, watching *Sordid Lives, Gladiator, 300,* or *The Birdcage* for the tenth time.

Country living's easier if you're resourceful and self-reliant, if you savor solitude and learn to take pleasure in small things: the shifting seasons, the changes in weather, big meals, good books, music, and movies. The frost on the windowpane resembles feathers. There's a new cheese at the local Food City, a new variety of Scotch at the liquor store. Joni Mitchell just released a new CD. The latest Netflix DVD has Viggo Mortensen naked. The sexily goateed FedEx man just delivered, unbeknownst to him, porn star François Sagat bound and gagged in the latest Titan video release *Fear.*

Come to terms with country masculinity, winnow it, take the best, and throw away the rest. Many of us, once we discovered our homosexuality, rejected traditional masculine activities, the ones so beloved of small-town folks dedicated to old-fashioned gender roles. Look again. You can be brave *and* nurturing, strong *and* tender. Many apparently mutually exclusive things are really not. Honor, loyalty, stoicism, and protectiveness are warrior virtues more than worth retaining. As besieged as the queer community is these days, we need all the warriors (male and female) we can get.

Many of us, influenced by media and the prevailing urban values
of the queer community, tend to hold country enthusiasms in contempt.
Look again. Pickup trucks are handy as hell, and damned handsome at
that. Whether live or televised, basketball, football, and baseball games
can be pretty pleasurable. The players are often sexy, the beer and hot
dogs cheap and tasty. Country music brims with top-notch guitar playing
and heartfelt lyrics. Along with Reba McEntire, Dolly Parton, and other
country divas so adored by drag queens, there's a passel of fuckable and
furry studs who apotheosize the concept of Sexy Country Boy, prominent
among them lean and luscious Tim McGraw; hunky goateed Chris Cagle;
burly blond bear Toby Keith; and adorable cublet Chris Young—all ripe
subjects for kidnapping fantasies and fodder for erotic fiction.

In other words, you don't need to be the sleek, smooth, slender, well
groomed, androgynous, and thoroughly domesticated city queer of many
an *Advocate* ad or TLA movie. You can preserve a little wildness, like the
rural landscape around you. You can be as beefy and scruffy as many a
country boy and still be thoroughly queer.

Adding gay erotic elements to a country life can be challenging, but
between the Internet and an active imagination, you can work wonders.
Try to picture what being a country queer of any stripe was like before web
browsing! It was an isolation that bred soul-killing loneliness, despair, and
suicidal thoughts. Now a few minutes on Firefox can net you a slew of
distant delights. Order BDSM gear—bondage tape, handcuffs, ball gags,
hoods, tit clamps, and other toys beloved of leather bears—from faraway
stores like Mr. S or JT's Stockroom. Buy erotic bondage art from countries
as remote as Japan. (Check out the amazing work of Gengoroh Tagame
for evocative, arousing images of muscle bears bound, gagged, tortured,
and raped.) If you're single or in an open relationship, hunt down partners
for long-distance flirtation. If you're lucky, you might even lure one into
visiting. Back to that guest bedroom and that cookbook collection. There
are lots of city-pent leather boys likely to relish a cozy weekend in your
B&D B&B, bound to your bed or treated to your home cooking.

If you affix a leather- or bear-flag sticker to the back window of
your pickup truck, you might meet friends or playmates even closer to
home. A note with a stranger's phone number or e-mail address might be

waiting for you beneath your windshield wiper when you're done fetching groceries and cruising the sexy young clerk at Food City. And being out to your neighbors is likely to net you advice regarding the location of local queers. Sociable small-town folks are often eager to introduce people with similar interests.

It takes imagination to infuse daily life—which tends toward the habitual, the boring, and the mundane—with erotic energy, whether you're partnered or single. It's even harder in the queer-sparse countryside, but, if achieved, it adds an edge and intensity that we leather bears cherish. Wear that chain-and-padlock slave collar beneath your sweater when you go to work, or the naughty BUTCH BEAR: HAIRY, HORNY, HUNGRY t-shirt you bought online. Slip in a butt plug for your workout at the local YMCA. Take pleasure in the weight of a chrome doughnut cock ring while attending the baseball game. Handcuff and bit-gag your partner before cuddling on the couch to watch the latest Netflix. Leave him hogtied and ball-gagged on the floor of the closet for an hour on Sunday morning, while the rest of the county sings hymns in church. Half of the pleasure of being a kink-buff living in a rural/conservative area is knowing how much you're getting away with and picturing the expressions on your neighbors' faces if they only knew.

Finally, save the money and take the time to travel, whether it's to the nearest small city for a bear- or leather-run, to San Francisco to check out the infamous bear bar The Lone Star, to DC to admire all the bare and hairy torsos during Green Lantern's Shirtless Night, to Key West for the clothing-optional, all-male guesthouses, or overseas to explore the leather bars of Vienna, London, and Berlin. Novelty is exhilarating, you'll see what you're missing, you'll admire the plethora of sexy city men, if you're lucky you'll bind, gag, and bed a few, you'll ravish a few restaurants too. Then you'll be ready to go home, where there are still trees and pastures, where things are slow enough for folk culture, tradition, and good manners to survive, where the nights are very dark and you can see the stars.

LEATHER-BEAR APPETITES

Stand naked before this morning's bathroom mirror, one week before your 48th birthday. Buddy, you're holding up tolerably well. All bear, that's for sure: salt-and-pepper beard, chest and belly hair, tribal tattoos, pecs and arms pumped up from weightlifting. Then there's the moderate belly, something you love on other men but never have been too enthused about on yourself. If it weren't for the bear movement, you well know that you'd be considered too hefty and old for anyone to want. As it is, you embrace the titles of Leather Bear and Daddy Bear with great gratitude; they're identities that have netted you many admirers.

From whence this belly, you growl, rubbing its curve. You're 220 lbs, heaviest you've been in all your life. You look best about 190, dammit. This thick physique, this run-to-fat metabolism you inherited from your father. You've spent the last thirty years falling in and out of diets; you love good food and drink too much ever to be thin. Ten years with John, ten years of his fine talents in the kitchen on top of yours (you, descendant of so many excellent country cooks), plus regular imbibing of wine, Manhattans, martinis, mint juleps, plus too much sedentary reading and writing—from thence this belly, this belly the furry solid symbol of memory, your body's stubborn, not-to-be-simply-shed memory of multitudinous good meals. Just this week, you and your husbear have whipped up hummus, tsadsiki, Southern eggplant salad, chicken and pork kabobs with mango chutney and pita bread, turkey-sausage-and-mushroom sauce atop radiatori. Next week, at your birthday celebration in Key West, Lord, there'll be shrimp,

Cuban pork, black beans and flan, piña coladas and Key lime pie sampled from as many restaurants as your limited vacation time permits.

Food and sex, what else is there? you are wont to joke with bear bravado. (Well, booze, of course. Booze, books, music, mountains, movies, forests, friends, and family. Does that cover it? Just about.) This morning perhaps—since John has just bought you both new mountain bikes and you're thus likely to exercise more often—perhaps you can get away with a big, fattening, unhealthy Southern breakfast, the kind of meal you grew up on and so forever crave, the kind midlife health concerns rarely allow. Buttermilk biscuits and sausage gravy, that's your specialty, one of John's favorites. It's what he deserves today, bless him, after the cock-sucking he gave you last night. Bears are all about appetite.

Quietly you pull on camo shorts, letting him sleep late. In the kitchen, barefoot, bare-chested, sipping coffee, you gather the ingredients. Cut Crisco into self-rising flour, the way your grandmother taught you, then add buttermilk. Knead the dough firmly, gently, the way you do a lover's beefy torso or crotch. Waiting for the biscuits to bake, fondle your nipples, still sore from last night's lovemaking. Rub your hairy, growly bear-belly, through the camo cloth tug your cock. Remember what flesh remembers, blessed history of men and meals, when hungers so sweetly converged.

—◊◊◊—

THE GREAT PASSION OF YOUR life, you must start with him, the few feasts you shared. Thomas is middle-aged now too, plump and even grayer than you. But today, with the scent of biscuits filling this house where you spend your life with John, not him, you want to see him now as he was then, when you wanted him more than you'll want anyone again, a short, well-muscled, thickly hairy cub with a sharp tongue, sharp mind, and impish grin.

It's 1991, and how you want to please him. Perhaps, if you give him enough, if you make love to him more passionately and perversely than anyone else ever can, perhaps he will leave his lover, he will stay with you, he will not leave town at summer's end. Here are the surprise gifts you bring to your assignations: carved wooden boxes, spheres of amethyst, books on the Kabbalah. Here are bottles of German wine, cream-cheese

Danishes, almond croissants, lemon squares. You present these tidbits to him like offerings, like the fruits of the harvest that your heathen ancestors used to lay inside stone circles, by sacred wells and on woodland altars, prayers of the supplicant for favor.

Today you sit on the deck with him, sipping Moselle. You are both shirtless in the balm of late May. Sun and the breeze-stirred shadows of maple leaves ripple over his bare chest, the rich brown hair over his heart. Soon you will buckle a black-leather, metal-studded dog collar around his neck and lead him inside. You will knot one bandana between his teeth, knot another over his eyes, rope him spread-eagle to the bed, and suck his nipples and cock. What you feel for him is what many feel for Christ, and, when you have him naked, bound, and gagged, a willing sacrifice, he is more beautiful in his submission than anything on earth. But right now you listen to him—how he loves to talk, how he loves how you listen— you listen to the wind in the leaves, you sip the wine and savor cream-cheese Danish, the buttery flakes scattering your belly hair. You feel the time together so rapidly running out. Young as you are, you somehow sense nothing will ever taste so sweet again.

Another day, deep into July, you are driving up the Shenandoah Valley, taking Thomas to his professional conference. Consummate liar, he's told his spouse that he's traveling with fellow students, but he's secretly here with you instead. The windows are down, summer air pours over your bare chest, Carly Simon's singing "These are the good old days." He's so desirable; it's such bliss to be with him. Despite the homophobic hooting of those driving by, he feeds you bits of blueberry scone, as if the two of you were truly intimate, truly spouses, not just fuck-buddies. You wonder if he loves you, and, if not, why not. It never occurs to you that the dangerous, needy, obsessive depth of your love is the very thing that makes it impossible for him to love you in return. And he is, for all intents and purposes, married. He's just having a little erotic adventure; he doesn't want some crazy poet to wreck his life. Nearly two decades later, when you are in his shoes, then, then, fool, you will understand.

So many meals you cook for him, hoping that your domestic talents might convince him what a perfect husband you could be. There's hummus rich with olive oil and tahini, there's kung pao chicken spicy with peppers and crunchy with peanuts, there's tabouleh he criticizes for lacking sufficient parsley. There's a feast to celebrate Beltane: chicken curry with rice, homemade puri and mango chutney, apple strudel with ice cream. You cook all day, because nothing is too much trouble in your quest to impress him. There could be orange-glazed pork loin, spanakopita, or sauerbraten with potato dumplings, but these are meals that the presence of his spouse, the limitations of your adulterous time together, never allow.

Thomas is a meal in and of himself, your communion wafer, your hirsute god-loaf. Again and again you bring the little bear full of honey to your trysts. Again and again you dribble clover honey over his hairy nipples, his balls, the head of his cock. As if he were a big bearish biscuit, as if he were something entirely edible, your own private banquet. God knows you want to devour him, but licking honey off his nakedness has to be enough. There are, inconveniently, laws against cannibalism, against abduction. You want to keep him bound and gagged in your basement till his beard goes gray. You want your cock up his ass and his chest hair beneath your tongue till the stars tarnish.

He leaves, of course, at summer's end. You cry in his lap, you shake his hand on your office steps, he walks away, he and his husband move to New England. Your heart is an ash pit; no one wants to fuck a man so full of grief. What is left but food and drink? Pleasures of the present, they help you momentarily to forget the past. They are simply and easily arranged; unlike the ravishing of a beautiful man, they do not require reciprocity or consent.

You are too shy and damaged to pursue romance or sex, so victuals must substitute. This is called sublimation; this is called gaining weight. Culinary tourism becomes the key to your emotional survival. Track down roasted octopus, retsina, ouzo, *melitzanosalata*, and *moussaka* in Greece. In England, savor hard cider, steak-and-kidney pie, fish and chips, spotted dick. In Scotland, there's single malt Scotch, haggis, and gooseberry fool; in Ireland, there's potato boxty, soda bread, and stout. Vienna is *Wiener Schnitzel*, *Käsespätzle* and *Linzertorte*; Zermatt is kirsch and *Raclette*; Zurich is huge *Riesenwurst*, *Rösti*, and *émincé de veau*. On a restaurant balcony in Lucerne, look out over the river and mountains, sip beer and cut into the local specialty, *pastete*, a pastry case full of veal, mushrooms, and cream sauce. You have come all this way to prove to yourself that wonders and delights apart from him are still attainable. For a few minutes, savoring the Swiss landscape, the wine, the food, you are truly happy; for a few minutes you succeed.

—⋙—

THESE BISCUITS, THESE HERE, NOW, in 2008, they are done. You slide them off the baking sheet, wrap them in a tea towel, snuggle them in a basket to cool. Start the gravy. Chop onion, heat milk, fry sausage. Reach out for what remains of 1995.

—⋙—

IN WINTER, A LETTER FROM Thomas after three years' silence. News of his move to the DC suburbs, his desire to see you. The affair recommencing during his husband's business trips in February and May. Touching, tasting, tying, sliding inside him again. Pilsner Urquell, homemade pizza, popcorn, Canadian whiskey. His tongue, nipples, cock in your mouth.

Now it is July. After two months overseas, you are flying into Dulles, eagerly meeting Thomas for lunch. The crepe myrtles blossom pink and white, Georgetown is humid and hot, his beard-shadow and the scent of his sweat madden you. He knows how much you love it when he doesn't shave or use deodorant. Lure him back to your friend's apartment. Give him the pewter quaich you bought him at Edinburgh Castle, the tiny bottles of Lindisfarne mead and Atholl Brose. Soon enough he is stripped, the hardness of muscle and softness of chest hair once more within your grasp. Soon enough he is blindfolded and bound, trembling and sighing on the unfolded futon. Sip mead from the quaich, drip honey-fire on his lips and brow, pour creamy Atholl Brose over his nipples and navel. Lick and lick, nuzzle and lick, as if you might burrow down into some sweet place inside he's never let you see. Soon enough you've both shot, he's untied, you are lying together sticky and spent, your beard musky with the aroma of his armpits and crotch. Your time is over, he must get home.

Making love, you've been spared the knowledge that you and he will never make love again. Now his necessity showers off your honey-wine and your scent. Embrace him one last time, walk him to the Cleveland

Park Metro stop. In a few months, there will be someone new in his life, there will be acrimonious e-mails back and forth, angry e-mailed good-byes. You will mourn, you will want to die, you will fuck around, you will meet John, you will happily settle down, you will never forget.

Twelve years pass. Then one winter night there he is, sitting with his latest husband in a San Francisco bookstore where you are reading your work, poems and fiction he inspired. It has been so long, he has become so gray it takes you a few minutes to recognize him. One of the greatest shocks of your life, but, even so stunned, you are sufficient Southerner to be polite, you are professional enough to read with some composure, even though what you really want to do is hide in the men's room and sob. He is smiling as if you are simply old friends; he's hoping to grab a drink and catch up. You are far too numb to manage that. Instead, you introduce him to your husbear, and then you flee. In the bar across the street, you order several doubles, Tullamore Dew straight up, you chat with friends as if nothing were wrong.

You will never be drunk enough. You will not sleep tonight. You will not want to touch or be touched for months.

What kind of freak are you? It's been over a decade.

—∞—

IS THIS PROTECTION, LEARNING NOT to worship but to play? Is this wisdom, now that men have become mere friends and fuck-buddies, not gods? See, romanticism expires, realism burgeons, but the feasts continue! They do not mean as much as they used to—nothing means as much as it used to—but they are perverse and they are delicious. What you have achieved is breadth. You are no longer capable of depth.

—∞—

RON'S A SHORT, STOCKY, AUBURN-GOATEED Top you've met online; his scene is tying up men in their leathers. This January weekend, he's driven down from Lynchburg despite impending snow for several days of play. You're dressed as he's ordered, in jeans, cowboy boots, A-shirt, and biker jacket. He's had you leave the jacket unzipped so he can play with your horny-hard tits. He tapes your mouth, ties your hands in front of you, ropes up your feet, wraps yards of tight white rope around your knees and torso. You are one happy fucking pig; it is so fucking hot to be this powerless. You grunt and struggle; he holds you down, laughing, kneads your pecs, rubs his cock across your face.

You spend the night bound like this. Toward dawn, a heavy snow begins. Toward dawn, as you'd hoped, Ron pushes your jeans down to your boots and kindly fucks you up the ass. In the morning, he unties you, strips you to your briefs, cuffs your hands in front of you, buckles a ball-gag in your mouth. "You promised me bacon and buckwheat cakes for breakfast, boy. Get to it!" he says, slapping your butt.

It is hard to break eggs, sift flour, and flip bacon while restrained, but you are in no position to complain. Soon, to your shame, you are drooling around the ball and into the batter. Ron grins—"Man, you're making a mess!"—wipes your moist, bristly chin and ties a bandana over the ball-gag to soak up the slobber.

It should be an Olympic event, flipping pancakes with cuffed hands. You grow deft at it. Now all is ready, the table set, the food steaming on two plates. Ron uncuffs you only long enough to recuff your hands behind your back. He cuts your heap of cakes into bite-size pieces, pours on the syrup, puts the plate on the floor, and pushes you to your knees. Removing your gags, he pushes your face into the food. "Go for it, boy. Chow down."

You gobble like a dog, your beard and nose glazing with syrup. Ron chuckles, nudging your butt with his boot. The snow continues to fall. You can check another fantasy off.

—∿—

WILL'S HALF YOUR AGE, BUT he's one of the best Tops you've ever known. Lean, smooth-chested—not your type at all—but the guy's super-smart, hugely hung, and he thinks a Daddy Bear with a furry man-rack, bourbon-and-biscuit belly, and graying goatee is the hottest kind of captive. What man approaching fifty can resist such blandishments, such ego-food? No one seeing the two of you knocking back pints together in local dives would imagine that, one, you both are queer; two, guys with such an age difference are fucking; and, three, the big butch bear, not the slender boy, is the bottom.

But here you are, sitting and sweating in the dark, bucked and gagged in Will's closet on a beautiful spring afternoon. He's told you you'll be enduring at least an hour in here, and you've meekly acquiesced. You're wearing camo pants, a camo hat, and black army boots: the guy not only has Daddy and bondage fetishes, he's into military gear too. You're bare-chested; a chain-and-padlock slave collar and dog tags hang around your neck, marking you as his property. The dowel tied over your elbows and under your knees cuts into your flesh; your ass aches against the hard wooden floor. You fight your bonds, you groan, you shout for help, you beg him to let you loose. But Will's cruel—one of the things you like about him—so all your muffled complaints will do no good. He's out there in the light, drinking bourbon and playing guitar. He'll get to you when he feels like it.

At last the music stops, the closet door's unlocked. You look up at him, your face furrowed with discomfort, eyes squinting in the sudden light. Old Civil War torture: this is a hard position to take for long, especially if you're more muscular than limber, especially if you've got a gut. Will stands over you smiling. He wipes the sweat off your brow, then squats down and begins to flick your nipples till they stiffen.

"Hands all right? Not numb?"

Shake your head, manage a muffled, "Fine, Sir."

"Happy?"

Grin into your gag, vigorously nod, grunt, "Yes, *Sir*. Yes, *Sir*." He knows how much you love this.

"Poor private. Bet you're hungry."

Suddenly the bandana's unknotted, pulled from your mouth.

"Look here, big man. Your favorite."

Krispy Kreme. The little bastard has fetched you Krispy Kreme doughnuts. You shake your head, grinning with disbelief. Strange places our lusts lead us. Will pulls off sugary chunks and feeds you tenderly. "Thank you, Sir," you whisper in between mouthfuls. Doughnuts will only plump you up further, but, bless him, your Sarge loves a furry belly.

"Here's something to wash it down," he says, lifting a glass to your lips. Bourbon. You suck down several healthy swigs. He knows how much you like to be buzzed during your captivity.

"Jesus Fucking Christ," you sheepishly mutter. "Bondage, bourbon, and doughnuts? I think I'm in heaven!" In answer, Will dips the bandana in the whiskey, gets it sodden, then stuffs it back in your mouth and knots it behind your head. When you bite down on the cloth, bourbon oozes into your beard and, dripping off your chin, moistens your belly and chest.

"Tastes good, huh? That'll keep you quiet while you're enjoying these." When Will pulls alligator clamps from his pocket, your eyes widen, you shake your head and start whimpering helplessly. He eases the metal teeth onto each nipple, tightens their bite till you gasp, tugs on the chain between the clamps till the tender flesh throbs and you're begging him to stop. Will would love to see tears roll down your cheeks, but he knows you're too tough for today's torture to break. He'll have to settle for your wild eyes, your futile moans. Some other day, perhaps, he'll have you sobbing.

Right now he's had enough of your pained pleas. He presses one hand hard over your mouth. "Shut the fuck up," he says.

Your eyes meet. "Take it and shut the fuck up." Nod, grit your teeth, fall silent. He smiles, tightening the clamps yet another turn, and keeps tugging and twisting till your eyes roll back in your head. One of these days he's going to bring blood.

"You got another half hour," he says, dropping the chain to dangle between your agony-swollen nipples. He straightens your camo cap, pats your head, then shuts and locks the door, leaving you alone to rock and struggle, to chew your whiskey-sodden rag, to suffer and sweat, drunk and grateful in the dark.

—⁓—

DAMNATION, ZACK'S HANDSOME. THAT BLACK beard, that burly body, that stunning smile. At last month's conference you were entirely mesmerized, finding it hard to speak to a man so smart, talented, and hot. You may be shy in person, yes, but you're bold as hell online. Now, after several weeks of back-and-forth e-mail flirtation, Zack's breaking up a long drive north by spending tonight with you and John.

You both know how to seduce a bear. Tonight start with chipotle salsa, guacamole and chips, then chiles rellenos and chicken enchiladas. Finally, serve homemade peach ice cream. John, knowing how infatuated you are, heads upstairs with his dessert, giving Zack and you some time alone. Your ice cream grows a little soupy as you and Zack begin to neck on the couch, as you pull his shirt off, then shrug off your own.

"Holy fuck," you sigh, recognizing the old reverence, pulling back from a beard-to-beard kiss to take the thick flesh of his fur-dusted pecs and belly in your hands. "I have *got* to tie you up."

"Fine," says Zack casually, smiling that amazing smile. "I need tied bad. Why don't you just feed me my dessert?"

"Hell, yes!" you growl, pulling rope from your baggy shorts pocket. In about thirty seconds, you've very tightly and expertly knotted Zack's hands behind his back, then helped him step out of his jeans and briefs. He is, of course, even more beautiful naked and bound. A few dripping spoonfuls end up in his mouth. Some of the creamy melt you pass from tongue to tongue as if it were semen. Some ends up in his beard, in yours; in his chest hair, in yours; on his belly, on yours. Two bears laughing and lapping, getting hard. This is easy, this is joyful. You haven't had a man this remarkable in a long time.

Now the ice cream's done. Time to tie a bandana between Zack's teeth. Time to lead him upstairs by his cock, push him belly-down on the bed. Time to eat his hairy ass for nigh onto an hour, cherish how he bucks and moans. John will join you soon, to suck Zack's cock, tug his balls, kiss his gagged mouth.

Sticky sheets, body hair, and beards matted with peach-cream and come: here are sacraments worth celebrating.

—⚬—

THE SAUSAGE GRAVY IS JUST about ready when John trundles sleepily into the kitchen. The scents of cooking have roused him.

"Biscuits and gravy? Great!" he mumbles, never too talkative before coffee.

Things are a little staid after a decade together. The two of you used to cover one another with olive oil and wrestle naked on a plastic sheet. He used to tie you to the bed and make you lick Sambuca off his cock. You need more of that. You need barbeque sauce nuzzled off thighs, cream of coconut lapped patiently from hairy butt-cracks, brandy sucked out of fuzzy navels, Key lime pie nibbled off torsos. You need to keep a little plastic honey-bear in the bedroom. Wealth and fame you do not have, but, thank the gods of lust and harvest, imagination your hungers have never lacked. You watch your husbear—the man who loves you, tries to control you, maddens you, protects you, pisses you off—as he snarfs up his breakfast. You thank the gods of fire, cock-sucking, ass-fucking, knot-tying, and the cooking cauldron for the power to satisfy appetites. You and he have years together yet, so many men and meals yet to share.

"Woof, this is delicious," he says, taking another big bite of biscuits and gravy. You fork up a rich mouthful, chew slowly, and smile. Good god, he's right.

715 WILLEY STREET

It betrays my country roots, how awed I am by this sight, a city steaming and gleaming in the rain. Chance or my host's careful choice, I don't know, but this Northern Kentucky hotel room must be the best in the house. It's set high within tonight's storm, overlooking the Ohio River and facing Cincinnati's riverfront, a complexity of bridges, interstates, and glowing office buildings. The scene's dramatic, the view's a privilege. I almost feel as if I've arrived, as if this is some fancy hotel room reserved for rock stars or visiting royalty.

No real star here. I've come to Northern Kentucky University at the kind request of a man who's teaching my new book *Loving Mountains, Loving Men* in his grad class on Appalachian Literature. I've spoken to his students and given a reading. His department has paid for this hotel room. I don't get a lot of these invitations—writing about gay people in Appalachia doesn't net me much money or attention—so it's nice to feel successful for an evening.

As exhilarating as the attention has been, I'm tired after the long day of driving, speaking, and then chatting with folks at the post-reading party. I'm glad to be alone now, happy to sit by this big window in the dark and watch the city glitter in the rain. The bed's king-sized—enough room for me and a couple of country-music stars, preferably Tim McGraw and Chris Cagle—but they're inconveniently not here, and I'm too exhausted to do more than cuddle anyway.

Lights in the river: like phosphorescent watercolors, yellow and blue, swirled over a black canvas. Cities: beautiful from a distance, a delight to visit, but I can't imagine living in one. I'm too addicted to solitude and silence, which this hotel room is at present providing. "Chris, Tim, time for bed!" I say, grinning at the foolish impossibility of fancy, heading to the bathroom to brush my teeth. I'm in my late 40's: the same decades that have allowed me a small literary reputation have diminished my erotic opportunities and, in consequence, deepened my fantasy life. Thus, these days, Tim and Chris are my houseboys. They don't get much cleaning and cooking done since they spend most of the time shirtless, struggling, sweaty, gagged, and bound back to back in my basement. Plus imaginary slaves aren't good dishwashers to begin with.

I'm lying in bed naked, relishing interior fantasy, exterior warmth and quiet, watching the veils of rain diminish, when it hits me.

Cincinnati. Cincinnati.

Last I heard, Allen was living here. Is he still here? Is he even alive? When you don't hear from a college friend for years, if you're a gay man of my generation, you can't help but worry and wonder about the worst.

The phonebook's huge, like most cities'. It takes me a while to find what I'm looking for, but there the name is. He's still on earth. It's not too late, so I call. Machine, not man. But for the first time in fifteen years I hear his voice. I speak into the phone, and somewhere my words are seized by magnetic tape on his answering machine. By this room I will leave tomorrow and never see again, the Ohio River runs by, making small sounds not audible at this distance. Across its rain-stippled black back, restless as history, the city lights spill their aspirations.

—m—

EVERYONE CALLED IT AUGIE'S, AFTER the owner. The official name was the Washington Café, at the bottom of Walnut Street, near the Monongahela River. Seedy and friendly, like most gay hang-outs outside large urban areas, with a low bar along one wall, a line of wooden booths along the other. Now it's a small art gallery, but for a few years in the late 1970's it was the only gay bar in Morgantown, West Virginia. It was the first gay bar I ever entered, at age seventeen, the spring of 1977. With only a couple more months of high school to endure before I graduated, I was getting an advance taste of freedom and university life by visiting my lesbian buddy Bill, a hometown friend who was attending West Virginia University. She figured it was time for me to glimpse some gay nightlife, so down to Augie's we went. I was excited to be in Queer Space for the first time, and scared too, afraid a horde of homophobes wielding baseball bats might burst in any second. Natural introvert, small-town boy in the city, I sat in a booth with Bill, listened to Joni Mitchell on the tiny table jukebox, and watched wide-eyed. I had never seen so many gays and lesbians in one room before.

Bill introduced me to several folks that night who would later become enduring friends of mine, and Allen was one of them. The son of a coal-miner, Allen had, like me, grown up in southern West Virginia, in Raleigh County, which adjoins my home county of Summers. He was tall and lean, with short, wavy light brown hair, a handsome, angular face, and large strong hands. It took me only that first evening to discover that he had the kind of quick, mercurial, wicked wit that so many gay men possess, a sharp intelligence I can never match, bulky Caliban that I am, but which I wholeheartedly savor. His whispered comments about this and that bar patron would have done Oscar Wilde proud.

Acerbic he could certainly be, but he was also kind. That evening, he did his best to make me, shy, unsure, shaggy-haired kid that I was, feel at ease. There was, to begin with, no major erotic chemistry between us, which allowed us to skip the complications of sexual attraction and move right into a simpler friendship. Immature men have real problems mixing erotic and platonic love—fucking a friend can ruin the relationship—but we were to be spared those dangers, for the most part.

When, in August 1977, I began my studies at West Virginia University, he and Bill were sharing an apartment in a broken-down old house in Sunnyside, Morgantown's student ghetto. I was living in Boreman Hall, a brick dorm on the Downtown Campus, with a clod-like roommate from Greenbrier County who decorated the walls with *Penthouse* pin-ups and did laundry at two in the morning. I've never been particularly patient, I've always cherished privacy, not to mention uninterrupted sleep, and, besides, I'd come to college not only to get an education, but to spend time with other queers, so it wasn't long before I was sleeping most nights on the lumpy couch in Allen and Bill's University Avenue apartment.

(*How did I stand it?* I wincingly ask myself at age 47. The answer: an 18-year-old back.)

Bill I'd gone to high school with. Allen I had only begun to know. Nevertheless, he never complained about my regular presence in their apartment. On the contrary. In I'd stump, rain beading on my leather jacket and in my sparse beard, and there he'd be, smoking and studying by the window or hunched over his sketchpad creating another amazing image with ink or watercolor. Far more cognizant of the gay world than I—in fact, more competent and knowledgeable in just about everything— Allen took me under his wing. He told me about gay bar etiquette, the fine points of cruising, the ins and outs of oral and anal sex. I hardly knew how to make instant coffee—I'd been spoiled by the good cooks in my family but had as yet learned none of their skills—but Allen was an old hand in the kitchen. He cooked us stews, baked macaroni and cheese, on snowy nights whipped up the Unofficial West Virginia State Dish—brown beans and cornbread. We played Joni Mitchell, Janis Ian, and David Bowie into the wee hours, sitting at the little kitchen table studying side by side: his Sociology and Costume Design, my British Lit and Aesthetics. With Bill, Laura, Cin and other lesbian friends, we'd bustle into the Fox—the latest gay watering hole now that Augie had died and the Washington Café had closed—where Allen would advise me on alcohol options like Tequila Sunrises and Harvey Wallbangers (a far cry from the neat Scotch I favor today) and coach my uncoordinated body in the various bump-and-grind dance moves appropriate to the thumping music of Donna Summer and the Village People. I had never danced with a man before, but Allen was a patient teacher.

We had our hard times. From this distance, both the pleasures and the adversities of college days seem unnaturally vivid, as if I stand in the gentle hills of the Piedmont looking back on a sheer mountain landscape I've recently passed through successfully but with some effort, a world far more dramatic and more difficult to traverse than the one I inhabit now. One night we returned to Allen's apartment to discover that someone had broken in and taken the few things of value. Another time, an anonymous someone called to mutter homophobic threats. Once, during that savage winter of '77-'78, when snow layered the ground in November and stubbornly remained, with regular supplements from the sky, till March, when I was constantly being haled by complete strangers to help them push their wheel-churning cars out of drifts, the heat in Allen's apartment failed for 48 hours and we ended up sleeping together in a completely unerotic attempt to avoid freezing to death. At the end of my first semester, Bill quit school and moved out; a charmer named Larry moved in, stayed a few months, then decamped to Florida with Allen's best blazer, leaving behind an enormous long-distance phone bill Allen ended up having to pay. I developed a huge infatuation on one of Allen's friends, Bob, a handsome and thoroughly superficial Italian-American guy from Weston, was far too shy to make my interest known, and then one night lay in agony on the couch listening to Allen and Bob make drunken, noisy love in the adjoining bedroom. I didn't speak to Allen for a few weeks after that.

Despite minor conflicts, we decided to become roommates, for I was hot to escape dorm life. By the beginning of my sophomore year, Allen and I were sharing the second-floor apartment at 715 Willey Street. That address now evokes futile nostalgia, a clichéd longing for the Lost Abode of Youth in which those inescapably middle-aged tend to indulge. During my brief returns to Morgantown, I sometimes drive past that house, and its present decrepitude reminds me both of the relative rapidity with which all I know and love is gradually leaving this earth and of that circle of friends—Allen, Laura, Cin, Kaye—who helped me survive my youthful despair, sexual frustration, and loneliness.

—w—

ODD WHAT RETURNS TO ME, almost thirty years later, poised here over my keyboard. I live in Virginia now, with John, my partner of ten years, in Pulaski, a small mountain town very much like the ones I grew up in. I'm publishing books, teaching university students. My beard and chest hair are full of gray, and just lately I have started to notice that same silvery glitter in the fur on my forearms. I have several gay acquaintances, not one truly close gay male friend. I haven't seen Allen in almost twenty years. Still, typing this, I find my way back.

Allen is preparing Cornish game hens, the first I've had. But before they're baked, the hens must dance. Allen's whimsical humor so often pulls me from my depressions. One minute I'm lying in front of our gas fireplace brooding over my celibacy and the cursed and unerring accuracy with which I desire men who have no desire for me, and the next, at Allen's suggestion, we are dangling the hens by their little wings and propelling them in a complex pas de deux across the kitchen table. They bow, they leap, they circle like passionate partners, the Ballet of the Dwarf-Fowl. Allen and I laugh till we hurt.

I'm sitting at the kitchen table making index cards to help me memorize dendrology facts more efficiently—maples have opposite leaves, black walnut leaf scars look like clown faces—when Allen, in one of his frequent prankish moods, slips up behind me. He gently hooks my nostrils with two fingers, pulls my face up and back while I grin and cuss, admires the piggy-nose configuration he's created, says "Oink, Oink, Pussy-Face!" then lets loose and bounds beyond the reach of my play-punch. Ever since my beard has started to fill in, he calls me Pussy Face. He also has elaborate jokes about how much I supposedly love to rim German Shepherds. We're boys from small towns in southern West Virginia: rank humor is par for the course.

"Oh Gawd, it's the Dana and Kaye Show!" I whisper, sticking my head into Allen's overheated bedroom. He's always turning the little heater in his room up and then sleeping under nothing but a sheet, even in the bitter winter weather. I drag him into my bedroom, where the window's cracked a bit even in January and quilts are heaped in layers upon the rarely washed sheets. "Now listen!" I urge, handing him the glass. He puts it to the bare wood floor, listens a minute, and grins. Even without the aid of the glass, I can make out "Oh....my....God.....Dana!" Lesbian love-making at its loudest. "We should invite folks in and charge for this!" I say, eager entrepreneur.

Allen's driving us back from Frostburg, Maryland, where we've dropped off Lisa, a lesbian friend. While there, Lisa's cronies coaxed me into trying my first bong. Pot is something I've smoked socially, but it's never really hit me before. Now, sitting in the passenger seat and watching the purple-gray mountains stream by, I'm so fucking high I hardly know where I am. It's scary as hell, though I try to act calm, fight back the panic, and just listen to the tape Allen's got playing. It's at this point in my chemical confusion that a helicopter appears in silhouette against the sunset's red West. Lord God, *I think,* am I hallucinating? Was there angel dust in that weed? Is my mind screwed up for good? *As casually as I can, I say, "Uh, man, look at that. Uh, what, uh..?" I'm afraid to say "Look, is that a helicopter?" because I'm half-convinced that he isn't seeing what I'm seeing, which would mean that my brain is ruined and I'll be trapped in Semi-Rutabagahood for the rest of my life. Allen says, "That's a sweet chariot come for to carry you home, you hopped-up cocksucker!" I choke, he laughs and pats my thigh. "Take a nap, Jeff," he says, and I do.*

It's a windy April evening. We've been listening to the house creak, sprawling on the floor in front of the gas fire, indulging in what is very expensive beer to students as poor as we are, the rare elixir Michelob (which, in my much later beer-snob days, I'll describe as a product that "ain't fit to douche a dog"). We're telling ghost stories—I have the drowned lady who haunts Bluestone Reservoir, he's got some kind of mine-disaster specter. "Well, I'm hitting the sack," says Allen, just about the time I'm thoroughly creeped out. "Sweet dreams," he says wickedly, closing his bedroom door. Trying to relax, I piddle around ineptly on my new guitar—Joni Mitchell's exotic tunings are challenging for a novice— then head for bed myself.

Shucking off my clothes, I slip between grimy sheets. I lie there in the dark, thinking about mine ghosts and monsters. The wind rattling the window screen right beside my bed isn't helping, so I grab a Kleenex, close my eyes, and start constructing a detailed fantasy about the beefy black-bearded boy I heartily and hopelessly covet in dendrology class. I've got a rag tied between the stud's teeth, his hands roped behind his back, and am lapping his hairy beer belly when something scratches the screen. I start, drop my dick, stare into the darkness. The scratching continues—I'm seeing four-inch-long claws—then a sinister something rasps, "Jefffff...." Suddenly the screen rattles and a white face is pressed against the window.

"Holy Fuck!!" I shout, leaping out of bed with a rapidly declining hard-on just about the time laughter starts rolling through the screen. It's that bastard Allen. He's climbed out of his bedroom window onto the top of the porch roof and crawled over to my window, all to see if he can make me piss myself. By the time he climbs back in, I'm poised to tackle him. We roll around for a while, laughing and cussing, before he pins me down. I'm the bearded, butch, aspiring leatherman, but he's always the one who wins our wrestling matches. He's always been stronger.

—m—

ALLEN GRADUATED AT THE END of that year. We parted uneasily. I was selfish and dominating, he was tired of catering to me, he said. I found other accommodations, with a rule-bound recluse I took to calling the Sterile Cuckoo. After a few months of his obsessive-compulsive behavior, I moved into a shabby two-room place on Falling Run Road and began what was to be a long series of years of living alone. Mutual friends informed me that Allen's social work degree wasn't of much use in the work world, and pretty soon I heard that he was living with his Aunt Lil near Beckley and working in a tollbooth on the West Virginia Turnpike.

We reestablished contact fast—rural Appalachia is a fairly hostile environment, so gay boys there need to stick together. Soon, during my summers home in Hinton, I would spend a weekend every now and then in Stanaford, the Beckley suburb where he'd grown up and where his parents and aunt still lived. Allen and I would drive an hour down the West Virginia Turnpike to Charleston, the state capital, and the Grand Palace, a gay bar of many years' duration, to gyrate on the checkerboard of the dance floor, an elevated structure lit from within, to drink cheap beer and to watch the big-haired drag queens cavort. As usual, Allen flirted with ease, while I avoided the guys I found attractive, far too insecure to introduce myself, much less ask them to dance. Allen, bless him, saved every other dance for me.

Worn out with hours of disco, we'd face a 2 am drive through the dark mountains of Kanawha, Fayette, and Raleigh Counties back to Stanaford. (We gay folks in rural regions will drive a long way for some precious time with Our Own Kind.) We'd sleep together—only once did cuddling lead to more, a quiet coupling with his aunt snoring in the next room, a little 69ing that left minimal morning-after awkwardness and was never spoken of afterwards. Put two young and perpetually horny gay men in a bed, and something's bound to happen sooner or later. From the perspective of middle age, I would say that's reason not for judgment but for celebration. Even in my twenties, the concept of *Carpe diem* made perfect sense to me.

Then those late-morning breakfasts courtesy of Mizz Lil, biscuits with sausage gravy made not from milk but water, along with eggs, juice, and lots and lots of coffee. Most folks from my neck of the woods, however modest their means, are superbly hospitable, and I soon learned where Allen had inherited his culinary skills. Nights we didn't drive to Charleston would be composed of stiff drinks and big meals, TV and gossip. Breathless as a Tennessee Williams heroine, Lil would tell tale after tale. Once she gasped, "I took my prescription to the drugstore, and, Lord God, it cost me fifty dollars for four pills. 'Fifty dollars for four pills!?' I said, 'I swan, I'm going to the liquor store, I'm going to buy a bottle of rum, I'm going to go home and have a rum and coke, I'm going to have a rum and coke if it hairlips the president!' I did, I said, 'Fifty dollars for four pills...I'm going to have me a rum and coke and I don't care if it hairlips the president!' Indeed I did, I said..." When, years later, I read Florence King's *Confessions of a Failed Southern Lady* in which she claims that many Southern women feel compelled to say things three times, I could only grin at the familiar rhetorical pattern.

—⋘—

HOW DID ALLEN AND I drift apart? I finished undergraduate school, then graduate school, lived in Washington D.C for a bleak and lonely semester, returned to West Virginia, and began teaching as an overworked and poorly paid instructor in the English Department at WVU. Allen saved his turnpike money and then returned to WVU for a degree in art. He settled down with a new lover, McCarty, in a Tudor-style house not far from my apartment. There we were in Morgantown again, but both so busy there was little time together. He took me down into the bowels of the maze-like Creative Arts Center a few times to show me his sculpture studio, and I attended his senior exhibit. After years of painting, he was focusing on sculptures now, creating disturbing constructs that often evoked the AIDS crisis—slate-gray boxes with shards of mirror and dangling bones. One he gave me, and it stood ominously in my living room until I moved to Blacksburg in 1989. It was too large to take with me; I gave it to McCarty. Their relationship had apparently been provisional from the first—Allen knew he'd be leaving, going to grad school—so McCarty was left with an apartment full of Allen's paintings and sculptures, while Allen moved on to Cincinnati about the time I got a new job at Virginia Tech.

How did we lose touch so completely? Both of us had new lives, in towns far apart. Neither was good at steady correspondence. I made a new set of friends in Blacksburg, fell wildly in love with a man already partnered, grieved terribly when he and his lover left town, then, desperate for consolation, slept around as much as possible. Eventually I met John. Eventually I got a postcard announcing an art show of Allen's in Cincinnati. In 1998, I sent him a copy of *Bliss*, my first poetry chapbook, but heard nothing back. Allen had always been the kind of independent friend who waited for invitations from others to jaunt out together but rarely initiated contact himself. I'm the proud sort who thinks, "Now it's *your* turn to get hold of *me*." I construct little tests for people, count things up, brood over tit for tat. Bad combination. "Well, fuck this," I thought, hoping for and never receiving a note from him gushing over the quality of my poetry. Laura and Kaye, when I saw them during vacation visits, always asked me about him but had never heard from him either. He'd moved to Ohio and simply vanished. "Well, that's what comes from living in the Midwest," I growled, more devoted to my mountains than ever.

—ɯ—

WHY HAVE I HAD SO few gay male friendships? I wonder this a lot in my middle years. I've had many good lesbian friends, quite a few good straight friends, but almost no close gay friends. There was James, someone I met through Larry, the handsome liar who'd left Allen with that unpaid phone bill so long ago. James and I had an on-again/off-again friendship for two decades. I envied him his string of desirable butch-bottom lovers, and he relished my envy, as well as the way my solitary charmlessness, like leaden foil, accentuated his gemlike charisma. Fallings out, years without contact, reconciliations…until, in Rehoboth Beach in the late 90's, over the pettiest of reasons, one estrangement finally took. More recently, there was David, who kept his careful distance at the same time that he relished my cocktails and I relished his eminently quotable wit. He left town recently, and he was palpably chilly to me at our last meeting, for reasons I have yet to discern. My only present gay male friends are Dan and Phil, though the relationship is long-distance now that John and I have moved to Pulaski. We share weekends of martinis and Manhattans, comfort food, and Netflix two or three times a year.

Am I too rural in my values to appreciate or be appreciated by most other gay men, who are largely urban and urbane? Am I too somber, the dark poet who stands in the corner brooding amidst the glittering party chatter? Too self-consciously butch, the token leather bear, the bearded BDSM guy who makes the vanilla types nervous? I don't want to talk about home appliances, the Tony Awards, Project Runway. I want to talk about mythology, country music, poetry, guitars, and pickup trucks.

Ah, too late to change. This ole dawg needs no new tricks. I have John, I have family, I have my work, I have sufficient friends old and new. Still, I look backward as often as I look forward, for the years behind begin to outnumber the years likely to come. I want those friends of my youth to know how much their help meant at that crucial point in my development. I want, if possible, to see them all again, faces creased by the same decades that have creased mine. Thus, after years without contact, that phone call I made from a Northern Kentucky hotel room, overlooking the subtle and ceaseless black flow of the Ohio.

Here's that phone call's answer, one evening a month later, here in Pulaski, with Hilda, our one local queer friend, over for dinner. I'm warm on Irish whiskey, we're all three full from another of my big, fattening country meals, relaxing in the living room, watching the cats chase one another, when the phone rings. It's Allen. He's using the phone number I left on his answering machine. Amazed, I carry the phone into the dark library and sprawl on the couch for a good twenty minutes, laughing, catching up, reminiscing, before John appears at the door, annoyed, pointing out what a bad host I'm being. "It's Allen, dammit!"—I'm a specialist in the subtle snarl—"You've heard me talk about Allen. I haven't seen him in fifteen years!" John cocks an eyebrow—he's a specialist at tacit disapproval—and returns to keep Hilda company.

I'm too Southern not to get off the phone fast—bad manners are indeed the ultimate accusation—but I've heard what I need to know. Allen's still sculpting in Cincinnati, piecing together a living at this and that (as artists often must), as healthy and vigorous and witty as ever. We agree that it's been too long, that we must set up a meeting soon. What's unspoken is that we're both approaching fifty. The time that might allow for reunions is dwindling fast.

—⚉—

AN INTERVIEWER ONCE ASKED ME what I missed most from my gay youth, and I replied, with only a little hesitation, "Dancing." I left behind my dancing days in 1989, when I moved from Morgantown, with its conveniently located downtown gay bar, to Blacksburg, where the nearest gay bar is in Roanoke, a forty-five-minute drive away. Living now in Pulaski, I only get to gay bars when John and I travel, to DC, San Francisco, New Orleans, and those bars are almost always bear or leather bars, where there's little to no dancing. I guess it's thought not butch enough.

I have a trifling secret. My partner doesn't know this yet, but I'll share it with you. When I lift weights in our basement—the Radon Gym, I call it, since the radon test results were declared "inconclusive"— in between sets, I shadowbox and dance. I always play loud music when I lift, usually Melissa Etheridge, and most songs have sufficient beat for me to move to. There I am, a beefy, silver-bearded, bald leather bear in A-shirt, camo shorts, and weightlifting gloves, an overgrown boy with pumped-up hairy chest, tattooed arms, and a sheepish grin. I twitch my hips, hump the darkness, and punch the air, my only partner/rival/ lover the wide-shouldered shadow moving along the wall. The few boxing moves I learned a while back at the Virginia Tech Boxing Club; the few dance moves are those same ones Allen taught me long years ago, when I was so young, so ignorant, so innocent, and so in need of the guidance he gave me. I never could master the complex disco steps at which Allen was so adept. He was always the better dancer.

NEGATIVE CAPABILITY IN THE
MOUNTAIN SOUTH

I t's an odd juxtaposition, I suppose: John Keats' grave in Rome's
Protestant Cemetery, and beside it, an Appalachian leather bear
come to pay his respects. The soles of my feet are burning from
long walks about the Eternal City, for I am determined to see all I
can in my short time here, and this grave is high on my list of sights not
to be missed. It's a beautiful, peaceful place. Cats sleep in the shade of
the monuments, insects buzz beneath the cypresses and umbrella pines,
lilies and roses bloom white and scarlet. I have come a long way to honor
this young English poet, whose poems I have loved for decades, who died
of tuberculosis at age twenty-four, exactly half my age. I owe him much.
His poetry helps me understand passion and mortality; his musings on
negative capability help me understand how I can love and hate home at
the same time.

Negative capability, said Keats in an 1817 letter, "is when man is
capable of being in uncertainties, Mysteries, doubts without any irritable
reaching after fact & reason" (1818). I take this to include ambivalence
and ambiguity, both of which I possess in profusion. Living with emotional
and mental uncertainties and contradictions, rather than insisting on and
striving for comfortable, simplistic resolutions, is how I have remained
very Southern and very queer and still retained my sanity.

That's another allusion to Rome, when I say I "love and hate" at the
same time. The phrase echoes the poet Catullus—*odi et amo*—musing
on how romantic love evokes intensities and extremities of contradictory
feeling (130-31). I would hazard that three things inspire, for many people,

those opposite extremes of love and hate: your family; your love object/
spouse/partner; and, more to the point of this essay, your homeland. In
other words, all that with which you are most intimate.

Homeland means, for me, the American South; more specifically, the
Highland South. It is no doubt a weakness, my inability to think with any
clarity on national and global issues. I am much more of a regionalist.
My region is my world, and I see as clearly in that microcosmic realm as
I see darkly in others. My region is the object of my fascination and my
passion, my love and hate.

—⁓—

I TURN FORTY-NINE TOMORROW. THUS I have several decades to look back on,
to trace the shifts between adoration and resentment, attachment and scorn,
admiration and fear, in the long relationship with my native region.

Here I am at age ten. The South means my family. My mother, a
Virginian, coaches me in consideration and politeness, determined to
raise me as a Southern gentleman, albeit in Hinton, West Virginia, a small
mountain town far from Tidewater gentility. My father, a West Virginian,
prods me to help him gather and chop wood, weed the garden, and gather
vegetables; he is constantly singing the praises of self-reliance and country
living. My grandmother dotes on me; she delights in feeding me her home
cooking, especially pies: custard, pecan, cherry, coconut cream. This is
the rural South of childhood comfort. It is sweet.

Here I am at age fifteen. Not effeminate but certainly not masculine;
asexual, really; a bookish, shy, quiet sort. My interests range among
such unconventional topics as the occult, Greek and Roman mythology,
and poetry. The devout Christians among my classmates at Hinton High
School are convinced I'm not only a weirdo but a hell-bound Satanist.
This is the small-town South of adolescent unrest and a growing sense of
displacement, a bad place for a nonconformist to be. It is sour.

Here I am only a year later, at age sixteen, realizing that I am not
asexual but homosexual. I'm reading gay novels, developing unspoken
crushes on male classmates, and finding companionship among lesbians
in my high school. For the most part, I am liked—several of my friends

are popular, and their light reflects on me—and my good grades make me an occasional object of admiration. But despite the myriad ways I have learned to conceal my queer desires, I consort with obvious lesbians and am no macho jock or collector of girlfriends, and so I am called "Faggot" every now and then. One day, without my knowledge, a football player classmate attaches a note on my back—"Kick me, I'm Queer"—which a more sympathetic classmate plucks off. One night, as I'm walking a female friend home, a man driving by shouts "Faggot!" When I give him a gesture of contempt, he stops the car in the middle of the street and punches me twice in the face before someone intervenes. This is the small-town South of contempt, violence, and danger. It is bitter.

Here I am at age eighteen, out of the South at last, albeit just barely, in Morgantown, West Virginia, which is just south of the Mason-Dixon line but which is, in terms of dialect and culture, certainly not as Southern as what I am accustomed to. I'm attending West Virginia University, getting degrees in English and Nature Interpretation, I have a passel of gay and lesbian friends, and there's even a gay bar to waste what little extra time and money I have looking for a Grand Love that never quite materializes. Ironically, now that I'm out of southern West Virginia, I miss it. Now that I'm getting unnerving tastes of adult independence and responsibility, I enjoy going home to Hinton on breaks to be coddled by my family and to gobble their home cooking. In Morgantown, I gravitate to others from the South, those whose vowel pronunciations match mine. In the North, I begin to identify as a Southerner. I become a passionate Rebel partisan and fan of Robert E. Lee, study the Civil War (i.e., the War of Northern Aggression), devour the works of queer Southern writers like Tennessee Williams and Carson McCullers, and try to learn how to make for myself Appalachian delights like biscuits and fried apple pies. This is the South from a distance, distance that allows out-of-focus forgetfulness. This is the expatriate's South. Its taste is sweet again, the flavor of nostalgia.

Here I am at age twenty-six, and nostalgia's syrup is even more intense. In search of gay community, I've moved to Washington, DC, to chase my big-city dreams. It's a complete debacle. I make next to no money teaching freshman composition part-time at snotty and unfriendly George Washington University. I have not one erotic, much less romantic, encounter in the few months I live there. My sensitivity to noise, my shyness and impatience make the crowds and traffic pure plagues to my senses. I read Thomas Wolfe's *Look Homeward, Angel* and ache. When I hear John Denver sing, "Take me home, country roads, to the place I belong...West Virginia, Mountain Momma," I get wet-eyed. Homesickness consumes me. This is the lodestone South, that pulls you home against your reason to a place where you can never entirely belong. It is bittersweet.

—∭—

I RETURNED TO APPALACHIA IN December 1985, glad to be done with DC Other than the occasional vacation beyond the region, I've lived here ever since. I have remained an avid devotee of many things Southern: Faulkner novels, country music, Civil War history, sausage gravy and biscuits. Teaching at Virginia Tech in Blacksburg, Virginia, has been helpful—university towns in the South are both of the region and not of it. Or, rather, in such towns you can have the South and much else besides, including a liberal atmosphere that, at least officially, finds open expressions of homophobia intolerable. Teaching courses in Appalachian Studies and Appalachian Literature has been helpful too, in consolidating my sense of myself not only as a Southerner but as an Appalachian. As I have learned more and more about the literature and folk culture of Southern Appalachia, I've been reminded of how much there is here to love and how much of who I am has been shaped by, and is dependent on, the Highland South. Mountain landscape, language, music, folktales, food—I am an ardent enthusiast.

So much for the many loves that make me feel as if I belong in the South. There are just as many hates, confusions, and fears that threaten every day my fragile reconciliation of Southern and queer identities. There are just as many days that I feel that I belong nowhere, neither in the gay world nor Appalachia. As I've already indicated, only a high tolerance for hopeless and irreconcilable ambivalence—Keats' negative capability—and my own innate stubbornness allow me to continue this balancing act. All that, and the fact that I can't conceive of a radically different identity or existence. Call this lack of imagination or the immobility of middle age.

So, not-belonging? My double identity has, to some extent, isolated me from a strong sense of cultural solidarity with the mainstream LGBT community. (Political solidarity is another matter; just because I don't feel like I have a lot in common with many other queers doesn't mean I shouldn't stand with them politically; I know the same rabid bastards hate us all and are striving to diminish our civil rights.) Other than those few bleak months in the suburbs of DC, I have never lived in or near a place with rich and varied queer culture. Living where I have, in relatively small cities and towns in Appalachia, has made me self-reliant, independent— I've had to be to survive—and forced me to develop a sense of self that has been influenced more by Appalachia than my fellow queers. At this point in my life I can take or leave queer culture when it is ever so rarely encountered and queer social opportunities when they are ever so infrequently offered (though, in this regard, it certainly helps to be an espoused, middle-aged homebody).

My Appalachian background and rural values have also made me fairly critical of many aspects of gay culture. When I browse through the *Advocate* or *Out*, much of what I see appears frivolous, effete, urban, and consumerist: Project Runway, the latest cologne, the newest spiky-haired twink singer, the hot new interior designer or hair-stylist. Most of it bores me. Most of it seems irrelevant to my life as a middle-aged leather bear in the mountains of southwest Virginia. This gap is highlighted when I go to the nearest gay guesthouse, in Lost River, West Virginia: the DC gays I encounter there seem no more impressed with me than I am with them. They display a cliquish, over-refined unfriendliness I think of as citified and elitist. In other words, the rough-edged masculinity and stoicism I absorbed from my native region cause me to regard many urban gays with dubious distance. (This dubiousness might be not only a rural versus urban issue; the schism could also be that between mainstream gays and leather bears.)

Certainly my attitudes toward effeminacy were initially shaped by my region. Appalachia, like many primarily rural places, puts a high priority on masculinity and ostracizes those males who don't measure up. A bookworm rather than a jock, a nerdish asexual rather than a stud, during high school I had gotten a taste of that ostracism. From the get-go I was certainly attracted to masculinity in others—local country boys, muscular comic-book superheroes, courageous TV cowboys, mythic Greek warriors—but I did not at first possess masculinity myself. I came to gender normativity late—like any behavior, it was learned—during my university years at WVU. Uninspired by the effeminate gay men in Morgantown's gay bars, I patterned my inchoate manhood, my erotic persona, on the country boys I'd grown up around and emulated my butch fellow forestry majors.

Unfortunately, like most young guys insecure about their manhood, I regarded effeminate men as unattractive and worthy of scorn. (Scorn behind the back, of course—I'm too much of a Southerner to hurt someone's feelings and be rude to his face.) Like the worst of straight men, I mocked my less-butch fellow queers. This is bad behavior—reactionary, provincial—I've grown out of slowly, through good friendships with effeminate men whose kindness, determination, and nurturing I've very much admired and through constant reminders of how obnoxious and dangerous macho behavior can be. Now that I have a firmer sense of who I am and have less to prove, I regard effeminate gays with respect, having some sense of how much stronger than I they've had to be to live their lives.

An ironic postscript to this development: I've recently encountered some fey gay men who regard my masculinity and my fascination with more traditional manhood as a symptom of internalized homophobia, as a cop-out, as passing. I end up wanting to say, pleadingly, pathetically, "But now I like you the way you are! Why can't you like me? Butch isn't always mean! Butch can be sweet!"

I am aware of another irony: most of my fellow country boys would regard my interest in ethnic cooking, poetry, literature, and mythology as enthusiasms as effete and useless as I regard the pleasures of many urban gays. (Not to mention what my fellow country boys would think of my passion for goatees, chest hair, and BDSM. But more on that later.) Here again I find myself wedged uncomfortably between worlds.

Living in that gap, I find that what I say today I might contradict with equal conviction tomorrow. Having pointed out that I am a queer mountaineer pretty much detached from the LGBT world, let me now say that, living as I do in southwest Virginia, I am occasionally queer-starved. In this mode, I take great pleasure in getting together with LGBT friends both near and far. In this mode, I plan trips to San Francisco, Key West, Provincetown, and New Orleans to suck up gay atmosphere and company. In this mode (oh, the fickle quicksilver shifting of chemicals in my brain), despite the aforementioned haughtiness of DC gays at the Guesthouse at Lost River, it's good to be around My Queer Kind there, and I resent the presence of straight people who invade the place. "Can't they keep to their own spaces and leave us alone?" I snarl, despite the fact that the straight couples are often friendlier than the gays. In this mode, the recent weeklong gay cruise of the Mediterranean I enjoyed with my partner John was wonderful. It was a magical alternative universe, with 3,000 queers and only a handful of straight folks...and they existed only to wait on us. It was a world I did not want to leave. Appalachia, with its overwhelming preponderance of heteros and their numerous and very often obnoxious spawn (I can't abide a loud, badly behaved child), was a home I had little desire to see again.

—◊—

WHAT I HATE MOST ABOUT the South I am not likely to forget, for I have a queer gadfly to remind me if ever I need reminding. I have known her since 1979. She is my best friend. She is the political theorist, feminist scholar, and women's studies professor Cynthia Burack. She is an expert on the Christian Right.

Cindy has been stinging me, for twenty-odd years, with gentle but constant reminders that I mustn't idealize my Southern homeland too much. A sometime resident of Washington, DC, she confesses to avoiding Northern Virginia, just across the Potomac, because of Virginia's conservative politics. She regularly points out how queer-hating the South can be, how viciously conservative its small-town values, what a hotbed of Republicans it is. Despite this, she and her partner Laree visit me here in Appalachia. (Luring them down with promises of homemade eggplant Parmesan generally works.) Despite my inescapably Southern nature, she loves me. But talking to her, I know what I most detest about my native region.

There it is, listed first among the mountain traits Loyal Jones lauds in his essay "Appalachian Values" (507-17). The others, the ones I very much embody and admire, include Attachment to Place; Sense of Beauty; Familism; Personalism; Neighborliness and Hospitality; Individualism, Self-Reliance, and Pride. Those are elements of the Mountain South that make me love it. Religion, the element that heads Jones' list, is what makes me hate it.

Kind, truly compassionate, liberal Christians? I have met a few, people that I suspect Christ would be proud to call his followers. But here in the mountains the variety of Christianity I have spent my life around is the intolerant, judgmental sort that encourages homophobia. I well remember the pious little shits who composed Hinton High School's Bible Club. I well remember the debate at WVU between members of the gay/lesbian student group I helped found and members of the Campus Crusade for Christ. I well remember gay and lesbian friends who were made miserable by the conflict they perceived between their desires and their faith. That kind of religion is, as far as I'm concerned, a poisonous, inescapable gas that taints the air of Appalachia.

These days, as busy as I am, it might be possible to forget the fact that I'm surrounded by devout Christians who are most probably inimical to LGBT rights here in Pulaski, Virginia, a small town near Virginia Tech where John and I have settled, primarily due to the cheap property values that allowed us to purchase a fine house. Of course there are an absurd number of churches in Pulaski, as well as a Christian bookstore. There's a goodly amount of bumper stickers displaying Jesus-fish and other expressions of faith. These evidences of religion I might, with effort, be able to ignore. But two things highlight for me the South's ubiquitous fundamentalism and its frequently expressed hostility to My Queer Kind.

One is my gadfly, of course. I certainly couldn't ignore the local Christian bookstore when Cindy dragged me into it. She was doing research for her work on the Christian Right; in particular, she was looking for the vicious little cartoon pamphlets created by Jack Chick, several of them over-the-top homophobic. I don't think she would have found them, except for the excited little growl I made as I rounded a bookshelf. "Oh, there they are!" she said eagerly, plucking a few from a rack by my elbow. I had to tell her that the growl wasn't my delight in finding Chick tracts—I hadn't even noticed them—but my pleasure in seeing a life-sized cardboard cut-out of a young man with an adorable grin framed by a brown goatee and a Biblical-times tunic cut low to show off his hairy chest. There we were, two queers blending in—with Cindy's polite and deferential manners and my bearded country-boy look and Southern vowels—while she looked for evidence of the Christian Right's hatred of queers and I wished the cardboard boy were a real man I could take home and top. "If They Only Knew" is a frequent mantra of mine.

Cindy's research has born fruit: she has just published a book about these issues: *Sin, Sex, and Democracy: Antigay Rhetoric and the Christian Right.* What I know now, having read it, is that the Christian Right is both smarter and crazier than I thought. They are careful to give insiders in their movement a much clearer and more honest expression of their true aims than any eavesdropping outsiders. They are devoted to squashing same-sex desire through the ex-gay movement, they think of LGBT folks as internal terrorists threatening the well-being of this country, and they are determined to "place the moral force and disciplinary resources of the state behind proscribing behavior deemed immoral and ungodly" and "to suppress freedom of expression and bad behavior on the part of disbelievers who, left to their own devices, might engage in the proscribed behaviors" (Burack 125-26). "The ultimate goal," says my gadfly, "—one that more often than not is not disclosed openly in political discourse—is placing believers in charge of the state and enabling them to consolidate a politics that will deflect God's wrath away from the righteous and prepare the world for the Second Coming of Christ" (Burack 126).

In other words, to quote Alayna, Cindy's and my masterfully satiric friend, they're "crazy as shithouse rats." Members of the Christian Right are certainly not confined to the South, but they certainly dominate it. I hate them as I would any natural enemy dedicated to my annihilation, which is to say that I hate a goodly part of my beloved region. I have no doubt that Cindy is correct when she says, "it is undeniable that traditionalist religious belief motivates most antigay bias and activism" (Burack 142).

Cindy has helped me both face and endure my own ambivalence by not only reminding me of the dangers posed by these "crazy fuckers" (to quote Alayna again), but also suggesting that one way to deal with such love/hate is to cherish Southern culture but detest Southern politics. She's too kind to point out that the culture shapes the politics, but it's a welcome out that I take every now and then when the internal inconsistencies get to be too much.

The second of those things that won't let me forget Southern conservative religion and its attacks on queer rights? In the process of writing *Loving Mountains, Loving Men*, my book about being both gay- and mountain-identified, I thought I had made some kind of peace with my biculturalism, to use the Appalachian scholar Helen Lewis's term. But in November of 2006, that delicate reconciliation of warring selves was blown all to hell when voters in the state of Virginia passed a constitutional amendment banning same-sex marriage, one of the nastiest in the nation. When I heard the outcome, I spat on the street. (How's that for a furious mountain redneck gesture?) Was I surprised? No. It still felt like my home had betrayed me.

My attitude toward the South has never been the same. It is angrier, more fraught, more defiant. For years I have tried to excuse the South's ugly conservatism, tried to convince folks outside this region that we're not all a bunch of ignorant hate-mongers and backward reactionaries. I'm tired of that fight. For years (especially before I settled down with John, whose family's from Massachusetts), I regularly used "The Y Word" ("Yankee") as a derogatory term, as Southerners sometimes do. Now, considering how differently certain Southern states and certain New England states have responded to same-sex marriage, well, I'm humiliated. Thank God for Yankees.

—∞—

WHO WAS HE? I HAVE no idea. He was simply a stranger in Pulaski's Food City whom I silently admired last week in the midst of grocery shopping.

At the time I was too swamped with lust to think of much, other than how I wanted him trussed up and naked in my bed. In retrospect, however, I see that many of the conflicts I've discussed above are reflected in my complex response to him. In memory, he embodies the loved, desired, feared, hated South.

Not for nothing the title of my book *Loving Mountains, Loving Men*, for those are two sources of the greatest beauty, as far as I'm concerned. And he was very beautiful, that scion of the mountains. It was hard not to gape and gasp. Just my type: a Southern country boy with dark brown hair and goatee, camo baseball cap, beard stubble shading his handsome cheeks, adding that rough edge I find so tasty. Broad shoulders, well developed chest pushing out the front of his tight white muscle-shirt. Tight denim shorts, furry legs. Muscular arms with spiky armband tattoos. What I couldn't see I instantly assumed: hairy chest, hairy belly, hairy butt.

For want of a name, let's call him the Food City God. Male beauty like his stirs up in me a storm of intense reactions. Needless to say, I desired him powerfully. Butch country boys are the kind I lust after the most, especially beefy ones with muscles, facial and body hair, and tattoos. Envy was as present as longing. I envied him his face and body. He was better looking and better built than I, not to mention at least fifteen years younger. I heartily wished that I were, once or now, that throbbingly desirable. It was clear from his confident little swagger that he knew what visual gifts he possessed.

I resented him. Straight boys (note the leap of assumption, based on statistical likelihood) around here tend to be conservative homophobes whose votes keep me and mine second-class citizens. I resented him too because, as fascinating as I found him, his body language made it clear that he hadn't even noticed me, and that wounded my fragile Leo-ego. Not that his indifference was a surprise; on the contrary, I've spent my life in predominately straight parts of the world hankering after men I can't have, but it's still an unwelcome feeling. I don't like to want men who don't want me. It makes me feel vulnerable, pathetic, powerless, and, lately, old. I suppose my libido is unusually strong: merely looking at a man that beautiful is far from enough. I wanted to ravish him, and, because

I couldn't, his beauty hurt me; I was both disappointed and relieved when he left the store.

I feared him. Somewhere inside I still think of myself as the pudgy, defenseless high school scholar who was punched one autumn night decades ago in downtown Hinton, not the man of some bulk, brawn, determination, and strength I've become, strength I've cultivated in order to survive in a place that often feels hostile. I was about his size, and he could not read my mind, so my fear was groundless. But I couldn't help guessing what he'd think of my desire for him. (Back to "If They Only Knew." Perhaps a T-shirt slogan?) Violent disgust is always the reaction I imagine, especially considering the compulsively kinky specifics of my leather-bear lusts. I.e., a man that hot I want to strip, bind, and gag. Once he's my consensual captive, I want to shower him with oral and manual ministrations both tender and sadistic, keep him tied up for a protracted amount of time, ride him long and hard, achieve mutual bliss, indulge in some serious cuddling, treat him to some good Southern food and drink, and keep him around for a few sweet days as my submissive, dog-collared slave. Beauty that staggering I want to abduct, dominate, protect, abuse, and possess, reactions not at all odd among BDSM Tops.

As a man imbued with many traditional Southern values, I admittedly feel embarrassment and shame for having such wildly unconventional desires; they certainly make me feel like a complete alien in Appalachia, a perverse monster. As a man who believes in free and polymorphous expressions of Eros, who considers himself part of the "safe, sane, and consensual" leather community, I also claim such kinky yearnings with a hard-fought pride and the conviction that any honest expression of the erotic is a rebellious political act in such a puritanical country. But the fact remains: an overwhelming majority of the Southern men I find most delectable would regard my desires as the height of wickedness and satanic sickness. Made aware of my fantasies about them, they would most likely direct toward me a desire equally fervent: to beat me to death. (Thank God for the bear movement, which has provided the world with gay men who look like the rednecks I crave but who do not possess their often repellant values. Let's hear it for big, hairy, butch guys who are kind and nurturing, not aggressive and cruel, and who are open to a variety of mutually delightful erotic experiences.)

At the same time that I viewed the Food City God as a dangerous and potentially hostile Other and as an unattainable erotic icon, I also felt a kinship with him. Despite our assumed differences (he *might* have been looking for a Daddy Bear to rope him up and top him, but I'm guessing my educated assumptions were accurate), we probably have a few things in common. We're both sons of the South. The things I love about this region—food, folk culture, landscape, etc.—I'll bet he loves too. So mixed up in that moil of feelings he evoked is brotherhood as well. He might not, more's the pity, be a willing receptacle for my pumped-up lust and aesthetic awe, but unwittingly he allows me to reify my "lover's quarrel" with the South, to borrow from a famous Yankee, Robert Frost (280).

—w—

I'VE BEEN GIVEN A BIRTHDAY epiphany. I'm finishing the first draft of this essay on my birthday, August 8, while listening to the soundtrack of *300*. Yes, I'm familiar with the charges of homophobia leveled at the film. I agree; parts of it are undeniably homophobic. There's a crack at Athens' "boy-lovers" (ironic, since man-boy love was a big part of Spartan culture), and there's the deliberate depictions of Spartans as super-macho and brave and Persians as effete, bejeweled, and sinister. It's one of my favorite movies anyway. (You know by now my high tolerance for internal contradictions.) I love Greek history; I love big battle scenes full of swords; I love doomed heroism; and, of course, I love Gerard Butler as King Leonidas, his black beard, fierce demeanor, and hard-muscled body (though I wish he hadn't shaved his chest for the role). I have a *300* baseball cap and T-shirt, not to mention a replica of Leonidas' sword in my considerable collection of long, sharp blades. But it's only today, composing this essay, that I realize— this is so obvious it deserves a "Duh!"—another reason why the film seizes me so deeply. Hmmmm, a small number of valiant souls battling a huge and hostile majority who wants to wipe them out... Cindy's discussion of the Christian Right has certainly given me new ways to relate to *300*. Here we are, fellow queers, defending the pass of Thermopylae. "We are everywhere" is a comforting LGBT slogan. Less comforting is the fact that *they* are everywhere. It is no exaggeration that, like the Spartans, those butch boy-lovers, what we stand to lose is freedom.

—ᴍ—

BISCUITS AND GRAVY, BEASTLY FUNDAMENTALISTS, the Food City God not bucked and gagged in my basement, Gerard Butler's beard, and now, to finish up, the errant route curls back to Keats. What negative capability comes down to in my longtime struggle to balance disparate selves is this: there are no answers, there is no lasting peace. I, like many other queer Southerners, will no doubt spend the rest of my life trying to integrate my many warring facets, sometimes feeling enriched by my two cultures, sometimes feeling torn apart, scorned, or dismissed by them. I feel sure of very little, as you might surmise by now. But I am sure of this: living without answers and in constant conflict either will make you a raving, maimed mess or will make you strong. Strength—physical, mental, and emotional—is something I've striven for all my life. After all, I got the message early in the Highland South: real men are strong, sissies and faggots are weak. Well, this faggot has learned to be, most days at least, strong. This kind of strength is a form of scar tissue, I suspect, but there it is, a valuable and unexpected byproduct, a diamond polished by pressure and heat, forged by my erratic vacillations between loving and hating home.

WORKS CITED

Burack, Cynthia. *Sin, Sex, and Democracy: Antigay Rhetoric and the Christian Right*. Albany: State University of New York Press, 2008.

Catullus. *The Poems of Catullus*. Trans. Guy Lee. New York: Oxford University Press, 1991.

Frost, Robert. *New Enlarged Pocket Anthology of Robert Frost's Poems*. Ed. Louis Untermeyer. New York: Washington Square Press, 1977.

Jones, Loyal. "Appalachian Values." *Voices from the Hills: Selected Readings of Southern Appalachia*. Second Edition. Ed. Robert J. Higgs and Ambrose N. Manning. Dubuque, Iowa: Kendall/Hunt, 1996. 507-17.

Keats, John. "To George and Thomas Keats." *The Norton Anthology of English Literature: the Major Authors*. Sixth Edition. Ed. M.H. Abrams. New York: Norton, 1996. 1817-18.

SURVIVING WINTER'S WOODS:
A TALK GIVEN IN VIRGINIA TECH'S
"FINDING MY PATH" SERIES

(for Irene McKinney)

B eing asked by Multicultural Affairs and Programs here at Virginia Tech to speak on "finding my path" is flattering. The underlying assumption in asking me to speak about how I have "discovered meaning and purpose in life," to quote from the e-mail invitation I received a few months ago, is that an audience can somehow benefit from hearing that story. To talk about "the journey to finding [my] career path" and "important life lessons" I've learned is to presume that, from knowing a little bit about my experience, listeners can glean some truths of use to them.

On this score, I am a little "juberous" (Appalachian for "dubious"), a little hopeful, a lot humbled. Much of the time I find it hard to believe that anyone's read anything I've published or could garner any kind of wisdom from anything I have to say. Self-confidence has always been elusive.

But, since I've agreed to be here (a poet rarely misses an opportunity to enjoy the attentions of an audience), first let me complain. This invitation comes at a bad time, since these days I am full of grave doubts about my "meaning and purpose in life." As an author whose work was originally inspired by a group of American writers called "the Confessional Poets," I write and publish material, both poetry and prose, that is very often bluntly (one critic has said "recklessly") autobiographical. So I hesitate only briefly before confessing to this room of some friends but mostly strangers that I am burning up with, riding full tilt into, wallowing piggishly amidst, the mythical, apparently inevitable Male Midlife Crisis.

What admission could be more banal? Really, what could be less interesting, more mundane, than a man in his late forties with a beard full of silver who's whining about his unsatisfied dreams, futile and unreciprocated lusts, nagging despair, undone deeds, and sense of professional failure, who whinges (that wonderful British verb) about how his elbow joints interfere with his weight-lifting, how his commuting derails his half-hearted attempts to stick to a regular biking schedule, how his committee work robs him of time to focus on his own writing? You didn't come here to hear about my "Slough of Despond," to use the phrase from *Pilgrim's Progress*. Well, be patient for a few more minutes, and we'll all get to a more comfortable, positive point.

The phrase "Finding My Path" suggests that said path has led to an edifying, comfortable, satisfying place, a place where deep yearnings have been fulfilled, hard questions answered, important accomplishments attained, and some peace achieved. When I was twenty-one, I expected (I think—who can remember exactly what one expected twenty-some years ago?) that middle age would indeed be such a time of serene accomplishment, of battles won and gloated over. It should be the well-deserved era not just of sitting but downright sprawling on one's laurels.

For some, this might be the case. For me, and many others of my approximate age, this is not so. We have our accomplishments, yes, and for most of us, we can say, with Mary Chapin Carpenter, "everything we got, we got the hard way." We can also say, with Steve Earle, Faust, and the rest of the perverse and restless species, "I ain't ever satisfied." Let me be perhaps uncomfortably honest, and, at the same time, step into the self-protective first person plural. Despite any material comfort we might luckily have amassed, we host depression, doubt, the slow and annoying erosions of aging, the comforting but tedious rounds of routine and domesticity, the abrasions of financial necessity, an aching and pointless nostalgia for lost youth, angers without easy outlet, the dulling of hope, and the receding of mystery and passion. The world is too much with us, to quote William Wordsworth. We have, by this point in our lives, been forcibly parted with many loved ones. Each of us could recite with ease longish litanies of loss. We are haunted by questions without answer, questions that have driven artists and philosophers for centuries. The wearisome Latin phrase is *Cui bono*: What good? What good is the mortal world when nothing strong and beautiful lasts? What use is desire, especially that which can never be fulfilled? What good is ambition when it is so often thwarted? What, if anything, can be learned from, salvaged from, fear or loneliness, or from the world's blatant and daily tragedies and injustices? We, to echo Dante, in the middle of our lives find ourselves in a dark wood. We are often not whole, not balanced, not calm, pleasant, or rational. Often we feel too much; we are too intense for our own good.

As you can surely tell by now, my father's ancestors, the Ferrells from central Ireland, the Manns from Germany's Palatinate, have bequeathed to me a tendency toward melancholy, a Northern European gloom. In addition, my native region has given me a wide streak of Appalachian fatalism. Rereading *Beowulf* lately in the Seamus Heaney translation, I can only shrug with affirmation when Beowulf says, "Fate goes ever as fate must." This is an attitude that, on bright days, leads to freedom; on grim days, to a pervasive sense of hopelessness. Here I think of Lee Smith's wonderful protagonist Ivy Rowe in *Fair and Tender Ladies*. Writing to her sister, Ivy says,

> Silvaney, I have been caught up for so long in a great soft darkness, a blackness so deep and soft that you can fall in there and get comfortable and never know you are falling in at all, and never land, just keep on falling…You know I used to have so much spunk. Well, I have lost my spunk some way. It is like I was a girl for such a long time, years and years, and then all of a sudden I have got to be an old woman, with no inbetween. Maybe that has always been the problem with me, a lack of inbetween. (193)

And as, to borrow from "The Sire of Sorrow," Joni Mitchell's musical take on the Book of Job, I find myself "all complaint," I cast up, despite myself, several life lessons I hardly knew I knew, as the whale ignominiously cast Jonah upon the sands. One: don't expect the struggle ever to stop. It merely takes new forms. Two: constant struggle will wear you down and wear you out, but intermittent struggle keeps you awake, productive, and alive. Three: suffering can lead us to empathy and compassion, to a deeper connection with the human race. As the narrator of James Baldwin's "Sonny's Blues" says after the death of his daughter, contemplating his estranged brother, "My trouble made his real." Four: art, whether it be literary, musical, or visual, can help us make sense of our lives and lend us a context in which to understand our struggles. Case in point, that compulsive list of allusions I just produced: Mary Chapin Carpenter, William Wordsworth, Dante, Beowulf, Lee Smith, Joni Mitchell, Job, and James Baldwin.

So, these small wisdoms aside, my path has led to a dark wood? Well, yes, this particularly bleak winter day at my desk, composing this talk, questioning my purpose, the worth of what I've lived and learned. But, well, no, not entirely. One of the great gifts of aging is this knowledge: that internal darkness, however deep and apparently endless, is not endless.

I survived long enough to learn that, and that knowledge has helped me survive a lot longer. I'd like to tell you now about someone who did not survive, a man I never met, and what I learned from his story. Then I'd like to tell you about the people and places that have given me light and hope even though—I am old enough to know myself, strong enough to be honest—my brain's chemical constitution tends toward light and hope's polar opposites.

A few years ago, my partner John and I visited the poet laureate of West Virginia, Irene McKinney, in her home near Belington, in Barbour County. A survivor herself, having recently endured a series of treatments for bone cancer, Irene was as full of vivacious intellectual energy as ever. Talk about a role model when it comes to dealing with adversity. It was January, so we stayed inside a lot, cooking, drinking wine, and talking, watching snow flurries whiten up the pastures. I was working on a new book then, *Loving Mountains, Loving Men*, a collection of memoir and poetry about being gay in Appalachia, and Irene, who'd kindly agreed to write a blurb for the book's back cover, had read earlier versions of it. Reading about my life reminded Irene of a friend of hers, and she told me about him. I have no idea whether his family would appreciate his presence in this talk, so I'll use a pseudonym and call him Jamie.

Jamie grew up in Barbour County. He used to play drums with Irene's guitarist son; together they built Irene's A-frame guest cabin on the edge of her property. He was a lot like me. He loved to make music, he loved to walk the woods. He was a great enthusiast of Native American culture, and he was devoted to his mountain roots. He was gay, and so his country-Catholic father rejected him. He suffered from great loneliness, for, as you might imagine, there's not a lot of opportunity for gay romance in rural West Virginia, a loneliness I myself had known for long years before I was fortunate enough to meet John. Thanks to this isolation, these burdens, he was seriously conflicted, as many of us are, straight or gay. Something went wrong, in his heart or in his head. Jamie became seriously depressed. When he was thirty-three, during a visit to Wilmington, North Carolina, he disappeared. He was found drowned in the Atlantic Ocean, an apparent suicide. To use the language of this speakers' series, he had lost his path.

That night, as John and I strode across rainy fields to Irene's guest cabin, I saw Jamie standing and waving at the edge of the woods, where fallen leaves collected against the wire fence that separated bare trees from January's austere pasture. No ghost, of course, just a poet's fancy. I'd seen no photograph, and to this day I have no idea what he looked like. But, erotic idealist that I am, I imagined a lean, good-looking young man in standard country-boy garb with an auburn beard and a big smile. I saw a younger version of myself, really. As I lay in bed, in the dark beside John, watching the gas flames of the heater flicker, listening to rain on the pitched roof Jamie had helped build, I thought about him, how similar we were: both mountaineers, both men who loved men. I know better than most what a difficult combination that can be. I know how hard it can be to continue when preachers and politicians condemn you and complete strangers revile you, how exhausting it is to live in a constant state of siege. I wished we'd met, split a few beers, gone four-wheeling together, made some music with his drums and my guitar, cursed the conservatives, shot the shit about the pains and pressures of being an Appalachian gay man. I grieved a brother I never knew, and wondered why, faced with similar pressures, he ended his life and I have endured to this gray-bearded age.

What saved me? Figuring that out might serve as a spring tonic of sorts to ameliorate the woods' winter darkness, and it would lighten the mood of this talk considerably.

My family saved me.

My mother taught me Southern manners, hospitality, and how to care for people unselfishly (the unselfish part is still difficult), all of which has made for fairly harmonious relationships with other human beings. I am a good friend, good colleague, good neighbor, good host, and at least a tolerable spouse because of these lessons. I am not entirely self-absorbed; I am honestly concerned about the welfare of other human beings, especially those who have been kind to me. (Those who are not kind to me receive the assiduous and patient attention of my considerable dark side.)

My father was much less interested in other humans than he was in the outdoors. He took me walking in the woods and fields of Summers County, West Virginia, where I grew up. He pointed out the trees, then pointed out the trash along the side of the road. From those walks came an abiding love for the natural world and a savage disgust at the way civilization is trashing the planet. Later, this early influence led me to a degree in Nature Interpretation and a dedication to Wicca, a neopagan religion predicated entirely on a sense of the sacred in Nature and in the rhythms of the seasons. More recently, my father's teachings have led me to a violent detestation of mountaintop removal mining and the wealthy politicians who allow that blasphemous practice to continue.

My father also brought me up to read. From his great favorites the American Transcendentalists, in particular from Emerson's "Self-Reliance" and from Thoreau's *Walden*, I learned to reject as best I could the restrictive dictates of society, to live with a sort of honest and defiant individualism. Daddy also encouraged me to share his vast contempt for the more intolerant brands of orthodox religion. When, at age sixteen, I realized I was gay, these lessons were to prove golden. It was easier to follow my heart's and my hormones' dictates with confidence and without guilt. What polite society and the church had to say about my erotic leanings was never much of a concern. "Whoso would be a man must be a nonconformist," claimed Emerson. And "What I must do, is all that concerns me, not what the people think." And "Society everywhere is in conspiracy against the manhood of every one of its members." And when my parents finally discovered my sexual orientation, they did not reject me, as Jamie's father did him. They did not turn cold and throw me out—all of which happens, be sure of that; I have heard enough painful tales from other gay people to know. After taking some time to adjust to this unwelcome fact, they accepted me wholeheartedly. My father, in fact, has published several op-eds and letters to the editor in West Virginia newspapers defending me, and the Lesbian/Gay/Bisexual/Transgender community in general, from pious homophobic attacks.

My grandmother and aunt saved me. They taught me the stories of my family, and this has helped me realize that I am not some emotional mutant, some inexplicable oddity, but one of a line of complex, passionate, conflicted people who will have his embattled time in the sun before joining his ancestors in the cemetery on that little hilltop near Forest Hill, West Virginia.

My sister saved me. From childhood we have been close, with similar values. Her good cooking has gotten me through many a heartbreak: it's amazing how much good biscuits, potato salad, and soup beans can mean when you're lonely and upset.

My tenth-grade biology teacher Jo Davison saved me. She and the circle of other young nonconformists to whom she introduced me provided me with a critical support group, letting me know that my love of poetry and music, my enthusiasm for black-bearded country boys like myself, were all fine by them. She came out to me as a lesbian, and then she lent me Patricia Nell Warren's *The Front Runner,* a novel about an Olympic athlete and his love affair with his coach, the book that made me realize I was gay. Gently she introduced me to the gay world, sparing me years of confusion and self-doubt. The openness I demand of myself now—an attempt to give young LGBT folks some sort of honest role model—I owe to her.

My friends saved me. For many years, as I moved from one unreciprocated passion to another (I had an amazing knack for falling in love with the wrong men), friends reminded me of what pleasures can be had in the absence of romantic or erotic success. Cin and I played guitar, Allen and I compared notes on men and danced at the local gay bar, Laura and I drove cross-country to San Francisco, exploring the Rocky Mountains, Mesa Verde, the Grand Canyon. These days, settled as I am with John (June 2007 will be our ten-year anniversary), spending time with friends is one of our great delights. Tiffany and Andrew whip up a complex Chinese feast, Dan and Phil join us at a gay-friendly guesthouse in West Virginia, Laree and Cindy show us around DC, Joe and Charlene stay over for a winter weekend abrim with good wine and ethnic cooking.

In particular, my friend Cindy has saved me. I have known her since Autumn 1979. Our lives have run along odd parallels: in love with difficult, hurtful people at the same time—Susan and Thomas—and then in love with supportive mates—Laree and John—and now comparing notes on the ups and downs of marriage. We have been lonely together, reveling in what small pleasures we could: eggplant parmesan, walks about the herb garden of the National Cathedral in Washington, DC We have hated together: George W. Bush, car stereos, obnoxious children bred with incompetent laxity, and, most especially, religious fundamentalists. We have pointlessly hankered together: I for country-music star Tim McGraw, she for actress Jessica Lange, a woman whose beauty makes even me, six on the Kinsey scale (i.e., completely queer), perfectly comprehend heterosexuality. Thanks to our long history, Cindy understands, without hesitation, who I am, as crazily contradictory and ambivalent as that often is. When I'm with her, I often think of French philosopher Simone Weil's saying, "The love of our neighbor in all its fullness simply means being able to say, 'What are you going through?'"

Literature saved me. I see myself, my passions and sufferings in Wordsworth, Keats, Yeats, Eliot, Whitman, and so many others. In particular, Sylvia Plath gave me a black-glass mirror in which to study my own dangerous intensities. When I encountered her work my senior year in college at West Virginia University, her late poems fascinated me. They showed me how art could be made from desolation and rage. Her work inspired me to attend graduate school and become a poet. Expressing my internal storms in writing has been one way to make sense of them and so to weather them. Though she and other fine poets I admire—Anne Sexton and John Berryman—ended as suicides, their poetry and my own artistic attempts have helped keep me from a similar conclusion. Reading and teaching Appalachian literature and gay and lesbian literature have also helped me understand my convoluted self by encountering in books the "hillbilly" and "queer" aspects of my identity.

Music saved me. The music my father raised me on—Beethoven, Brahms, Puccini—as well as the popular music I listen to these days delights, invigorates, and redeems me. Joni Mitchell, Carly Simon, Melissa Etheridge, Mary Chapin Carpenter, Tim McGraw, Kathy Mattea, Keith Urban: their voices have lent me fire and transcendence on the most ashen and miserable of days, and the lyrics of their songs show me refracted versions of my own troubles. Playing guitar, piano, or mountain dulcimer soothes and centers me. Singing along to favorite CD's, I, to quote Joni Mitchell's "Hejira," "see something of myself in everyone / Just at this moment of the world / As snow gathers like bolts of lace / Waltzing on a ballroom girl."

My native landscape saved me. Often, due to my difficult brain chemistry, my psyche's boundaries feel perilously thin. I am unusually sensitive to noise, to bustle. Cities abrade me. As much as I love to visit them—for the most part to ravish their bookstores and ethnic restaurants, to a lesser extent to visit their gay bars and luxuriate in the presence of My Kind—I cannot tolerate urban areas for long. I soon feel overstimulated, invaded, endangered. The rush, the traffic, the crowds turn me surly, paranoid, and impatient fast. But the countryside—Thomas Hardy's "far from the madding crowd"—is another matter. Living in small towns among the mountains, as I have for most of my life, has kept me sane. The natural world is never far. The hills rise protectively about me. I can see the stars. Commuting back and forth between Pulaski and Blacksburg, I can study the seasonal changes in meadow, woodland, hillside, and creek. I can bike through the countryside down the New River Trail, take in the view from the top of Draper Mountain, drive the tortuous emerald bends up to Mountain Lake and look out over the crests of the Alleghenies.

Universities saved me. I hope to emulate my father, who is reading and writing nonstop at age eighty-five, by spending my life in a constant state of learning and creating. I teach because I want to keep learning. I choose fresh materials for my classes with some regularity so as to read new stories, new poems. I have been connected with universities in some capacity, either as undergraduate student, graduate student, instructor, or professor, since I entered West Virginia University in August 1977, and that connection has kept my mind active, hungry, and enthusiastic. The liberal atmosphere of university towns has made living in Appalachia as an openly gay man a lot easier than it could have been. Mine is an unusual combination of diversities—"the Mountaineer Queer"—that might not be understood or appreciated off-campus but which is apparently valued by the university community. Thus my presence here today.

Romantic and erotic failure saved me. This seems counterintuitive, to say the least, since they also made me want to drive my pickup truck into the side of a mountain. But, past the initial and very lengthy suffering, with serious contemplation (great gift of the introvert) I learned a great, great deal. I learned how much turmoil can fuel poetry. All of my first poetry collection *Bones Washed with Wine* and much of my second collection *On the Tongue* were inspired by a particularly agonized affair I had in the early 1990s. I learned that yes, one can love with the deep and half-insane passion one sees in novels like *Wuthering Heights*, and it is a blessing to have the capacity to feel that dangerously and deeply, no matter what the price (and the price will be as deep and devastating and sometimes far lengthier than the love). I learned that, for some of us, our hearts lead us to those who are incapable of or thoroughly uninterested in reciprocation. In other words, I learned that my heart can betray me. I learned that some of those who feel themselves beloved will take just as much as you are willing to give, but that casual acceptance of gifts does not evoke in them any sense of obligation or even gratitude. I learned that, for many of us, such passions, as is claimed so often in sentimental song lyrics, truly do come along only a few times in a lifetime, and that is good, for otherwise we might all die young. I learned that those loved so passionately and then lost will haunt you inescapably for the rest of your life, but being haunted is not a bad way to live. It is certainly an artistically productive way. I learned that, once you survive the loss of such a muse, that any other pain you encounter will be, if not small, then smaller, in contrast. You can look up at the gray tsunami of suffering foaming and cresting, about to break over your head, and say with confidence, "Well, I survived that, so long ago. I am certainly strong enough to survive this."

My partner John saved me. He has created a safe space, a home, in which my overly sensitive soul might escape the world's hostilities. He lends me support, humor, pleasure, and comfort. He somehow tolerates my mood swings, roving eye, and regular rants. We enjoy fine meals, quiet time by the fireplace, trips to San Francisco, Hawaii, Prague, Scotland, Scandinavia. Despite the hateful amendment passed last fall in Virginia, outlawing any form of same-sex marriage, we are married in every important sense of the word. Stupidity and prejudice have robbed us, and those like us, of legal recognition or benefits, but that only gives me reason to remain ornery, defiant, and outspoken in my protest.

So, to everyone's relief, perhaps most especially mine, though this talk began as lament, it ends as a procession of blessings, a paean of thanks. As natural as it is for me to focus on what is lacking, what has been stolen, it is certainly salutary to remind myself of what is present still, what has been rescued, what makes continuing worth it. I write this, speak this, in order to give gratitude some enduring shape, so that, when the bleakness returns, I have my own words as evidence, as reminder, as driftwood for the drowning.

I want to finish with my lost and unmet brother Jamie. His body was returned to his native Barbour County for burial. Irene told me about his funeral. It was a mixture of folks who might not come together in any other context: gay people, mountain people, Native Americans, Catholics, and musicians. There, personified, were all the wildly disparate elements of his psyche, paying their respects, sitting down together in sadness, sharing a groaning board of funeral food. Those many identities must have seemed to him hopelessly fragmented and irreconcilable, as he stood there on that North Carolina beach staring at the welcoming waves. My guess is that, had he had all that I have been blessed with, he might have been able to give himself more time. Had he encountered as much kindness as I, he might have been kinder to himself. Had he lived longer, that slew of apparently incompatible shards could have been fused. Amalgamated, they could have provided an incredible, if always difficult, depth and richness. Unfused, they caused a fragmentation that destroyed him.

I understand fragmentation, the centrifugal forces that invite us to fly apart. As a child, I found a praying mantis egg case on a japonica bush in the backyard and kept it inside a vented jar. I remember the hatching, all those tiny insects crawling from what appeared to be a chunk of brown Styrofoam. I cannot forget that seething, how, trapped together inside the glass, they turned on one another, how rapidly cannibalism began. Even at that age, I sensed a metaphor for the deep and potentially destructive divisions of the human brain. Standing here in the winter wood, I can feel those opposed selves grappling for dominance in the dark inside my skull. Nevertheless, living the examined life that Socrates suggests, I know what has saved me and continues to save me, and now you know it too. Loved ones, literature, learning, music, and mountains: they have given me the strength to give myself time, and that time has given me a self strong enough to survive myself, survive the world, and to speak what I know. I speak to those like me, the dark and divided ones, those waiting in winter light, light the cold silver-gray of magnolia buds, those sad ones mesmerized by the swirl of snow, those hesitating, desolate, at the edge of the forest, the edge of the ocean. What I say is *Stay*.

LOVING TIM;
OR,
MY PASSIONATE MIDLIFE AFFAIR

Let's start with fantasy, since that's where most fruitless passions lead. It's a mountain cabin high in West Virginia's Potomac Highlands. Autumn night, flickering fireplace. Tim and I are playing guitar together; our voices blend nicely. We're both a little buzzed on the bourbon I've been pouring us. About the time the full moon rises over the eastern ridge, Tim pulls his guitar off his shoulder, stretches, then grins at me in the firelight. "Whatcha in the mood for now?" he asks.

Even after our several years together, I'm a little shy. "Uh, there's some leftover apple pie…" I begin.

Tim pulls his T-shirt over his head. He knows how much I savor his hairy chest. "Let's save the pie for breakfast. Tonight, how 'bout you tie me belly down on the bed, stuff a rag in my mouth, and ride me till we're both sore?"

"Hell, yes!" Now I'm grinning too. The gleeful frankness of his hunger for submission has always delighted and amazed me. I unshoulder my guitar, shrug off my shirt, and pull Tim to me. Beautiful lover, complementary longings. This is the life I've always dreamed of.

—⚡—

I AM PRONE TO CONFESSION. Sylvia Plath and Anne Sexton, members of the "Confessional School" of poetry, were among my first literary role models, so my poetry has always taken an autobiographical bent. I have published poems about having a secretive affair with a man behind his

195

spouse's back, poems about sodomy and sadomasochistic sex, poems about my hatred of right-wing politicians and fundamentalist Christians and my fantasies of slaughtering them with one of the many sharp blades in my sword collection. But this most recent confession I have saved for prose. Poetry tends toward the concise; prose allows more expansion. I need room for this confession: there is much to admit.

Here it is: though I am turning 48 in a month, though I am contentedly settled with John, my partner of ten years, I am having a passionate midlife affair with the most desirable man in the world.

Well, not an affair, really. As attractive as it would be to claim that, it would be fiction, and the genre of creative nonfiction demands truth, so I must stick to less attractive fact. The fact is I am tormented by an unrequited passion, much like those with which I frittered away my frustrated youth. The object of this ardor doesn't even know I exist. He is more indifferent to me than Beatrice was to Dante, than Laura was to Petrarch, than Maude Gonne was to W. B. Yeats. This indifference only makes me want him more, for it is the inaccessibility of Muses that deepens their mystery and erotic power.

He is, in fact, married to a beautiful and talented woman and has three daughters. He is a superstar in country music. You have probably heard of him. His name is Tim McGraw.

Why would I confess to such a pointless infatuation? This is the problem with the use of honest autobiography in published works: you run the risk of looking like a fool in front of many people and becoming the object of mockery. But passions, however quirky and absurd, are never unique. Writers operate under the assumption that what we have felt, others have felt. In writing about our own mental and emotional convolutions, we not only try to make sense of those sometimes intolerable internal contradictions but also offer ourselves as representative men and women, in whose images readers may see something of themselves. To be this breed of writer takes ego, takes guts. Because the literature that has most nourished me has been that which reveals the follies, lusts, rages, and despairs of the heart, the dark niches, the disturbing, hard-to-talk-about, hard-to-admit passions, this is the kind of writing I aspire to create. The fact that many widely admired contemporary authors do not tackle these subjects, relying instead on a facile, distanced cleverness, is simply proof of the emotional cowardice of our age. As for myself, I take my cue from brave role models like Plath and Sexton.

This apologia aside, in scrutinizing my Tim-Passion I hope to discover the sense in its apparent senselessness. Passions always have a point. Even unrequited or aching from afar, they serve some function. And aren't we all expert at yearning painfully for what we can't have? What of you, whoever you are holding this essay now in hand? (To adapt Walt Whitman). You! My reader, my double, my brother! (To borrow Baudelaire.)

—ɯ—

THE OBNOXIOUS ALARM CLOCK GOES off at 7 am, several hours earlier than John and I would prefer to rise. But I have to teach today, and John begins telecommuting at 8:30. We lie there, groggy, gathering our energies. "Tim!" I shout into the morning gloom. "*Tim*!! Coffee!!"

Yes, I'm calling my imaginary houseboy. John's used to it. He knows I enjoy weaving whimsical erotic fictions. Sometimes he even plays along. As he's admitted, my crush on a man I'll never meet is far better than the real-life affairs many middle-aged married men fall into.

"Dammit," I mock-snarl. "Where *is* that boy?! He never gets anything done around the house! He's bucking for a paddling for sure!"

"Didn't you leave him bound and gagged in the basement?" John queries matter-of-factly, sitting up and pulling on underwear.

"Oh, yeah. Right." I grin at the delicious image and head downstairs to turn the coffee pot on.

—ɯ—

I WRITE THIS ON A Macintosh laptop lent me by my department. The screensaver is a photo of Tim. (I say "Tim" rather than "McGraw" since lust, even unreciprocated, creates an illusion of intimacy.) He's squatting on a rain-puddled city rooftop, in one of those awkward positions so many photographers must think of as artistic. His signature black Resistol cowboy hat is cocked over his eyes, though the handsome angles of his face and his brown goatee are visible below the brim. He's wearing black cowboy boots, tight jeans, and an A-shirt that shows off the leanness of his torso and belly, the slight curve of his pectorals, the moderate muscles of his arms, the tattoo of a cross on his left arm, and the dark hair matting his upper chest.

Sometimes, when my students come into my office for one-on-one conferences, they notice this image, since my laptop is always open on my desk. I come out to all my classes—it's a grass-roots political act that I hope makes a difference in how my students perceive and respond to LGBT people—so these students already know I'm openly gay by the time they glimpse my Tim screen-saver. They are therefore certainly not shocked; they are probably mildly amused but too polite or politic to show it. Perhaps they are a little disconcerted that a middle-aged academic is so obviously a creature still ridden with desire. If their eyes wander during our conversation, they will also see various Tim fan paraphernalia displayed here and there around my office. There are several "Tim McGraw and the Dancehall Doctors" baseball caps, several photos, several country-music magazines with Tim on the covers, a copy of Tim's *Greatest Video Hits*. Here again, I am taking a risk by being honest about my lust. Surely, seeing all this, some students will mock me behind my back.

I keep these images around me for several reasons. First of all, Virginia Tech, though relatively liberal itself, is located in a very conservative area and is, like most institutions, composed primarily of straight people. Thus I think it does folks good—and serves an educational purpose—to have a very open queer around (and what is more openly queer, short of public fucking, than the visual evidence of one man's desire for another?). It's also a nice blow against the stereotype of effeminate, fashionable urban queens to have that open queer be a burly, bearded Appalachian who loves country music and his 4x4 pickup truck.

The other reason Tim adorns my office is that he is a reminder of beauty. Long ago I read Andrew Holleran's novel *Dancer from the Dance*, in which one character writes to another, "As Santayana said, dear, artists are unhappy because they are not interested in happiness; they live for beauty." Beauty is something that is harder and harder to achieve or maintain in one's own face and body as one ages; and as one ages, it is harder and harder to find a beautiful partner for erotic experience. For

LGBT folks, the difficulty is increased immeasurably by that damned 90%/10% ratio. What, for instance, is the likelihood that the remarkably handsome twenty-five-year-old cashier at the local Food City here in my small mountain town would 1. be gay, and 2. be attracted to forty-seven-year-old me? The laws of averages are always working against the fulfillment of queer lust.

I keep images of Tim around because two-dimensional beauty is far better than none. His presence, even in mere photographs, serves to remind me that I am still able to experience wonder, awe, and desire, elements of depth that daily life does not often provide uncoaxed.

—ɯɯ—

SURROUNDING MYSELF WITH EVIDENCE OF this particular singer's fine looks, however unmet, distant, and inaccessible he might be, has given me an interesting glimpse into the world of the country-music fan. It has also made me ponder the function of star-worship and erotic icons. I am a fan and a star-worshipper, yes, as has been made clear, but I am too much of an intellectual not to analyze these phenomena even as I participate in them. To be in the world, but not of it: that's the perpetual position of the writer. It is often in the liminal spaces that one is most able to see and speak clearly.

How fan clubs functioned before the Internet, I do not know. Newsletters, I suppose. These days, however, every star has his or her webpage, with a wide variety of merchandise with which one can proclaim one's enthusiasm. To John's tolerant amusement, I have collected a good number of fan items over the last few years. There is, for instance, the Tim McGraw sticker on the rear window of my pickup truck. I'm assuming that most folks here in Appalachian Virginia who notice this sticker must simply assume that I'm a big country-music buff, since the erotically radical concept of one hairy, goateed country boy lusting after another hairy, goateed country boy is too far from their stereotype-constricted ken. So far, I'm glad to say, no tire-slashings to report.

Other Tim items I possess, listed as "Accessories" on the website store, are a key fob and a coffee cup. On the fob, the friendly expression on Tim's face makes him look at least somewhat accessible, someone you might want to share a pitcher of beer with. There are the usual Resistol, sideburns, and goatee, and his shirt is unbuttoned almost to his solar plexus. This is a man who gets overheated a lot, perhaps? Actually, his publicists or image coordinators or dressers or whoever decides these things are very fond of showing off Tim's hairy chest, which is a blessing for body-hair enthusiasts like me. His shirts—in photos, on TV, in concerts—are almost always unbuttoned a good bit. How odd it must be to have professional PR people manipulating you and your image for erotic appeal. I imagine ridiculous but no-doubt realistic conversations during photo shoots. Photographer, demanding, urgent, sensing the ultimate album cover: "Tim, unbutton some more. Fluff that chest hair. Smolder for me!" Tim, tired, petulant, wanting to get home to wife and kids: "Ah, man, give me a break! It's chilly in here. The damn air-conditioning is up too high."

On the topic of Tim's man-rack, as I like to call it, if you look closely at the cover of *Live Like You Were Dying*—and you can bet I have looked at it very, very closely very, very often while growling and grunting with lecherous appreciation—whoever has arranged the man and his half-open black button-down shirt has even given us the tiniest glimpse of nipple... I think. I keep looking, but, like distant horizons, it fades maddeningly in and out of view. Whoever designed that CD cover is both an artist and a sadist.

One last, and this time annoyed, man-rack observation. Despite all this torso teasery, it is almost impossible to find photos of Tim completely shirtless, other than a few coyly blurred images in his CD liner notes that I pull out and drool over every now and then. Since I am a chest-man and since I am so wildly infatuated, I respond to this paucity with my favorite Internet-surfing activity: trying to find bare-chested pics of him. (Naked is too much to hope for.) As much of a sex symbol as he is, you'd think there would be more photos along this line, but I suppose he's trying to straddle the fence, so to speak, between Hot Country Stud and Respectable Family Man, a combination that article after article cites as the major basis of his appeal. (I, of course, would prefer far more of the former and next to nothing of the latter, but more on his wife and kids later.) So far, all I've found is a very small number of pics (immediately downloaded) of Tim wearing nothing but nylon shorts, playing basketball with his band. Yes, he's as lean, muscled, and furry as I would have hoped. I only wish I could append those precious images to this essay so that you too, to borrow Millay, could look on beauty bare. Of such images is habitual onanism born.

Back to fan "accessories." The fob I keep my home and office keys on, which means I carry Tim around wherever I go, and he spends the day—I can't resist the lewd joke—close, very close to my crotch. How many elements of our lives are sad substitutes for what we really, secretly desire? Then there's the coffee cup—Tim's looking stern, clad in shiny black aviator jacket and A-shirt, with several days' growth of beard stubble (one can't help but speculate how it would feel against one's face) between his goatee and his sideburns. The joke here is that every morning I sip rich, stimulating, sweet, creamy liquids from Tim. This is what writers do: we make words stand in for the thing itself.

Then there is the Tim McGraw Calendar. The latest, 2009, is hanging in the sunroom of this house John and I share, here in the small mountain town of Pulaski, Virginia. Thus I pass Tim, like an icon at a roadside shrine, several times every day. Sometimes I jokingly speak to the image, in the same way that those who live alone speak to themselves, half-seriously, half-humorously. "Good morning, beautiful," I whisper, on the way to the kitchen. "Hey, baby, I'm home," I say, throwing down my backpack and heading for the bar to fix John and me end-of-the-day martinis. "God *damn*, ain't you *hot*?" I growl, after imbibing a few of those martinis.

Most of the calendar photos also show off the habitually exposed, bewitching and hirsute V of his cleavage, and in a minority of the shots he's dressed in the casual clothes most country boys would wear. Most others, however, present him in absurd, highfalutin, citified "club wear." Again, I imagine the conversations. Wardrobe queen, coaxing: "Tim, *darling*, just slip into this silk shirt. Isn't it *exquisite*?!" Tim, reluctant, weary: "That damned thang? You have *got* to be kidding me, buddy. Where's my black T-shirt and camo pants?"

Finally, there are the clothes that fans can buy off the website: McGraw Wear, as it's sometimes referred to. Being, like most mountaineers, a boots-jeans-and-T-shirt-wearing guy accustomed to informality, I own, by this point in my several-years-long Tim Devotion, quite an assortment of T-shirts bought off the site. Most sport Tim's handsome face, and sometimes his body, shown off by tight clothes of flattering fit (though a physique that perfect doesn't really need flattery, just simple display, to be eye-catching).

Sometimes, I must admit, I question the advisability of wearing shirts that bear a face and body better looking than mine. The contrast must surely work against me. Still, at least twice, to my wild and disbelieving delight, colleagues, studying my T-shirts, have told me that I look like Tim. On both occasions I was ready to pay them good money or treat them to filet mignon in return for such a compliment. I'm afraid the only physical features Tim and I share are our race, our sideburns, our goatees, our general hairiness, and the fact that we're tattooed and muscular. Otherwise, to use queer parlance, he's an otter (lean and hairy) and I'm a bear (beefy and hairy). Being a sex symbol and a public performer, he's in great shape; being a sedentary academic, I'm in not-so-great shape around the middle, though vanity insists that I keep the chest and arms up with semi-regular weightlifting.

This is, by the way, one of the big problems of same-sex desire: it encourages competitive comparison. Thus, sometimes the hot men you desire are a blow to your ego not only because of their disinterest in bedding you but also because their erotic appeal palpably dwarfs your own. Apparent perfection is always thus. When I stand in museums staring at Greek statues of Apollo, Dionysus, or Hercules, part of me is stiff with lust mixed with aesthetic awe, and part of me is horrified at how far from the ideal my body has fallen (not that it was ever particularly close to the ideal to begin with). One both craves the beautiful and resents it for highlighting the world's (and one's own) flaws.

Along with T-shirts that carry simple images of the star, there are two other categories. Some celebrate specific albums, such as *Set This Circus Down* (his best CD so far, in this fan's opinion) or *Live Like You Were Dying* (the title song's the best tune he's yet recorded). Others play off the well-built, athletic, masculine image Tim embodies, with slogans like "McGraw Athletics," "McGraw Wrestling," and "Tim McGraw: Real Good Man." Most designs, after a several-year run, are discontinued, and the newest designs, as of this writing, have leapt in price from $25 to

$35, a fact that has sadly convinced me that I own enough McGraw Wear. Tim, I love you, but enough is enough. For $35, I would expect not only a T-shirt but at least a French kiss.

What I'm wondering is whether men other than lusty queers who want to ravish Tim buy these shirts. Are gay country-music fans such a significant subgroup that their desires are taken into consideration in marketing plans? Is Tim more than a hot guy a hungry bear like me wants to make his house-slave? Could he be a role model of sorts for straight male fans, guys who wish they possessed his charm, talent, and sex appeal?

—⟋⟋⟍—

CONVENIENT SEGUE TO A THEORY of mine. Fans buy items that remind them of their beloved stars for the same superstitious reasons that some savage tribes ate the flesh of their slaughtered enemies or the wild animals they brought down in the hunt: to take on their *mana*, their power. And, further, some fans imitate their favorite stars in order to incorporate what they admire and desire.

This is probably obvious to just about everybody. Much has been said about famous figures and the ways they have influenced how we dress, speak, act, even kiss. As for myself, I know that I have half-consciously patterned my appearance and my behaviors after men I have lusted after and/or looked up to, starting with the mountain men of my hometown and continuing to present-day public figures I admire. In this context, I think of Jack Malebranche's controversial book *Androphilia: A Manifesto*, which most of my gay friends would excoriate but which I pretty much relished reading, despite certain ideological differences of opinion. Malebranche complains about effeminacy in the gay community, discusses how masculinity is a learned behavior, points out that many traditional male values are well worth possessing, and encourages the butcher sort of gay men to "[b]uild a pantheon of productive role models. . .who embody manliness," who are worth emulating.

Yes, I would put Tim McGraw on my list of recent role models. He is a man I admire and look up to (even though he is eight years my junior). From what I can tell at this distance, he's not only incredibly handsome, charismatic, desirable, and well built, the qualities that first caught my eye and libido, that combo I call "eminently fuckable." He also seems to be, from all I've read and heard, smart, talented, loyal, dedicated, determined, and kind. Unlike the almost equally sexy Toby Keith, Tim's politics are appealingly liberal. Even Bill Clinton has spoken approvingly of Tim's plan to one day run for governor of Tennessee. Plus, he appears to be masculine in a secure, relaxed way, in a world where masculinity often takes aggressive, ugly, destructive forms. His music bespeaks someone not afraid of emotion, someone who honors deep feeling in a nation so often afraid of it.

It is, by the way, this appreciation of the inner as well as the outer that makes what I feel for him more than mere lust but an actual passion, albeit directed at a public persona rather than someone I'm acquainted with. "Can you love someone you don't really know?" I used to ask myself in the roiling midst of my adolescent infatuations. Well, yes, since we don't completely know anyone, and romantic and erotic love is so often based on illusion.

So, a man worth emulating. Here lies a complication innate in some same-sex desire. Handsome men who fire me up, do I simply want to make love to them? Or do I want to *be* them, or, at the very least, be like them and so take on some of their manliness and their attractiveness? All of the above, in my experience. Growing up, trying to figure out how I could become a man in a world where gay men were so often expected to be craven effeminates, I learned masculinity from men I desired, in the same way, I'm assuming, that straight men learn masculinity from other men they simply admire. I was attracted to muscular men: I began to lift weights. I was attracted to men with facial hair: I grew a beard. I was attracted to men who wore jeans, leather jackets, baseball caps, flannel shirts, and boots: I began to wear the same.

I do not know if there is an essential self, as some philosophers and theorists claim. But I do know the self shifts in ways large and small. Large ways: I am more compassionate than I used to be, more confident, less needy. Small ways: like many rural men who, consciously or not, take their fashion cue from Nashville, since I've become a serious country-music aficionado I wear more cowboy boots and cowboy hats, common enough attire here in Appalachia. My favorite hat is—you guessed it—a black straw Resistol a lot like Tim's, which John bought me for Christmas several years ago. Tim might have bad taste in beer—he has done TV commercials for Bud Light, and I often, in my drunk and randy moments, have been heard to say that "that boy needs a big Daddy bear to truss him up and teach him a few things about good brews"—but he has superb taste in head gear. In a store full of cowboy hats, the black Resistol's the variety I would have chosen even without the Tim Imprimatur. Tim and I are both into playing up a streak of bad.

An amusing aside involving Tim-hats. Once, in my department, I was comparing notes with a work-study student on Tim's multitudinous charms. It's common knowledge among fans that he wears cowboy hats, dew-rags, and baseball caps all the time to hide his receding hairline, and this student confessed that, as delicious as she found him, as much as she'd like to get hold of him, he'd lose his appeal without the hat. Bald spots and thinning hair just weren't her thing, she explained (and this to a professor with a shaved head). I didn't have the heart to tell her that Tim, if bedded, would be hard pressed to keep that Resistol on during the energetic thrashing and bucking of sex-frolic.

You might attribute my Tim Emulation to a neurotic's shaky ego or a queer's frightened need for camouflage in the hostile provinces. Perhaps. Perhaps, wearing this Nashville-inspired garb, I want merely, briefly, to belong. As an intellectual, a poet, a pagan, a BDSM enthusiast, a gay man who has refused the lure of the city and has remained in my native region, I have spent my life feeling marginalized. It's a pleasant change of pace to be nothing unusual, simply one of many rural men at a country-music concert, at a baseball park or farmers' market, or driving my pickup truck down mountain roads with Tim's latest CD blasting from the stereo. That sense of belonging is an illusion, I know, since the country boy/redneck is only one of my many conflicting selves, but I savor it when it comes. It provides a pleasant respite from the much more common feeling of being at odds with the world.

—∽∾∾—

"TIM! *TIM!*" I SHOUT. "WHY haven't you done the laundry?"

"Haven't seen him around," John says casually, tapping at his laptop.

"*Damn*! He's run off. He's run back to that *hoor*!" I curse, beginning to sort the colored clothes from the white.

Well, every great love story has to have conflict. The problem with this particular passion is not only that Tim and I have never met, but he's married to the stunningly beautiful country-music star Faith Hill and they have three adorable daughters. Damned big obstacles. Yet another huge inconvenience of being a man who lusts after men, including members of the heterosexual majority: you are often the exact physical opposite of the sort of creature your desired one desires. Faith Hill and I have as much in common physically as a hummingbird and a baboon.

In the running fiction of my hot but complicated affair with Tim, I must, of course, bitterly despise my rival Faith. I habitually call her "That Hoor," taking the unconventional spelling and pronunciation of "whore" from a character in Lee Smith's novel *The Devil's Dream*. I'm especially apt to hurl that epithet Faith's way when I hear her singing, "I'm the lucky one." No shit! Going home to that face and body every day? *Hoor*!

The other line I use against Faith in mock-fits of jealousy is one reported to me by my best friend Cindy. One evening she was dining at a gay bar/restaurant called Union Station in Columbus, Ohio. There were music videos playing on huge screens, apparently a regular feature of the place. During one particularly steamy video, the musician Nelly was gyrating passionately with a scantily dressed seductress. Suddenly a slender black queen in the audience, apparently as enamored of Nelly as I am of Tim, rose to his full, statuesque height, pointed a tremulous finger at the woman on the screen, and shouted with outrage, "That bitch stole my man! That *bitch* stole my *man*!" It's a line too priceless not to borrow. Faith, you bitch, you stole my man!

Well, okay, outside of the amusing fiction of my illicit and adulterous affair with Tim, I admire Faith Hill almost as much as I do her husband. They are two of the few open liberals in the overwhelmingly conservative country-music world. Much to my delight, they gave Bush holy hell in the inexcusably sloppy aftermath of Hurricane Katrina. When, about that time, a journalist pointed out to Hill that she didn't seem to be a typical country-music star, Hill said something to the effect of "I don't *want* to be a typical country-music star." Good for you, you hussy, you hoor! These days I'm buying Hill's CD's for the same reasons I'm buying the Dixie Chicks' work: the music isn't entirely up my alley, but the politics surely are.

—◊◊◊—

SO, AFTER YEARS OF THIS fond fascination, on October 10, 2004, Tim and I found ourselves together in the same room. That did not, of course, mean that I was close enough to touch, smell, or taste him. Sight and hearing, the less intimate senses, were the only ones satisfied. I was one of about 13,000 heated-up, seething fans crammed into the Civic Center Coliseum in Charleston, West Virginia. Since I am an inveterate introvert and hater of crowds, my mere presence there was proof of my passion. We—there was indeed a sense of unity in such shared devotion—waited through an hour and a half of opening acts: the Warren Brothers, followed by Big and Rich. Then the musical foreplay was done, and out he strode.

Yep, there he was, not merely a recorded voice or a photograph, but the man himself, the man who, of all famous figures, I find most desirable. John tells me that I began grinning like a love-struck adolescent or an asinine fool as soon as Tim appeared, and I retained that expression of moony delight till concert's end. Nevertheless, reader, I did not ravish him. I am, I assure you, not writing this from the cozy confines of a jail cell or padded room. The laws of social propriety and the laws of the land (pesky legal concepts like kidnapping and rape) kept me in my seat, not to mention John's firm hand and the presence of security personnel. Denied the opportunity to act, I was reduced to mere observation, trapped in So-Near-But-Yet-So Far, envying psychopaths and criminals whose skewed worlds give them an amoral sense of entitlement that encourages them to simply take what they want.

Tim was dressed, not surprisingly, in very tight jeans and a loud, psychedelic, gratifyingly half-unbuttoned shirt, with obligatory cowboy boots and Resistol. His distant figure was replicated on large video screens, which I tried to ignore, despite the better view, simply because I can see video images of him any day. Seeing him in person, albeit half a coliseum away, wasn't something I was likely to enjoy again any time

soon. He began with "How Bad Do You Want It?" which seemed like
a cock- or cunt-tease's ultimate question, one very much pointed at the
audience. The answer was all around me: *Real Bad!!*

I had forgotten what ear-piercing notes the female throat can produce.
Here were thousands of women, young and middle-aged, entirely in heat.
Before I saw the frenzies of that evening, I had thought my passion for
Tim was a little crazy and a lot perfervid. But compared to the female
hysterics on display that night, my infatuation seemed relatively moderate.
I felt like a well-behaved satyr among rabid maenads. Every twitch of our
Nashville Dionysus's thigh, every shift of his ass, every self-conscious
Elvisesque move sent these women off. A few brazen vixens even became
stage interlopers. One was gently escorted off-stage, another eluded
security long enough to get to Tim before he even knew she was there.
She insisted on a handshake before she was removed. If I had gotten that
far, I would at the very least have torn off his shirt, but, then again, my
Eros is rougher than most.

Since I couldn't abduct the man, I studied him, intellectual analysis
being one of few legal responses left to me in that situation. He was an
interesting mix, or, rather, his stage persona was, since I'm in no position
to really know what he's like. Some of him seemed down-to-earth, sweet,
earnest. There was even a little endearing insecurity: he joked about
being twenty-five, then admitted he was thirty-seven; he wondered how
many more years he'd still be able to get in jeans that tight. He also came
across as cocksure, a deliberate tease: every once in a while he'd pull up
his untucked shirt to give the lucky galleries, those shrilling banshees, a
glimpse of his no-doubt-sweat-sheened belly. During "Back When," he
punctuated the line "when a screw was just a screw" with some lewd
hip-pumping, as if he were fucking the air. Several maenads, weak with
impalement fantasies, must have nearly swooned at that point. I must
admit to being less maddened by this movement, since Our Boy brings
out the Top in me, meaning I'm more interested in fucking than being
fucked.

At any rate, his deliberate erotic manipulation of the crowd seemed
to me both exciting and slightly contemptible. I would have preferred
someone less conscious of his appeal, with less deliberate trading on

his physical charms. But how could I have expected such innocence? How could he not know his erotic might in the face of all that hysterical adulation? How could he not know it, use it, and revel in it? Wouldn't any of us, fortunate enough to have that power? Certainly most of us in the audience attended that concert as much for his Flesh as his Word, as much for his sweaty, hairy décolletage and firm butt as his very fine music. The man has made untold amounts of money because he's not only talented, he's sexy.

Throughout the duration of the concert, intellectual observations such as those above coexisted with a kind of rapture I rarely feel now that I am staid and middle-aged, a sort of ecstasy that precluded any attempt of mine to keep still. I danced in my seat, I sang along (quietly, so as not to bother folks nearby), I tapped my feet on the floor and pounded my fists on my knees. I was intoxicated and entirely happy. Huge, enthusiastic concerts can be soul-shaking in the way that ancient Greek drama is believed to have been. Concerts are our modern Bacchic revels, explosions of poetry, sexuality, beauty, and community.

Perhaps, then, the wild audience adoration that night was entirely apt. Apropos, perhaps, that idolatry, the flowers thrown like offerings onto the stage, as if this small-town boy from Louisiana were indeed a Messiah, a god in human form. His body's proportions did remind me of the way Christ has been depicted in many painted crucifixions—something about the relative size of the shoulders, chest, and hips. Tim even seemed aware of the semi-religious nature of the audience's reverence. When he sang "Drugs or Jesus," at one point he briefly mimicked the form of Christ on the cross: feet together, arms spread out, head thrown back. An intentionally evoked parallel, slightly shocking, and particularly maddening to a man like me, a leather bear with a penchant for muscular, hairy, bearded, bound-down saviors. Perhaps stars like Tim function for us the way pagan gods did for the Greeks and Romans: perfected versions of ourselves but with recognizably human traits, powerful, beautiful, mysterious, distant, the subject of many oft-repeated tales. To use Platonic language, they appear to be closer to the Ideal Form than the rest of us, a reminder of what is possible. Not for nothing that word *star*.

Gods give us a sweeping sense of community, if they are any good at all, and several of Tim's songs did that, even for me, the king of anomie, the perpetual outsider, the brooder on the edges, the Grendel of Appalachia who so rarely feels he has anything in common with anybody. There I was singing along with those thousands of strangers, first to the lyrics of "Live Like You Were Dying," while our handsome Christos was bathed in blinding white light, and later during an encore song, that great tune "The Cowboy in Me," which actually ends with a statement of commonality, "I guess that's just the cowboy in us all."

The concert ended, for me, with the erotic high point of the evening, the climax, if you will. Tim sang the last note of "Cowboy," the band continued the melody, and Our Star strode across the stage toward the side exit....*my* side of the stage, praise Eros. Yes, his last, most ruthless tease: as he left, he completely unbuttoned his no-doubt sopping shirt, the bastard. There was a split-second's glimpse of hairy torso and belly—too far away to relish the flatness of the belly and the muscled curves of the chest, damn it—then he turned and headed down the corridor backstage. Halfway down that corridor, he pulled off his shirt entirely. There was the smooth, pale, inverted triangle of his bare back—broad shoulders, small waist—gleaming above his denimed ass and long legs, and then he was gone. Theophanies are not only rare, they're evanescent. That's why they're treasured.

—⁓—

WITH THE DEITY VANISHED, THERE were only other cultists to study as John and I left the coliseum. All around us, straight couples were passionately necking. No doubt the women, all afrenzy over Tim, were turning to their less godlike boyfriends and husbands for substitute satisfaction, to serve as solid earth to ground that crazed electricity. One sexy young man sporting a dark goatee, sideburns, black cowboy hat, and half-opened black shirt was trading very nicely on his resemblance to the star. He'd arrived with a conservative-looking, prim girlfriend, but during the concert he'd begun flirting with what my father would call a clutch of whoresomes, in particular a blonde with a pink blouse and huge breasts. By the concert's end, the conservative girlfriend had disappeared, probably in high dudgeon, Baby Tim's shirt was completely unbuttoned, revealing tastily furry chunkiness, and he was kissing on the rapacious blonde. Then the whole crew—hunk and four whoresomes—left together, probably to some illicit nest nearby. No doubt there was much Tim-inspired fucking going on all over the Kanawha Valley that night.

It was late, nearly midnight, by the time John and I got home and hit the sack. I hoped that sleep that night might bring sweet visions of Tim naked and grunting beneath me, but what sleep I got was dreamless. A tongue on my goatee—the cat's—woke me around 3 a.m. Tim's songs roiled around in my head, along with leftover adrenaline, keeping me awake for hours. I thought of him somewhere not terribly far away, in some hotel room or on his tour bus, fast asleep, naked or in briefs, snoring softly perhaps, musky with exhaustion. I thought of those middle-aged women who had surrounded me in the bleachers of the coliseum, women about my age, overweight and married like myself. I thought about the look in their eyes as they watched Tim. If the unrequited desire in that coliseum could have been harnessed, it might have powered the Eastern Seaboard for months.

I know why those women felt what they did because I felt it myself. We might love our husbands and cherish the lives we share with them. But one life is not enough. One man is not enough, though monogamists are loath to admit it. Habit makes even the most beloved things banal. Wanting Tim, we want what we can never have, and that ache for the unattainable keeps our erotic potentials awake. Middle age dulls us, there is so little left that inspires passion, and so we relish reminders of how fervently we once felt, how intensely we once loved. We want proof that we can still feel and yearn deeply without having to wreck our settled lives. Tim, who will forever be far from our lips, our arms, our groins, is, unlike many objects of desire, harmless. He spices up our banality, whets our time-blunted blades, gives us fire without consequence. His perfection is an illusion, certainly, one permitted by our ignorance and his media-blurred distance. In our minds, we know this. But our minds, if they are wise, like patient and doting parents, allow our hearts a few paltry illusions. Such an infatuation is an ideal answer to midlife restlessness (though I would also recommend infrequent frolics with fuck-buddies, if at all possible).

Our fantasies teach us about what we need, who we really are. It is, I realize, no coincidence that my fascination with Tim McGraw began to develop when it did: about the time that my relationship with John had moved past the initial honeymoon fuck-a-day phase and into the comfortable routine of coupled life, about the time that I realized that I tended toward neither domesticity nor monogamy. What my Tim-Love, however tongue-in-cheek, tells me is that, like many men and women who are brave enough to be honest about their emotional needs, I crave both the emotional comfort and security evoked by the familiar and the passion and excitement evoked by the novel and the inaccessible. I want John and Tim, marriage and affairs…or at least the pleasant distractions of extramarital desire, fulfilled or not. Yes, I want to have my furry beefcake and eat it too. For the deeply passionate, the world's inadequate. Imagination allows us to have what reality denies us: thus my frequent Bondage Weekends in the mountains with Tim. And, for those of us lucky enough to have understanding partners, open relationships allow us to enjoy the sort of adventure and variety that defuse erotic dissatisfaction. (Members of the Religious Right are welcome to throw up their sanctimonious hands in dismay. They don't know what they're talking about. I do. I've lived this life, and it's a healthy way to live.)

—⁊⁊—

MY TIM-LOVE'S ONGOING, CERTAINLY, NOT to be banished by the rational dissection exhibited in this essay. Just last week, listening to *Tim McGraw and the Dancehall Doctors* as I drove to Roanoke, I was engaged in heated dialogue with Tim. He sang, "Comfort me." I grunted, "Oh, yeah, you bet! *I'll* comfort you, buddy!" He sang, "I'll show you how a real bad boy can be a real good man." I sighed, "Hell, boy, you don't even *know* bad yet. I'll show you *bad.*" Anyone in the truck cab with me would have accused me of psychosis. I would argue for the catharsis of private playfulness.

Recently, indulgent John bought me an issue of *Redbook* to add to my Tim Cache. Shared interests can make weird bedfellows: there I was browsing through a magazine that contained articles on "Summer's best dresses" and how the use of make-up can create the appearance of "a big cleavage." Tim's on the cover, wearing another half-unbuttoned shirt. Inside, wedged among womanly articles and surprisingly frank fiction ("She felt his rough hands through the gauze of her tunic. 'Tell me what you like.'"), is a good interview with Tim and Faith, detailing their life together, their children, and their favorite comfort foods. It turns out that, like me, they're big fans of down-home Southern cooking like fried chicken and country-fried steak. I'd already read somewhere that Faith's sweet iced tea is renowned.

The latter detail inspires this sad admission: I dream about Tim every now and then, but it's never erotic. I'm not tying him to my bed, or taking his furry nipples into my mouth. No, in my dreams I'm visiting Tim and Faith in their country home, enjoying their Southern cooking, that legendary sweet iced tea, and the summer breezes on their patio. Tim and I are not illicit lovers, just buddies hanging out. Very disappointing. In other words, even in dream I can't make love to him. Even my subconscious seems to be trammeled with strict rules of proper Southern behavior: *don't rape someone else's spouse.* I've had to settle for the wish fulfillment of waking dreams: Tim's been the occasional Muse of my erotic fiction. I'm glad straight men don't read gay erotica; otherwise I would have been slapped with a restraining order by now.

The future of my passionate midlife affair? I have a long history of such infatuations, I must admit, indicating that my fickle loins might sooner or later aim their arrows elsewhere. Before Tim, after all, there were Tom Selleck in *Magnum, P.I.* and Joe Lando in *Dr. Quinn, Medicine Woman.* Lately the country-music singer Chris Cagle has given Tim some competition: Tim's a little lean for my taste, Chris is a beefy bear of a guy, more my type. Then there's Gerard Butler, the black-bearded Scottish actor in *300* and other action flicks. All fine fantasy houseboys welcome to fight for my favors. To twist another Walt Whitman phrase, I am large, I can love multitudes. As long as I retain my obsessive nature, however, I suspect Tim will have a place in my stable.

A part-time Luddite, I must still thank technology, with its ability to make the remote at least semi-present, for its kindness in making Tim available in one dimension or another. Though I wildly covet a virtual reality system that would provide me with long weekends of Tim-Humping, it has not yet been invented. So I must settle for CD players, which allow me access to his voice, and the convenient mechanism of video players, which give me new angles of audiovisual admiration. They flesh out the man, so to speak, though touching a television screen is no more satisfying than stroking a photograph. There's the *Greatest Video Hits* DVD, as well as television specials I've recorded on VHS tapes. In the last few years, Tim's acting career has added new fuel to my longing and new DVDs to my collection. Tim plays a bearded, hostile sheriff in *Black Cloud*, a (sadly clean-shaven) cowboy father in *Flicka*, a son-abusing drunk in the fine football movie *Friday Night Lights.* As fond as I am of Tim, his character Charles Billingsley in the latter film was so hateful I wanted to backhand him. A testament to Tim's skill. The man's a pretty good actor, which makes me wonder if there's anything he can't do. Make love to men, I regretfully conjecture.

Watching Tim play Billingsley in *Friday Night Lights*, I stumbled upon an epiphany, one that will lead to my last, albeit lengthy, observation, my last attempt to make sense of all this lustful nonsense. To my eternal gratitude, Tim/Billingsley appears sweaty, disheveled, and shirtless in one intense, very well acted scene that lasts long enough to allow one an unhurried study of his chest- and belly-hair patterns. That's not the epiphany; that's simply the reason I bought the DVD. The epiphany began with this: constrained by the demands of his character, Tim couldn't play Tim McGraw the Country Music Star, the man everyone envies and admires. He had to play Billingsley the vicious redneck, a man meant to be detestable and pitiable. Gone was the neatly trimmed goatee: instead there was several days' worth of beard stubble. Gone were the slick concert outfits: instead there were scruffy blue-collar clothes. Most noticeably, gone was the ubiquitous black Resistol; instead there were the receding hairline and big bald spot Tim compulsively covers in every other public context.

Was I disillusioned? Was I surprised? Did I fall out of love? Well, no. I'm not stupid; I recognize hype even as I admire the result of it. What that role stripped from Tim McGraw was the layers and layers of media gauze, film, scrim, cloud. I admired him for taking such an unappealing role, to be honest, for he knows better than anyone how much of what he is is due to cunningly arranged hype, and there must always be some danger in stepping out of that romantic mist to be seen more clearly, or at least to be seen differently.

After *Friday Night Lights*, after years of lengthy scrutiny, what I see in Tim McGraw is just another moderately handsome good old boy, the kind of guy I grew up around, the kind at least part of me has been patterned after, the kind I'm still attracted to the most. What I see, beneath publicity's gloss, is a man who embodies Southern small-town values, yet who's also experienced and well traveled, a complex mix of the cosmopolitan and the down-home.

This is the kind of man I've always wanted to be, and the kind of man I have in many regards become. Tim, *c'est moi*? Well, he's better looking and more talented, and his yearly income would make mine a pittance in comparison, but buddy Tim and I have a lot in common. We're Southerners, musicians, writers, liberals, beer-swillers, and home-cooking chowhounds. This is part of the fascination for me. Tim is Jeff Squared or Cubed. Erotic attraction, especially if it's heterosexual, is often depicted as the magnetic pull of the Opposite, the Other. Clearly, though, the magnetic pull of Like to Like is equally valid in many lives. I'm not simply talking about the desire of one man for another, but the desire of one man for another with a similar gender style, with a similar way of being a man.

I'm risking the accusation of narcissism here. In common parlance, narcissism is thought of as an unnatural love for oneself, but any psychologist can tell you differently. Just the opposite, in fact. We study the mirror in order to make sense of our own wounds, our shaky sense of self. So, the epiphany at last, this final confession, a fact it's taken the writing of this essay to figure out: when I pattern myself after men I admire, when I desire men who are something like me, when I love Tim from afar, I guess I'm trying to love myself. The latter job is much more difficult, since I know myself so much better than I do him or any of the country studs I see on the street, at Lowe's or Wal-Mart. I know my own neuroses and selfishness, my impatience and rage, my many contemptible weaknesses, my forgetfulness and incompetence, my slew of clamoring, rabid hatreds. I am one of many imperfect realities I find hard to love. In fact, the concept of loving myself has always seemed to me an outlandish idea, as impossible a task as if a midget were called upon to accomplish the Twelve Labors of Hercules, though I'm glad to say that my partner, family, and friends don't seem to find the task as daunting as I do.

Maybe my infatuation with Tim, a man somewhat like me, is both silly diversion and salutary exercise. Perhaps anything that deepens one's capacity to love, even my entirely imaginary and tongue-in-cheek "passionate midlife affair," is beneficial. Perhaps, by the time Tim and I have aged enough to have entirely lost our looks, I will have matured somewhat, mustered some honest affection for myself. Perhaps then, one nostalgic winter afternoon with nothing to do but dig up old mementos, I will sort through his CDs and photos and then drop him a note, writing as if to some beloved lost with my youth, "I wanted you in your handsome prime, when every fine thing was yours. We never made love. We never even met. But you enriched my life, you made me feel passionate and young, your music and your good looks helped me survive dark times. You helped me with that lifelong task of learning how to love the world."

Now I'm imagining two white-bearded men in cowboy boots and hats splitting a pitcher of beer. If Tim insists, I'll even agree to Bud Light. This vision's a long way from hirsute leather-sex in that imaginary mountain cabin where we began, but not a bad way for an unrequited passion to end. It's a rendezvous of which even Faith might approve. Hell, she's welcome to join us, as long as she brings along some of her homemade fried chicken and sweet iced tea. After the beer and fried food, we'll need the sugar and caffeine to stay awake.

BINDING THE GOD

(for Patricia Nell Warren and Patrick Califia)

I

The fascination goes far back. Probing memory, what I first find is an illustrated book of Bible stories for children in the optometrist's office in Lewisburg, West Virginia. My parents, both liberals, free-thinkers, and agnostics, bless them, kept me fairly insulated from orthodox religion and the narrow-minded Baptists that surrounded us in Southern Appalachia, but they didn't stop me from picking up that colorful book in the waiting room. God, how old was I? Ten? Leafing through that book, was I even then admiring the bearded men in robes, the savior with long hippie-hair? The savior in a loin cloth, stretched out and nailed down, the muscles of his chest and arms swelling, his hair falling down around his bare shoulders? Did the illustrator bother to give him chest hair, belly hair, nipples? I can't remember, but I hope so. Did the child I was think about how the savior tasted and smelled? Did I want both to wield the nails and also kiss his bleeding feet and comfort him? I hope so. If not, it wasn't to be many years before all those desires would well up in me like a mountain spring.

My sadomasochism might not have consciously kicked in by that age, but I know I was an occult enthusiast by then. I reveled over vampire protagonist Barnabas Collins' exploits on the ABC-TV gothic soap opera *Dark Shadows*. I spent my pubescence and adolescence reading huge tomes about pre-Christian religion, books like the abridged edition of

Sir James George Frazer's *The Golden Bough* and Robert Graves' *The White Goddess*, along with classics like Margaret Murray's *The God of the Witches* and Gerald Gardner's *The Meaning of Witchcraft*. These interests, needless to say, made me a complete freak in my hometown. Everyone who knew of my occult proclivities (and everybody knows everything about everybody in a town that size) assumed I was a Satanist. The Baptists were especially nasty and judgmental, and I responded to them with unconcealed hatred (still do).

The Catholics, well, there weren't many of them around, and the few that were—mainly folks of Irish descent—impressed me with how private and dignified their approach to faith was. Unlike the Baptists, with their pompous, sanctimonious high-school Bible Club and their revivals, their pamphlets, and their church camps, the Catholics I knew never pushed or proselytized. I appreciated that. I also appreciated their sense of ritual, for I'd been to a couple of Christmas Eve Midnight Masses with friends. Catholic observances reminded me of the incense, robes, altars, and chalices of witchcraft and ceremonial magic. The drinking of transubstantiated blood reminded me of how much I relished *Dark Shadows* and *Dracula* movies. My readings in Wicca had pointed out the ways in which the Virgin Mary was the sanitized Catholic version of the pre-Christian Mother Goddess (the Egyptian Isis, after all, being the first bearer of the honorific "Queen of Heaven"). Jesus, on the other hand, was the latest in a long line of sacrificed gods, in the tradition of Tammuz and other Green Man vegetation deities who spring to life with forest greenery and garden grains in the spring, reach maturity and fullness in the summer, and are sacrificed beneath scythe and frost in the fall. The nearness of Christ's supposed birthday and the birthday of the sun god on the Winter Solstice was just too much of a coincidence. I felt somewhat at home in Catholic churches when I translated their icons into pagan equivalents, glimpsing the Old Gods beneath the Christian facade.

As if being a Wiccan in the Bible Belt weren't enough of a predicament, when I read Patricia Nell Warren's novel *The Front Runner* during my sophomore year and realized I was gay, that uncomfortable epiphany made things even more difficult. Another secret to try to hide, though, with the recognizably lesbian friends I had, that secret didn't stay concealed much longer than my paganism. Now the Baptists despised me even more. Other than spending time with my lesbian buddies, I kept to myself, escaped into ancient Greece through the queer-friendly historical novels of Mary Renault, and dreamed of the day I would graduate from high school and get the hell out of Hinton.

But the most inconvenient facet of my identity had yet to surface... or, rather, I had yet to acknowledge it. By the seventh grade, I was jacking off, and the images that aroused me the most involved beautiful men struggling in restraint, strong men forced to submit and to suffer. There were the comic-book images of my favorite heroes—Batman, Tarzan, the Flash—tied up by villains. There were the stubble-rough cowboys on TV always getting overpowered or outnumbered or knocked out, only to end up bound and gagged, doing a lot of sweating and struggling in their bonds and making a lot of muffled noise. There were, ubiquitous in southern West Virginia, those Christian images of the crucifixion and the events leading up to it: the muscled, half-naked man bound, tortured, beaten, suffering on the cross.

Why did these perverse images carry so much erotic power? I didn't know (still don't). I only knew that this was another secret I'd damned well better keep to myself. Nevertheless, despite my confusion, by the time I was in high school, I was, in fantasy, vigorously wrestling down and tying up a few of the younger, handsomer substitute teachers. My bearded buddy Mike, only a year older than I but already possessing the muscles and body hair of a man—in daydream I would strip him to the waist, chain him to the wall of a garage, and gag him with a dirty cloth. I would beat him till he bled, till his body was wracked with sobs. The blood tasted good licked from his broad back. (I was, after all, not only a Wiccan but a vampire aficionado). Other times—already a Voracious Versatile, as I jokingly call myself these days— I would take off my shirt, tie my feet together with laundry cord, wrap cord around my chest, and imagine being the powerful, heroic prisoner of some dangerous Western robber.

Even as I filled Kleenex after Kleenex, I was convinced I was sick. Don't most leatherfolk for a while? Such desires had no context. They were shameful, twisted, not to be shared. Sometimes, seeing the way that bondage was portrayed in movies and television shows—always in scenes of nonconsensual violence—I feared that my aroused response to these scenes was proof that I was on my way to becoming a crazy kidnapper or a psycho killer.

Despite my guilty confusion, however, I sensed in these fantasies an almost spiritual power, a religious mystery. Seeing the relationship between BDSM (what we called S&M in those days) and Catholic imagery was a real help in solidifying this sense of the sacred and escaping my self-hatred and self-doubt. In this regard, Patricia Nell Warren saved me again. I'd fled to West Virginia University by then. My freshman year, inspired by Warren's gay biracial biker Vidal Stump in *The Fancy Dancer*, I started wearing a black leather jacket to the local gay bar but still had no real understanding of what my regularly savored fantasies about hot men bound and gagged could possibly mean. Then, in the autumn of 1978, I read Warren's *The Beauty Queen,* a novel based on Anita Bryant's campaign against gays and lesbians in Dade County, Florida. Two of the book's queer characters were leather-wearing cop Danny Blackburn and his lover Armando. Both were big, masculine guys, the kind I wanted to be, the kind I wanted to love. In Chapter 7, the lovers visit "the little St. Francis of Assisi Church on Wade Street" and pray together in the candlelight. Danny recalls "the guilty pleasure that he felt in parochial school. . .when he read in the prayer books about the torments of the martyrs" and was "enthralled by this fusion of pain with love." After they worship, they return to Armando's apartment, where Armando is stripped and chained down to the bed, and Danny pushes pins through his nipples. Armando suffers like a saint, like a savior, and Danny lies "beside him with the next pin, devastated at being both the instrument and the witness of this passion. There was no desire to hurt Armando, nor pleasure in it. He was the flaming angel. He was almost God, willing it to happen and knowing it so intimately" (Warren 155-157).

Reading that book, relating to Danny and Armando, getting my first glimpse of the leather community—where bondage and suffering involved not madness and crime but mutuality, love, and passion—so many disparate pieces came together for me on a deep, unspoken level. My sadomasochistic fantasies. Christian images of restraint, torture, suffering, endurance, redemption. The relationship between the spiritual and the erotic, a connection most people I knew would find sacrilegious.

Given courage by these revelations, I began to identify as a leatherman (well, leatherboy at that point—I hadn't tied anybody up but myself) and sheepishly began to admit my bondage interests to queer friends. When the film *Cruising* came out in 1980, like many gay men I boycotted it for its negative depiction of S&M aficionados as dangerous killers, though newspaper articles describing the film gave me pause, making me wonder what kind of world I was getting myself into. (Years later, I would guiltily rent it and get hard seeing a young Al Pacino, in a maddeningly brief scene, naked and hog-tied.) In my junior year, I ran across a guy who was very much into BDSM, but I wasn't really attracted to him, plus I really didn't know what I was doing, plus he was what I've since learned to call a pushy bottom, so our evening together was a major disappointment as first leather experiences go: silly, not sacred, and uninspiring enough to end up in my repertoire of cruelly satiric tales told for friends' amusement.

It was the summer of 1982, just before I started graduate school in English at WVU, that a handsome, flirtatious, red-moustached bartender named Steve finally gave me a chance to experience firsthand sex that felt sacred. I'd studied Steve for weeks, and the beauty of his face and body seemed as close to the presence of deity as I'd ever experienced, other than brief and solitary moments of transcendence I'd experienced in the natural world. Having read *The White Goddess* years before, I was heavily influenced by Robert Graves' belief that the poet's inspiration comes from a beautiful human muse who serves as the embodiment of the goddess. It was hardly a leap for me, then, to see beautiful men as embodiments of Wicca's Horned God, the deity of masculine energy, wilderness, and untrammeled sexuality, and of the Green Man, the god of vegetation who is sacrificed in the autumn, the muscular Savior—God immanent in bread or wine—whose body is devoured by his worshipers. Steve inspired in the lonely, horny, passionate boy I was a crazy, violent, devouring reverence. I wanted to bind him, gag him, suck him, fuck him. I wanted to eat him, drink him, incorporate him, make him a part of me. Like an Aztec priest, I wanted to hold his heart in my hands. That ache for fusion, for union, reminded me of Aristophanes' myth of love as recorded in Plato's

Symposium: two halves of a previous whole yearn for completion, and sexual desire is a manifestation of that yearning.

I was lucky. For a few weeks, before he moved on to greener pastures, Steve wanted me too. One evening I rode home with him. He lit tiny votive candles around the room. He pulled off his clothes in that flickering shrine, that stuffy bedroom down West Virginia Avenue. Oh yes, he was my Christ in the Candlelight. I tied his hands behind his back with a belt and knotted a dark blue bandana between his teeth. I sucked his big cock, chewed his hard nipples, reddened his ass with my palm, ate his smooth, perfect butt—white as a communion wafer—and I fucked him for a long time. I had found my religion that night, I knew without question, lying beside him later, watching him sleep, wishing I could keep him prisoner forever. Here was the Muse, the God, the Savior, manifested in this beautiful nakedness snoring softly by my side. I was the priest, the Roman soldier wielding the whip, the nails, and the spear, and the sinner redeemed by tasting the Sacrificed God's bound body, his moustache, his armpits, his nipples, cock, asshole, spit, and semen. Theophany had become not intellectual abstraction but physical and emotional experience. My heart swelled with gratitude as I rose to quietly snuff the candles out.

Graves differentiates clearly between the human embodiment of the Muse—often fickle and inaccessible—and the spirit of the Muse herself. I was to learn that the hard way, as Steve moved on to other men and then out of town. I mourned as only a passionate, despairing young poet can, but I was to find that Muse manifested in another man soon enough. In graduate school, I fell in love with Paul, who slept with me once and led me on for years. In literature classes, I studied the tradition of courtly love, the troubadours, the passion of Dante for Beatrice, of Petrarch for Laura, of Keats for Fanny Brawne, of Yeats for Maude Gonne. I read metaphysical poetry that effortlessly mingled the sexual and the sacred and called on Christ as the Divine Lover. Aching for Steve and later for Paul, I sat in Catholic churches staring at the beautiful bearded man suffering on the cross. I lit candles and whispered prayers that the God might return again and offer himself to me as a willing sacrifice. Though Christian concepts of sin and salvation were not ones to which I subscribed, I could certainly grasp how suffering and endurance might serve as paths toward spiritual and emotional maturity, and I knew even then that, if I were in need of redemption, my devotion to beauty—human, natural, and artistic—would be what would save me.

Writing lovesick poems about Steve and Paul and browsing again through Robert Graves' description of the muse in *The White Goddess*, I finally, belatedly, began to see how not only Christian iconography but related elements of neopagan religion might provide a much-needed mythic framework for BDSM. Graves hypothesizes that two powers, the God of Light—the Oak King, ruler of the Waxing Year—and the God of Darkness—the Holly King, ruler of the Waning Year—fight for the favors of the Goddess, a poetic mythology that has been since adapted by many Wiccan groups to celebrate the changing of the seasons. Light falls to darkness on the Summer Solstice, dark falls to light on the Winter Solstice, much like the Zoroastrian battle between light and dark that influenced early Christianity. Rival males fighting for a female was all too heterosexual for me, of course, but seeing those opposing gods as locked in a brotherly, loving struggle, that was another matter. As if Jesus and Satan were each to strip to the waist and wrestle away, till one overcame the other, bound him, and took his sweaty pleasure on top.

Graves gave me, in addition to this seasonal dualism, a crucial paragraph that summarized all my perverse fascinations with bondage, devouring, vampirism, sacrifice, and crucifixion. (Surely, in my adolescent first experience of Graves, I read this paragraph. Who knows how it might have, on some unconscious level, prepared me for my obsessions to come?) In his chapter "Hercules on the Lotos," he describes how Hercules, the sacred king, the lord of light, is, at midsummer, "made drunk with mead," led into a sacred stone circle where an altar stands, and behind that, an oak lopped to form a T, a makeshift cross. He is bound to the tree in a "five-fold knot which joins wrists, neck and ankles together," which sounds like a rigorous hog-tie to me, and then sacrificed. His blood is caught in a basin, much like a primitive chalice, and "used for sprinkling the whole tribe to make them vigorous and fruitful" (125). Here is the literal sacrifice that leathersex makes metaphoric, as Catholic communion makes metaphoric Christ's command to partake of his flesh and drink of his blood. Finally

I had a spiritual framework—reconciling, in my mind at least, Christian and pagan imagery—in which to comprehend sadomasochism.

Lonely, for the most part celibate, I spent the rest of my grad-school days teaching freshman comp and studying for my master's comprehensive tests, in my sparse leisure time reading Larry Townsend's *The Leatherman's Handbook* and bondage stories in *Honcho*. When I graduated with an M.A. in English, my creative thesis was composed of love poems to Steve and to Paul, my erstwhile Muses. To this day, no Catholic but still a cherisher of relics, I have, hidden in a dusty box, the blue bandana, never washed, that, over twenty years ago, I knotted between Steve's teeth and which, in the course of his trussed-up, rapturous struggles, grew soaked with his saliva.

As a priest presiding over sacrifice, I had a true vocation. After graduate school, it was time for me to take my turn as the suffering god. Jim was not a lover, just a fuck-buddy in Beckley, a well-built, deeply closeted country boy with a thick accent and a closely cropped beard. It took only one play-session for him to admit that he preferred the dominant role to the submissive. I'd been almost exclusively a Top for years, but, as a true hedonist always ready to test any path toward pleasure and into intensity, I consented to bottom. When next Jim and I met, I was the Christos, naked, anointed with my own sweat, hands bound behind me, bandana knotted between my teeth, grunting and helpless as Jim propped my calves on his shoulders, put clothespins on my nipples, and gently pushed his condomed cock up my ass. Now I was the holy one, I was the one beautiful and desired. Now I knew how they felt, the heroic, handsome ones, the demigods and warriors whose fates led them to helplessness, to suffering, to crucifixion and penetration. Wicca holds that God/dess is in each of us, and that night, being topped by Jim, I felt my divinity inside, rather than projected outwards and honored in another. My role was not that of active worshipper but passive sacrifice, the god of the fallen stag, the scythed wheat, the crushed grape, Christ nailed gasping to the cross, Odin hung moaning on the World Tree.

II

Now I know what I am about. I am a collector of holy images, a participant
in rituals of submission and surrender. I will be ruthless priest and helpless
god as often as I can, before age dries up my sap and heaps wet earth over
what's left of my bone-fire.

—∿—

He meets me here when his lover's at work. It begins as experimental
Sex Magick, invoking gods to descend into flesh, to wrestle and love
through us. We drink wine, light candles, strip in the midsummer heat,
press our young, hairy torsos together. He is the most beautiful man I've
ever touched, and, were I able to choose my own endless heaven, it would
be making love to him forever. I tie him spread-eagle to the bed, blindfold
him, and buckle a cock-gag in his mouth. Then I sit back, sip Rhine wine,
and study his struggle. He groans, tugs at his ropes, then falls back into
acquiescent silence. Slowly, his cock grows hard, aroused by his own
helplessness. He looks like Christ stretched out and crucified. I run one
reverent hand over his forehead, taste the sweat on his temple and in the
hairy cleft between his chest's hard curves. I feast on a joy greater than
any I've ever known. This love is meant to be, I know. This love will
save me. I do not know that, by the Autumn Equinox, he and his lover
will leave town. I do not know what agony and loneliness, greater than
I've ever known, will seize me then. I do not know that, in statues and
paintings—the Stations of the Cross, the captive Christ bound, whipped,
or nailed to his brief death, St. Sebastian's body strapped to the tree and
pierced with arrows—in the churches of Sligo and Salzburg, the chapels
of Bruges and Brussels, for decades I will continue to see the lover I lost.
All I know is that a love as deep and reckless as this is bound to wrap my
heart in thorns.

—∿—

Appalachian summer solstice, the basement of a mountain cabin, and
Hercules is about to be bound. "Get naked," commands Everett, and I

do, stripping down to salt-and-pepper body hair and a steel cock ring. It's hot outside, but the dark air here beneath the house is damp and cool. He pushes a wooden stool against one of the posts supporting the ceiling. "Sit," commands Everett, and I do. Using yards and yards of Wal-Mart rope, he ties my wrists and elbows together behind the post, secures my chest and shoulders to the post, then my thighs and ankles to the legs of the stool. "Let's get you a little drunk," he says, grinning, and pours out a big glass of red wine from a bottle he's fetched for that purpose. He holds the glass to my lips and I drink, I gulp. Most of it I get down, some of it trickles out of the corners of my mouth and runs down my chest. This continues till the bottle's done and I'm light-headed.

"Time for your gag," says Everett. The head-harness is a complex collection of black-leather straps and metal rings, with a fat black rubber ball Everett pushes between my teeth and buckles in place. With a few more cords, he ties the head-harness to the post so now I can't even move my head more than a few inches in any direction. He's got clamps on my nipples and is merrily tugging them and tightening them and savoring my pained groans when his husband Glenn descends the basement stairs.

"He's tough. He won't talk no matter how bad you torture him," jokes Glenn.

"He does seem to be one happy pig," Everett says, adding some weights to the clamps. He pats my head, licks the ball in my mouth, and strokes my very hard cock. "Nice, nice..." he mutters. "Okay, we're gonna be outside working on that damn-ornery electronic gate. If you get into trouble, shout. I'll leave the door open. We'll hear you. We'll be right outside." I nod, and they're gone. Behind me, beyond my line of vision, the door to the driveway creaks open. I can hear their voices fading into distance, then the sound of hammering as they start on their task.

It's dim and quiet in here. I can't turn my head, but light from the open door behind me falls across the boxes of wine bottles, the leather sling in the corner of the basement. The post is cool against my bare back. My nipples are moving from fiery pain to dull ache. I test the ropes around my wrists, then those around my elbows and my torso. As experienced as I am, I can work myself out of a lot of roped-up situations, but not this time. If I really were a kidnap victim, held captive in this isolated place,

I'd be shit out of luck. As much as I curse and tug, the ropes don't give an inch. I'd forgotten how good Everett is at what he does. Giving up, I settle back, content at being totally helpless. I chew the ball in my mouth, and pretty soon spit wells up and drips over my goateed chin, drops in slow strings onto my chest and belly. Pretty soon my chest hair is soaked with my own saliva. I close my eyes, sink into my wine-buzz, and hear the small sounds of insects in the weeds beyond the door, the murmur of Glenn and Everett talking over their work. I have no choice but to sit here in the dark, in the humiliation and helplessness I've asked for, at the "still point of the turning world," as T.S. Eliot put it in *Four Quartets.* Later, in an hour or so, Everett will return. He'll make me hurt, with any luck. He'll jack me off, then count the feet that my congested lust arched. He'll let me loose, and by then I'll be sore and stiff and ready to be freed. But right now I'm alone, fully aware of my tightly trammeled muscles, my steady heartbeat, the drip of cool spit on my belly. It's Midsummer, and I am bound down like Hercules, like Christ, here at the sun's height, my body a small banked fire, thrilled with its own brief, intense heat.

—⚏—

"THERE'S A LITTLE JESUS FOR you," John jokes, nodding toward the stage. He knows what kind of man heats me up. We're in the Dutch town of Alkmaar this sunny August afternoon, and there's an outdoor festival going on near St. Lawrence Church. A band of young guys is making evocative, electronic music: one plays a hurdy-gurdy and one a bagpipe, but the musician that John points out is the accordion player. He looks to be in his mid-twenties. Even from here I can see chest hair curling over his T-shirt top. He's an otter: lean, with a closely cropped black beard and long black hair falling past his shoulders. Here's Christ again, bending over his instrument, swaying to the tune, and here I am, entirely fascinated, briefly unaware of all the world but this furry young man on the stage.

    Christ look-alikes always bring out the Top in me, the ache to overpower and dominate, but I'm almost fifty, and, more and more frequently, the scruffy saviors who attract me are young enough to be my sons, as is today's object of futile longing. My long-haired accordion player is most likely straight and certainly not interested in submitting to a man of my age and knotty inclinations. Thus, loving Christ's human manifestations in the rough and tender way I want is a passion that, to my regret, recedes year by year from possibility into fantasy.

I sigh and pull my eyes away. I have spent my life desiring with great intensity what I cannot have. John leads me to a café along the side of the church, where we sit in the sun sipping coffee and devouring Dutch apple cake. I can't see the stage from here, and that's a relief. I don't like to look long on beautiful men who are utterly inaccessible; it maddens and saddens me.

In the real Alkmaar, I'm chatting with John and planning a trip to Haar Castle. Maybe we'll tour the Maurithaus in The Hague to see the Vermeers, or track down some *rijsttafel*, or buy cheese in Gouda or ceramics in Delft. John and I have been together almost ten years. I love our life, our shared passions, our home, our pets, our travels. Despite the lacunae inevitable in any marriage, I expect we'll spend the rest of our lives together.

In another Alkmaar, one less secular, less solid, in fact entirely fantasized, Jesus stands before me in the sanctuary. The dim church smells of burning wax, lilies, incense. I take him into my arms and kiss him, I stroke his thick hair, fondle a nipple through his T-shirt till he's gasping with gratitude. He bows his head in surrender. I pull his sinewy arms behind his back, rope his wrists and elbows tight.

When I have him helpless, I unsheathe the dagger. Staring at the steel blade, he begins a soft whimper. I cut off his shirt; it rends like the temple's fabled veil. I pull off his jeans, then carefully slice off his briefs. Now he's naked, trembling in the chilly air of the sanctuary, his long dark hair falling about his face. In the restlessness of votive candlelight, his chest and belly are black with fur, his beard-framed lips are full and red, his brow is smooth and white. I lift him into my arms, stretch him out on the altar like a feast, an offering, a sacrifice. He lies on his side, panting, while I bind his crossed ankles together.

"Please..." he whispers. I know what he wants, and I oblige, stuffing his mouth full with the fragrant cloth I've cut from his loins. Gently I roll him onto his back. I strip, climb upon the altar, and lower myself on top of him. His eyes are long-lashed, wet, and wild. I kiss his chin, his gag-taut lips, his eyelids, cheekbones, and forehead. His cock is hard against my belly, and he mumbles muffled prayers into his gag as I bend down to take that thick flesh on my tongue. The packed cloth will keep his sobs down as I chew his nipples till his body gives me blood, as I hoist his legs over my shoulders and push into him, take him hard till tears streak his face. Upon our conjoined nakedness, stained-glass light will spill, ruby light, then darkness, then light again, as clouds surge and flicker over the sun. Sighing, rocking, sweating, suffering: this is how we enter eternity.

ABOUT THE AUTHOR

Jeff Mann grew up in Covington, Virginia, and Hinton, West Virginia, receiving degrees in English and forestry from West Virginia University. His poetry, fiction, and essays have appeared in many publications, including *The Spoon River Poetry Review, Wild Sweet Notes: Fifty Years of West Virginia Poetry 1950-1999, Prairie Schooner, Shenandoah, Laurel Review, The Gay and Lesbian Review Worldwide, Crab Orchard Review, Best Gay Erotica, Bloom,* and *Appalachian Heritage.* He has published three award-winning poetry chapbooks, *Bliss, Mountain Fireflies,* and *Flint Shards from Sussex*; two full-length books of poetry, *Bones Washed with Wine* and *On the Tongue*; a collection of personal essays, *Edge*; a novella, *Devoured,* included in *Masters of Midnight: Erotic Tales of the Vampire*; a book of poetry and memoir, *Loving Mountains, Loving Men*; and a volume of short fiction, *A History of Barbed Wire,* which won a Lambda Literary Award. He teaches creative writing at Virginia Tech in Blacksburg, Virginia.

More fine titles from
Bear Bones Books

Nonfiction

Edge: Travels of an Appalachian Leather Bear by Jeff Mann
Bears on Bears: Interviews & Discussions by Ron J. Suresha

Fiction

Bears in the Wild: Hot & Hairy Fiction, edited by R. Jackson
Bearotica: Hot & Hairy Fiction, edited by R. Jackson
The Limits of Pleasure, a novel by Daniel M. Jaffe
Spring of the Stag God by J.C. Herneson
Bear Lust: Hot & Hairy Fiction, edited by R. Jackson

Discover more at
www.bearbonesbooks.com.

CPSIA information can be obtained at www.ICGtesting.com

261037BV00001B/56/P